Uncle Jimmy
Elder Care or Elder Abuse?

C. W. Smith

This book is dedicated to the memory of Dr. James H. Smith; his wife, Iris Smith; and his son, James A. Smith.

[12]And Jesus went into the temple of God, and cast out all them that sold and bought in the temple, and overthrew the tables of the moneychangers, and the seats of them that sold doves,
[13]And said unto them, "It is written, My house shall be called the house of prayer; but ye have made it a den of thieves."

Matthew 21, verse 12-13, KJV

Contents

Preface

The National Academies estimate "between 1 and 2 million Americans 65 or older have been injured, exploited, or otherwise mistreated by someone on whom they depended for care or protection." Additionally, the Academies note that "the proportion of the population aged 65 and older has increased dramatically since 1950. Between 1950 and 2000, the total population of the country increased by 87 percent, the population age 65 and older increased 188 percent, and the population 85 and older increased 635 percent. These trends will likely be accentuated by the aging of the post-WWII Baby boom generation."[1] Simply put: The American population is living longer. The older we get, the more susceptible we are to elder mistreatment. Elder care is in demand, and we have reason to fear that elder abuse is on the rise.

A former New York State Investigator for the Medicaid Fraud Unit, Thomas Cassidy, notes that the worst elder abuse crimes that he has seen are committed by unlicensed care-givers, and he urges people in need to hire elder-care through a reputable agency that can provide appropriate oversight.[2] The consequences of a lack of oversight in this industry can be tragic.

What happens when oversight uncovers mistreatment? Who stands up against it? For many, it's just easier to avoid conflict, and walk away.

When I think about my uncle's final years, it's painful to imagine what could have been done when "this" happened or what should have been done when "that" happened. Please learn from our mistakes. Consider Uncle Jimmy's final years as a case study to analyze how so many people in the community, while not guilty of any crime, failed to stand up for what was right at a time when my uncle truly needed help. It is difficult to divide people simply into "good" and "bad." I suspect it is true in most cases that there are relatively few people actively committing crimes, and a similarly small percentage of people on the "front-line" actively fighting the good fight. Most of the population stays on the sidelines with a quiet mouth. If the majority stands up for a just cause, we can prevent evil deeds from occurring. If we stand by idly, perhaps hoping someone else will do the dirty work, those who would carry out misdeeds can do so freely.

Uncle Jimmy
Elder Care or Elder Abuse?

1. Blood and a Polygraph

"I never seen that much blood in my life, just to come out of somebody. It just was running. It just was running out, running out." Uncle Jimmy's former caregiver testified, after his death.[1] How did it come to this?

.....

Sometimes true stories are hard to believe. Perhaps even more difficult if the author is writing about his own family. Maybe even more so if the author claims a church's leadership acted inappropriately. As I relay these facts to you, it seems like a twisted plot for a Hollywood drama, even to me.

I make one assumption: That my father, the family member closest to my uncle when these events occurred, was telling the truth. I know some people are not as comfortable with that assumption as I am. I asked him to take a polygraph test on the subject. He did. According to the polygraph examiner:

> Professional Evaluation and Opinion
> It is the professional opinion of Andrew Goldstein, Multi State Licensed and Certified Polygraph Examiner that after careful review of the multiple charts collected that there was a non deceptive result to the truthfulness of the specific issue test questions....[2]

2. The Beginning

Dr. James H. Smith (Uncle Jimmy) was born in 1907, but this story begins before that. His father, William T. Smith, Sr., was born in 1873 and was raised in poverty in Canetuck, NC. William lived across the Cape Fear River from Woodford Farm in Columbus County, North Carolina. On that farm was an old farmhouse that was built circa 1831. As the story has been passed down, William wanted to live in that farmhouse. He worked his way through dental school and began to practice in Wilmington, North Carolina, about 30 miles from the farm he fell in love with as a child. By 1910, he had raised enough money to make his dream come true by purchasing Woodford.

By 1915 William had six children, four sons and two daughters, including James H. Smith. William's dental practice ensured that James and his siblings would never have to endure the same poverty he did. They spent summers at Woodford throughout their lives. In 1942, my great-grandfather, William Thomas Smith, Sr., sold the farm to his son, James, for $10.[3] This was a very good price, even in 1942. The family understanding was that Jimmy could manage the land, and profit from farming and timber, but he would preserve Woodford for the family.

A Thanksgiving reunion at the farm became a tradition for my great-grandfather's entire family. This tradition continued non-stop even after James bought the farm from his father. During my childhood, I spent every Thanksgiving at that farm house.

Of course, there was a lot more going on in Wilmington, North Carolina in the last century than just a family buying a farm and throwing Thanksgiving parties. The city had seen incredible growth, and, at times, incredible tragedy. There have been race riots and reconciliation; incidents of anti-Semitism and religious acceptance; gender identity intolerance and understanding. You might describe it as the best of times, and the worst of times, but, even at the best times, there are people harboring prejudice, and sometimes, tragically few standing up to end those prejudices.

I grew up in Wilmington. I attended the New Hanover County Public Schools. My paternal grandfather, my father, and I all went to the same high school. I'm a third generation Wildcat. The building that my grandfather attended class in still stands, but there are differences now. When I went to New Hanover High School it was a racially integrated school. When my ancestors went there only white children could go to school there. Williston was the school for non-whites.

Some things in Wilmington are the same, however. The forced integration of public schools did not bring perfect racial harmony. Racial slurs were not uncommon in school and recreational contexts when I was growing up. I wish I could say that I never used inappropriate language, but this book is about the truth – good, bad, or ugly. The truth is I was a part of the racial disharmony in Wilmington in the 1970s and 1980s, and I didn't even know it. I told jokes that included what my peers and I thought was "racial humor." I told jokes that made fun of homosexuals. I never gave much thought to how damaging these social stereotypes could be to my friends, family, and larger community.

When a teenager wants to fit in with his peers, he acts the way his peers expect him to act. If the expected action is telling inappropriate jokes, the youngster will likely tell an inappropriate joke. Why does this behavior persist into adulthood?

Today, Wilmington is a bustling small city. It seems huge to me compared to the 100,000 or so people that populated the city and the surrounding county when I was growing up there. I'm sure the contrast is much more evident to older generations. My father recalls a time in his childhood when he saw a woman pumping her own gas on a Sunday morning and thought he had "seen it all."

This is the setting for Dr. James H. Smith's final years. A beautiful small city, dealing with racial tension and reconciliation, homophobia and enlightenment, economic growth, and, at times, moral decay.

3. Moral Decay

It has never surprised me that a person can reach a point in life where he has been pushed around so much that he feels compelled, or justified, to commit a crime. What has surprised me is how often these criminal acts are not resisted by the community, frequently being greeted by silence. We study large historical examples, like the rise of Adolph Hitler, or the admonitions of Dr. King regarding "good" people's silence in the face of wrongs, but the same phenomenon can happen on a small scale in any community.

When we study Nazi Germany, we focus on the leadership: Hitler, Himmler, Goering, Goebbels, and their brethren. We spend a little less time discussing the German resistance, often represented by Oskar Schindler, Dietrich Bonhoeffer, and Colonel Claus von Stauffenberg. We spend very little time on the population from which the Nazi leadership drew its power. Some Germans took up arms to fight for their nation, willingly or otherwise. Many others simply kept their mouth shut when they might have spoken out. Think about who might have been able to steer that angry population away from war? What role could churches have played?

.....

Most of us think of religious groups as organizations that stand up for right against wrong, but you can't have religious extremism without religion. In 1095, Pope Urban II initiated the crusades by calling Christians to war against Muslims to reclaim the holy land with a cry of, "God wills it!"[4]

Some recognized corruption in the early Catholic Church. In 1517, Martin Luther initiated the major push of the Protestant Reformation by challenging Papal authority in writing, sparking intra-Christian wars.[5] Many Christians believed that the Church was using undue influence to scare people into paying cash for salvation. After hundreds of years of religious wars and corruption, Martin Luther was among those who stood up against a system that had brought many a king to his knees. Martin Luther would risk much to try to push his religion back up to the moral high ground. This founder of the Lutheran Church, possibly the most progressive church of its day through Luther's efforts, wanted to repair the wrongs that he saw occurring in the Catholic faith. His primary concern was indulgences or buying

4

salvation. A closer look at Martin Luther reveals that he wasn't squeaky-clean either.

Galileo Galilei was Catholic. He fathered multiple children out of wedlock, but that was not uncommon for the time. This would not have put him at odds with the Catholic Church. In his era, even the Pope fathered children out of wedlock.[6] Galileo would be brought before the Inquisition, instead, because he asserted that the Earth rotates about its axis and revolves around the sun. Galileo was imprisoned for his "crime" and stayed under house arrest until his death in 1642.[7]

.....

What does this ancient history have to do with Dr. James H. Smith, and what does this ancient biblical history have to do with his church, the First Baptist Church of Wilmington, NC? Should we doubt that modern churches, surely more enlightened than those ancient churches, would always stand up for what's right?

In Dr. Smith's lifetime, the Christian church did not stand up unified opposition to Hitler. As one example, on July 20, 1933, on behalf of Pope Pius XI, the Reichskonkordat was signed.[8] This treaty between the Vatican and the Nazi government increased the prestige of Hitler's regime around the world. The church condemned Galileo in the 17th century for supporting Nicholas Copernicus' discovery that the Earth revolved around the sun, but it wasn't until 1992 that Pope John Paul II issued a declaration saying the church's denunciation of Galileo was an error resulting from "tragic mutual incomprehension."[9]

Science isn't the only thing the modern church is struggling with. In the U.S. alone, over 16,787 people have come forward to say that they were abused by Catholic priests as children between 1950 and 2012. The Catholic church was believed by many to have been slow to take active steps to end this abuse.[10]

Modern abuses are not unique to the Catholic church. The Bureau of Alcohol, Tobacco, and Firearms raided David Koresh's Branch Davidian compound in Waco, Texas on February 28, 1993. The U. S. government intended to serve arrest warrants for possession of illegal firearms and explosives. A review of Waco events published by the Justice Department in October 1993 concluded that, "Evidence suggested that Koresh had 'wives' who were in their mid-teens, that Koresh told detailed and inappropriate sexual stories in front of the children during his Bible study sessions, and that Koresh taught the

5

young girls that it was a privilege for them to become old enough (i.e., reach puberty) to have sex with him."[11] Koresh fathered 12 children by several "wives" who were as young as 12 years when the children were conceived.

In another American religious conflict, a tax accountant and leader among the Fundamentalist Church of Jesus Christ of Latter-day Saints, Roulon Jeffs, used his social and religious position to marry women as young as 12, continuing this until he was as old as 85. When he died, one of his sons took over a leadership role and tried to take control of some of his wives.[12]

What amazes me about these events is not that a few people believed that they were chosen by God to lead, but that thousands followed them faithfully even as their communities suffered. More recently, and perhaps a little closer to home, for some, 380 Southern Baptist leaders and volunteers have been accused of sexual misconduct.[13]

.....

Is there religious fundamentalism in Wilmington, NC in the modern era? In 1989, the First Baptist Church of Wilmington decided to distance itself from the Southern Baptist Convention. In the words of an Associate Minister at the First Baptist Church:

> In a business meeting, held on October 15, 1989, the Church decided it was time to make adjustments in the way it was financially supporting the Southern Baptist Convention. The convention was being firmly controlled by a fundamentalist regime. Seminary presidents were being fired or forced to resign because of unfounded reports of liberal theological learnings. Threats were made to leaders of Baptist agencies and mission boards. The Baptist Joint Committee on Public Affairs was being de-funded by the convention.[14]

Among the problems cited by the Associate Minister are the Southern Baptist Convention's views on the autonomy of each individual church, the inerrancy of scripture, and the ordination of women. The solution that the First Baptist Church arrived at was to reduce the money it sent to the Southern Baptist Convention. According to the same Associate Minister:

[In 1989] Eighty Five percent of the membership chose to by-pass the Southern Baptist Convention. The other fifteen percent of the membership wanted to continue supporting the Convention and their wishes were granted. ... For the next ten years an even smaller percentage of the church chose to support the Southern Baptist Convention and they were allowed to do so without being made to feel uncomfortable.[15]

By January of 2001, the First Baptist Church of Wilmington had voted to remove the Southern Baptist Convention from its list of supported organizations.[16]

Dr. James H. Smith attended services at the First Baptist Church. His church's Associate Minister, quoted in this chapter, was Reverend Jim Everette.

4. The Lawyer

Another member of the First Baptist Church was Otto K. Pridgen, Attorney at Law. He was born in Wilmington in the 1920s. His parents both had about a 6th grade education. His father was a third-generation Baptist minister.[17] It may have been a rough start for a young man growing up after the Great Depression in a society that couldn't financially support the underprivileged and might not have chosen to do so even if wealth were available.

Otto Pridgen had friends and family who helped him through his education. An uncle who graduated from Wake Forest University supported him and inspired him to attend a program that allowed him to graduate from Wake Forest with an undergraduate degree and a graduate degree in Law in 6 years.[18]

In a "Living History" interview with Professors at the University of North Carolina at Wilmington, Otto recalls his close friend and classmate Lonnie Williams. Otto and Lonnie were in the Wake Forest Law School graduating class of 1953.[19]
About his education, Otto recalls that:

> As a practical matter, they did not teach you anything about how the court system worked, about how you would fit in or anything about it. It was a total disconnect. It was pure theory. I had nothing really to guide me when I started practicing law.[20]

Otto moved back to his hometown, Wilmington to start his law career. He reflected on his return:

> Well as I said, there wasn't any bread and butter. I discovered to my surprise that the people I had known for many years, they were family friends that had encouraged me to go to law school, one of them was owner of a large grocery store. Well it wasn't large, it was just a grocery store over here in what we called Brooklyn, it was the north side. And his customers were all black. He'd always say, "Can't wait for you to get out of law school. I had to send three people down to see Bill Rhodes last

week. Soon as you get out, I can keep you busy boy." Well after I got out of law school, you know how many people he sent to my office? How many do you think? … None.[21]

His first 5 years or so, he only made about $50 to $75 a week, if that much.[22] He described the law practice as "a very thin business" in those days. Reading Otto Pridgen's history leaves me with the impression that, if you weren't connected to influential people in Wilmington, you couldn't find work there in the field of law. Pridgen described the situation for a law practice in Wilmington circa 1953 as follows:

The practice of law was controlled by about three law firms. They had all the clients who were able to pay for legal services. The John Stevens law firm, and there was a son-in-law law firm around here in the CP&L building and they were the two biggest firms. Of course, Wallace Murchison had his firm that was getting started at that time. Outside of those three firms, there was not a lot of… maybe a couple more firms. There was Josh James and his brother Murray. They had an insurance business. Dudley Umpfred[1], Willis Kellam[2], his father-in-law, had a tie in with the people of savings and loan. They got all their legal work. In those days it was a closed shop as far as getting any kind of title work. You had to be on what they called the "approved" list. Banks did not make any loans whatsoever on houses. The real estate, well the construction of houses would never have happened if it was up to the banks. The banks did not lend 10 cents on a house loan. The beginning and the thing that created the savings and loan associations and they started these nickel and dime operations in offices this size – was the fact that people wanted to borrow money to build houses and the banks wouldn't lend them any money. So they just started tiny organizations with people putting in $50 and $20 and this kind of thing into this tiny bank. Osden Bellamy[3] for instance had his savings and loan in the office over here at the Odd Fellow's building. Osden

---

[1] Possibly Dudley Humphrey
[2] Possibly Woodus Kellum
[3] Possibly Marsden Bellamy

was an old guy, he was one of the one of the aristocratic Bellamy family, Osden was about 80 at the time I started practicing law. He was very eccentric. He would not talk to you face to face. He would always talk to you with his back, he'd look out the window and talk to you. He was also county attorney, but out of his law office, he operated a savings and loan association.

["Unregulated, you could just have one on your own?" The interviewer asked.]

Well I don't know how much regulation there was, but he had one. Of course most of his borrowers were colored people. Nothing wrong with that, they had to have houses too. But what I'm saying is, coming around to, if when I started I wanted to be a title attorney, I couldn't be. I couldn't be a title attorney. I wasn't approved by the savings and loan.[23]

…..

Frustration with the class system in Wilmington law firms seems evident in Otto's comments. On the necessity for partners in a law firm, Otto notes that "when you're an only child, you don't need a lot of partners. You're a world of your own and you're not afraid to tackle the world or whatever (laughter). You're your own circus. I did not…I've never had any partners, nor have I felt a necessity for one."[24]

By 2002, Otto Pridgen had been in the legal profession in Wilmington, NC for nearly 50 years. When he started out, according to his own comments, the established lawyers didn't consider him to be a threat to their businesses. After a half century in the business, Otto Pridgen asked a law professor at a seminar why they were pumping out so many lawyers. He claimed they were "flooding the profession, and this is not good."[25] Otto describes himself as no financial threat to his predecessors and suggests that the influx of lawyers of the new millennium were making it hard for more experienced lawyers to attract clients.

Otto seems to suggest that he was treated as an outsider in his chosen profession. He still had his church. The First Baptist Church is where Otto Pridgen met Dr. James Smith.

5. The First Baptist Church of Wilmington, NC, I

Greater and more lasting are the intangible evidences of the heritage of this congregation than are the tangible proofs around us. All around are unseen harvests in the sowing, which today's congregation pray will bring forth comparable yield in the years that lie ahead.

Helen E. Dobson
-Our Living Strength

The chapel of the First Baptist Church of Wilmington stands at the intersection of 5th and Market. The plot of land that the church stands on was purchased early in 1858, and ground was broken on the construction of the current building circa 1859, two years before the American Civil War erupted.[26] The Reverend John Lamb Prichard was the leading pastor of what was then called the Front Street Baptist Church. [27] Rev. Prichard travelled to "Richmond, Baltimore, Washington and other cities, examining models and consulting architects with a view of securing the best plan possible for what would thence be known as the First Baptist Church of Wilmington, North Carolina."[28] It is estimated that the reverend raised fifty to sixty thousand dollars for the construction of the church.[29] This must have been quite an accomplishment in 1860, particularly during the economic uncertainty leading up to the American Civil War. Rev. Prichard kept a diary including details about the construction of the new church. In reading his diary, one gets the impression that fundraising and political tensions were quite high on his list of concerns:

> November 1859 – "I am about to start once more to solicit aid to build a house for the Lord. O Lord, the gold and silver and the hearts of men are thine. Thou canst dispose them alright. Help me for Jesus' sake to succeed this day."

> (No Date) – "Wrote a piece for each of the daily papers in behalf of the new church enterprise. Saw several members in relation to subscriptions and secured $700.00 before 2 P.M."

> August 15, 1860 – "Late in the afternoon I walked again to the church. They have just commenced the vestibule wall. The

11

outer walls are up now to the height of the gallery, soon the gallery will be raised. O Lord, help us build and pay for this house and give it and ourselves to Thee forever."

November 15, 1860 (5 months prior to war) – "Went to the new church. It has grown some. But O, I feel so sad at the thought of the troublous times. Lord, shall the work cease? O, let it not, I pray thee!- I feel profoundly the importance of this crisis in political matters. O God, forsake us not. Give us men for the times."

December 21, 1860 – "Walked 'round the church. At work on west side, turning arches over the windows. – Heard cannon firing at the news of the secession of South Carolina."[30]

When I read the Rev. Prichard's eloquent words, I get the impression that there was something truly spiritual and magnificent happening in Wilmington at the corner of 5th and Market. I also notice that this celestial endeavor was tied to current events, both political and financial. Rev. Prichard never got to see the completion of this new church. War and Yellow Fever struck the inhabitants of Wilmington in the 1860s. The former delayed the construction of the church, and the latter claimed the life of Rev. Prichard on November 13, 1862.[31]

Fundraising wasn't a problem unique to Rev. Prichard's endeavor. Even in the earliest record of the Baptist community in the Wilmington area that I found, the collection of funds is mentioned. Meeting minutes from an 1808 Cape Fear Association meeting indicate that a newly constituted Baptist church was in fellowship in Wilmington. Peter Smyth, the reverend of this early church, reported 20 members and paid 10 shillings into the association treasury.[32] Between 1831 and 1833, the membership of this church had grown from 53 to 89.[33]

In 1864 (after Rev. Prichard died), Rev. W. M. Young, from Scotland, was hired full-time. Wartime financial fluctuations drove his salary from $6,000.00 in 1864 to $10,000.00 in 1865 and back down to $1500.00 in 1866, presumably due to the wartime inflation and eventual collapse of the Confederacy. The church that Rev. Prichard started was finished under the leadership of Rev. Young on May 1, 1870. Fundraising continued through the completion of the church, but

12

fundraising wasn't enough to complete the construction without loans. The church incurred a debt of at least $5,000.00 to finish the work.[34]

After the completion of the construction, finances remained tight. Resolutions on duties of members were set up. Time, money, and talents were expected to be donated or members would be declared guilty of covetousness and would be subject to church discipline.[35]

Between 1909 and 1915, the First Baptist Church paid off its debt.[36] Between the two world wars, the First Baptist Church was contributing to the Southern Baptist Convention's "Seventy-Five Million Campaign."[37] Fundraising also continued for the expansion of the First Baptist Church itself. A new Sunday School building was constructed at a cost of $71,000.00, and the church incurred debt again.[38]

Rev. Sankey Lee Blanton led the congregation of the First Baptist Church from 1936 to 1946. Rev. Blanton left the First Baptist Church in 1946 to assume the head position in the Department of Religion at Wake Forest University, which was then in Wake Forest, N.C.[39]

The First Baptist Church congregation continued to grow. By the 1980s, the church built an activities center at the corner of Independence Blvd. and Canterbury Rd. in Wilmington, about 3 miles from the main church building. In 1983, the congregation exceeded 1500 members, and it is recorded that 51,319 people participated in programs at the First Baptist Church activities center.[40] My brothers and I were three of those participants in the 1980s. We played basketball and baseball in a church league that used the First Baptist Church Activities center for games. The First Baptist Church has certainly made positive contributions to the Cape Fear community.

The quote leading this chapter refers to the First Baptist Church. In Helen Dobson's words, "Greater and more lasting are the intangible evidences of the heritage of this congregation than are the tangible proofs around us." There is certainly intangible evidence of the heritage of this congregation in the world today, but is there evidence of anything sour coming out of the church? When I read Helen Dobson's book, I only find the good things that the church has created.

.....

Reverend Jim Everette, Associate Pastor of the First Baptist Church, published another book, A Heritage of Hope – A History of

First Baptist Church, Wilmington, NC, 1808-2008. In the introduction to his book, Reverend Everette quotes Dr. James Wind's words:

> "The congregational historian's tasks are to ferret out all the plotlines contained within the life of a particular congregation, to select the important ones, and then to connect these filaments of story with those that stretch beyond it into the familial, denominational, social and religious histories."[41]

At the time of publication of Rev. Everette's book, my family had just been embroiled in a civil lawsuit against the First Baptist Church regarding Uncle Jimmy's estate, so before I read his book, I found myself concerned about whether this "congregational historian's" writings would be fair and balanced or would paint a picture of history that favors the Baptist Church. I wondered how he would decide which plotlines are important as he ferrets them out. I wondered if this would be a true history of the Wilmington community or if it would be a sanitized version. I was encouraged (but still skeptical) as I read on through his introduction to find:

> One may desire to paint the history of First Baptist Church as a masterpiece of the perfect "bride of Christ," but he must be honest with himself and his readers to tell the truth, even when it may expose his blemishes... [quoting Richard J. Evans]... "Good historians do not preselect the evidence according to their point of view."[42]

There is one recurring theme in his book. Fundraising challenges seem to be at the heart of every endeavor. The title Reverend Everette chose for his book matches the name given to the First Baptist Church's most ambitious fundraising campaign ever, "Heritage and Hope," which ultimately raised about 3 million dollars for the church's budget.[43]

As I continued to read Reverend Everette's plotlines, I was glad to see that the Reverend did not skip over what I believe to be one of Wilmington's most awful eras. In 1898, a horrific riot[4] rocked Wilmington. During Reconstruction, many black officials had entered

---

[4] Many references call this the Wilmington Race Riot. Better labels for the event may be Coup d'état, or race war.

government offices in Southern cities. Wilmington was no exception. One thing that set Wilmington apart from many southern cities at that time was that white people were in the minority. In 1898, white gangs in Wilmington started a campaign to run black officials out of town. Guns and torches were the tools the gangs used. Many black Wilmingtonians were killed.[44] I suspect many black Wilmingtonians were afraid for the lives of their friends and families.

A few months before the riot, Reverend Calvin S. Blackwell left the First Baptist Church in Elizabeth City, NC, to lead the First Baptist Church in Wilmington, NC.[45] The congregational historian, Reverend Everette, dutifully quotes this pastor's words, which were published in the November 13th 1898 Raleigh News and Observer:

> Sometimes special emergencies arise when evil-doers become the common enemy of the community. The community must put forth its hand and execute justice at first hands. There is purification by breezes, but sometimes nature sees fit to use a whirlwind. The violence of the whirlwind may destroy some things, but who will say it was not good as needed, that it was not ordered by God. The fact that a few negroes were shot was a mere incident. You can't make an omelet without breaking a few eggs. The primary purpose was not to kill but to educate.[46]

Reverend Everette further relays that it was reported by the News and Observer that Calvin Blackwell told members of First Baptist Church that "God and the white robed angels fought against the devil and his black robed angels and God prevailed and banished the black leader and his deceived ones and there was peace in heaven."[47]

This newspaper quote and a single paragraph are the extent of the negative press Reverend Blackwell receives in Reverend Everette's book. In his subsequent paragraph Reverend Everette continues, "Though he had his personal flaws and prejudices, Dr. Blackwell was said to have been an orator of the first rank." Through the next *two pages* Reverend Everette writes a miniature biography describing Reverend Blackwell as a seemingly admirable man. In these pages Reverend Everette tells us that Reverend Blackwell's "evangelical appeal was so effective that there were better than two hundred forty additions to the membership of First Baptist during his four years as pastor... His respect among the teenagers lead the congregation to begin a new ministry of Christian service training called Baptist Young People's Union during his pastorate. The objective of this ministry was to assist teenagers in discipleship as they grew in grace, learned how to lead others into a personal relationship with Jesus Christ, and... [Reverend Blackwell] proceeded to present what may be the boldest motion concerning finances ever brought before the congregation...." A record would be made public that would note which congregation members were pledging donations to the church and which members were not. It would also note which members were keeping up to date with their pledges.[48]

If I were a congregational historian writing a history of the First Baptist Church in Wilmington, I would have focused more on the fact that an outspoken racist was trusted by the congregation to educate their teenagers. I would have made the point clear that it was a very scary time in American history when human beings could be murdered, and the community's religious leadership would focus on fundraising instead of human dignity. Perhaps he was just trying to paint a complete picture of the man, but to me, violent racial segregation has more historical significance than the fact that the Reverend was a good fundraiser. If I were writing that chapter of history, I would have spent far more than a few paragraphs discussing how the Reverend analyzed destruction in the community. I probably would not have spent two pages discussing how he filled the coffers at the church. I did not write that chapter of history. Reverend James E. Everette, III did.

6. The First Baptist Church of Wilmington, NC, II

While I was disturbed at the focus of those pages in Reverend Everette's book that dealt with Reverend Blackwell, I commend Reverend Everette for recognizing the fallibility of his church throughout its past. He has obviously done vast research, and it must have been difficult for him to find imperfections in the history of his beloved "bride of Christ." In my research for this book, I was afraid of what I might find about my own ancestors. My great-grandfather, William Thomas Smith, was a member of First Baptist Church. I don't know when he moved to Wilmington, or when he joined that church, but he was born in 1873. He would have been about 25 years old during the Wilmington Race Riots. He could very well have been one of the 240 new members that joined during Reverend Blackwell's leadership of that church.[5] I was afraid that I might find out that my great-grandfather had participated in some of the atrocities that occurred in Wilmington. I was hopeful that I might find a historical record that showed that he stood up against or at least spoke out against those who committed atrocities. So far, I have found no such record. I imagine he, like most, was just an apolitical citizen trying to get through hard times.

The amount of research Reverend Everette must have done to write so much detail about the church is remarkable. Reverend Everette goes into fantastic detail about many events in the church's history. As an example, Reverend Everette notes the first deacon's meeting in 1957 led by Reverend Gregory in which he planned to lead the church through 18 months of intense evangelism across Wilmington, and he notes the need for parking spaces and room for Sunday school expansion.[49] Reverend Everette tells that Reverend Gregory was concerned that the growth of the church was causing the congregation to become impersonal for some. Reverend Everette includes detail about how Gregory replaced the church's annual picnic with a fish fry to spice things up a bit. Reverend Everette's ability to relate anecdotes

---

[5] I estimate that Dr. William T. Smith Sr. (Uncle Jimmy's father) joined the First Baptist Church circa 1917, 19 years after the riot.

in great detail is never more apparent than when he tells the reader who the most famous cooks in the church's Kitchen Committee were.[50]

As I read more of Reverend Everette's book, I perceived a change in the level of detail he used to describe his church's history. In a chapter entitled "A Heritage of Hope Into A New Millennium," Reverend Everette announces his arrival at the First Baptist Church in the third person. Everette goes onto the payroll of the First Baptist Church in the summer of 1990.

In 2003, the First Baptist Church had the chance to buy a large property that bordered the chapel. This was not just any neighboring property. This was the New Hanover County Law Enforcement Center, which covered about half of the block that the First Baptist Church inhabits. The property was also the home of seventy-eight parking spaces which, as Reverend Gregory noted, the church had been seeking since 1957.[51] In Jim Everette's words:

> In August of 2003, the church waded into a property expansion effort that became a public football that was fumbled back and forth between New Hanover County officials, private investors and trustees of First Baptist Church for two years. The New Hanover County Board of Commissioners accepted an offer from the church to purchase the building that formerly housed the New Hanover County Law Enforcement Center. The church offered to buy the fifty-nine thousand square foot building for one million dollars. Four members of the seven-member Board of Commissioners agreed to accept the offer. However, a few disgruntled members of the community created chaos by claiming the deteriorating building was worth much more money than what the church offered and that the building should be made available for public auction. After two years of wrangling over whether the church had a binding contract with the county, First Baptist Church – with the devoted lay leadership of Carlton Fisher, Berry Trice and Claude Arnold – became the official owners of the building on July 17, 2005.[52]

If you want to know who cooked at the First Baptist Church parties in the 1950s, you may find what you are looking for in Reverend Jim Everette's book. If you want to know the details of the church's million-dollar transaction that involved commercial real estate in the heart of downtown Wilmington, only about five years prior to the 2008 publication of his book, you should probably seek a different reference. Reverend Everette's text offers little information about that controversial purchase. Here are a few more details:

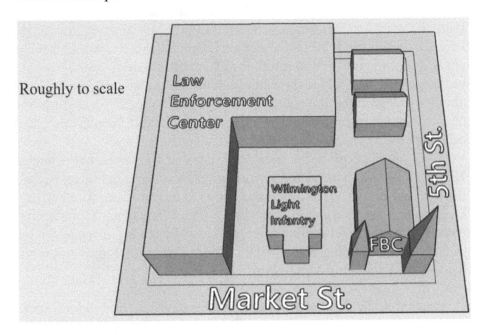

Real Estate was scarce on the block where the chapel sits. The church shared a city block with the Wilmington Light Infantry Building, two residential lots, and the New Hanover County Law Enforcement Center. In its quest for expansion, the congregation started to seek property outside that block. In 1958, Dr. Bertram Williams recommended that the church buy a property that was for sale across Market St. from the church.[53] The church purchased that residential property and used it as a Youth Activities Center. In 1963, with the help of a wealthy Wilmington resident, Hugh McRae, the church started plans to buy eight acres about 5 miles away from the chapel that would one day become the Activities Center.[54] That same year, one of the residential lots was sold to the church and converted to classrooms. The previous year, Reverend Gregory had been communicating with the owner, an aging Dr. Sidbury, about purchasing the house. Dr. Sidbury contracted with the church such that the church could pay for the house over three years. In the second year Dr. Sidbury, in declining health, agreed to defer all future payments if the house was given his

19

family name. According to Reverend Everette, Dr. Bertram Williams recalled Dr. Sidbury saying, "The annual payments are to be deferred until I inform you that I need the money."[55] The expansion of the First Baptist Church continued.

As early as 1989, the First Baptist Church was communicating with the City of Wilmington about buying The Wilmington Light Infantry building.[56] Before the First Baptist Church. would have a chance to buy the Wilmington Light Infantry building they would purchase the New Hanover County Law Enforcement Center.[57] At about the same time, the church trustees voted to legally transform the church into a non-profit corporation to "protect itself from the prospect of a lawsuit."[58]

Construction of the Law Enforcement Center had finished in 1979. The county completed the project with a "limited budget" of 4.3 million dollars.[59] By 2002, the New Hanover County Sherriff's Department had outgrown the nearly 131,408 square foot facility, including a two-level parking garage.[60] As the county discussed what to do with the building an editorial in the Wilmington Star News made the following comical suggestion:

> Widely scorned as an abomination of bricks, out of place and out of scale, the jail has been little but trouble since a fancy out-of-town architect inflicted it on quaintly historic us... The county could dump the monstrosity offshore as an artificial fishing reef. Or rent it for touristy boutiques. (Incarceration Mall?)
>
> But apparently the county would prefer to sell the place, assuming somebody is willing to shell out $6 million for a handyman's special equipped with 209 unburned beds in 28 cells and possessing no front door.[61]

The author of that editorial (and many others) had no love for the appearance of that building. Even though the property had a tax value of 10.4 million dollars, the county estimated that to tear down the building would cost 2-3 million[6].[62] The county arrived at a 6-million-dollar listing price. On the 14th of August 2003, the First Baptist

---

[6] Another estimate of the "book value" of the property was $3 million, still well above the church's $1 million dollar offer.

Church submitted a 1 million dollar bid to buy the 6-million-dollar property[63] and noted the possibility of using it to house the homeless.[64]

There were some problems with the Law Enforcement Center that the county commissioners and potential buyers would have to negotiate; the Law Enforcement Center shared a heating and cooling system with court houses on an adjacent block, was linked by underground tunnel to the courthouse allowing prisoners to move from the jail to the courthouse securely and housed the local 911 emergency center. A plan to move the 911 call center to Marketplace Mall had failed because the mall was not "a seismic-proof building."[65]

Amid what might be considered the largest real estate boom this country had experienced to date the First Baptist Church made an offer 5 million dollars below the 6 million dollar asking price. That offer did not include any assistance to replace the courthouse heating and cooling system and would have required New Hanover County to pay $4,000.00 per month to the church for the use of the 911 center.[66]

County Commissioner Julia Boseman responded, "My only problem is the $4000 rent." Boseman voted to make a counteroffer to the church which would accept all the terms except the $4,000.00 per month rent. The Chairman of the County Commissioners, Ted Davis, was disturbed that some of the Commissioners were willing to move ahead with their counteroffer before public opinion was heard. While some in the community supported the sale to the church, others felt that turning the facility into a homeless shelter would be "detrimental to downtown Wilmington." Chairman Davis and Commissioner Nancy Pritchett voted against making the counteroffer. Commissioner Boseman's vote to make the counteroffer won the majority.[67]

The Wilmington Star News reported that, under the county's bidding procedure, when the church accepted the counter offer a 10-day waiting period would begin to allow someone else to make an upset bid. The county would be required by law to accept an upset bid as long as it was at least 5% over the original bid.[68] Once subsequent offers were accepted, the 10-day clock would be reset, and bidding could continue. Theoretically, the price the New Hanover County taxpayers could have gotten for their Law Enforcement Center could have grown close to (or over) the 6-million-dollar listing price.

Developer Gene Merritt was informed of the 5% rule and made an offer of $1,050,000.00[7] for the property (and offered to maintain the 911 center free of charge for up to 2 years). This bid was exactly 5% over the First Baptist Church's offer. Mr. Merritt said that he was not bidding to spite the church (I wonder who suggested that he was), but he believed a more appropriate place for a homeless shelter could be found, and the property seemed like a "very attractive development possibility." He also believed that he could tear down the eyesore of a building for less than the 2-3 million dollars previously estimated.[69]

The Bidding continued after Gene Merritt's bid. Jim Quinn, a Wilmington City Councilman, announced Friday August 29, that he planned to submit a resolution to purchase the jail from the county. The City of Wilmington was looking for a new police headquarters at about the same time the county was planning to move theirs. Councilman Quinn called the Law Enforcement Center the "perfect location" for the new police headquarters. Councilman Jason Thompson agreed that the purchase was a good idea. There was some dissention among the city leadership. Councilwoman Laura Padgett thought that it would be best for the city if private developers "do what they do best and develop the site." Mayor Pro Tem Katherine Moore said that the Law Enforcement Center "…wouldn't work for a Law Enforcement Center."[70]

The Wilmington City Council eventually voted to make an offer with a 5 to 2 vote. Councilwoman Laura Padgett and Councilman Frank Conlon voted against it. While Councilman Quinn convinced the board that it was a good idea for the city to buy the property, he was unable to convince them that a jail was the best use for the property. Some wanted to use the property for city offices and to go ahead with a plan to build a police headquarters elsewhere. According to the Wilmington Star News Councilman Peterson "couldn't sit idly by and watch the county sell the Law Enforcement Center [to Gene Merritt] for $1 million. He said the property is worth much more than that."[71]

If the City of Wilmington made an offer, it could halt the bidding process. The municipality's bid would not be subject to the upset bid laws.[72] By early September, County Commissioner Julia Boseman had changed her mind about selling her constituents property for $1 million. She stated, "Now that it's been open up to bid, I think

---

[7] On August 30th, the Wilmington Star News reported that Merritt's offer was $1,052,000.00. This was not his original offer.

it's worth a little more than what we've been offered."[73] Her motion would not go through. The ball was already rolling.

It must have looked like the sale of the Law Enforcement Center to the City of Wilmington was inevitable, but the First Baptist Church had other ideas. When the church made the first offer, the ten-day clock started. Gene Merritt made his offer and believed he reset the clock. The City made its offer approximately 15 days after the church's original offer.[8] If Merritt's offer was valid, the City would have been well within the window of opportunity to make their upset bid, but the First Baptist Church found a different argument. Gene Merritt, relying on advice from the county finance director and a county attorney, did not know that the statute that governs these bids would require a bid to exceed the original by 10% of the first $1,000.00 plus 5% of the remainder. This would mean that to out-bid the First Baptist Church, Merritt would have had to bid $1,050,050.00.[74] Merritt's Million-plus was fifty dollars short. The First Baptist Church argued that, since more than ten days elapsed between the time their original offer was accepted and the first valid upset bid, they had a binding agreement with the county to purchase the property for 1 million dollars. Merritt believed that the church knew about this and quietly let the 10-day clock expire before bringing their argument to the county's attention.[75]

Law Enforcement Center Timeline (2003)[76]
Aug 14th: First Baptist Church bids $1,000,000.00
Aug 18th: New Hanover County makes counteroffer to church's bid
Aug 19th: Church accepts county's counteroffer
Aug 21st: Ad for upset bid published, with 10 days ending Aug. 30
Aug 28th: Developer Gene Merritt bids $1,050,000.00
Aug 31st: Ad for upset bid published, with 10 days ending Sep 9
Sept 2nd: City of Wilmington votes to make a bid
Sept 4th: First Baptist Church reveals Mr. Merritt's bid error.

The New Hanover County leadership had some egg on their faces. Commissioner Julia Boseman pointed out that the contract with the church was not signed yet, but the First Baptist Church maintained that they had a verbal agreement that was binding. Chairman Ted Davis and Commissioner Boseman both sent letters to Reverend Mike

---

[8] Other developers were said to be preparing offers.

23

Queen asking him to back off his claim and allow the bidding process to re-start more fairly. Boseman used the phrase, "What would Jesus do?" in her letter. In his letter, Davis urged the church to "do the right thing" and allow Mr. Merritt to submit a correct bid.[77] The First Baptist church would not relent.

On October 6, the County Commissioners voted 3 to 2 to overturn their decision to sell, claiming that the contract was not valid because nothing was signed.[78] As the legal battle rumbled on, other possible uses of the old Law Enforcement Center were considered. Local Judges wanted to keep the building for court-related functions.[79] Some suggested that it remain a jail and be used to house overflow from the new jail and/or be rented out to other counties in need of jail space.[80] Gene Merritt proposed an idea that might allow the church and the county to divide or share the property. He offered to do a six-month study, free of charge, to explore the possibility. The plan would have included more parking than was already present that would be free of charge to the congregation on nights and weekends. During the business day, the property would continue to generate revenue for the New Hanover County taxpayers. The Church's Board of Trustees published a news release stating they would not pursue legal action "at this point in time." Reverend Queen stated, "The fact is, we still believe we have a contract with the county."[81]

The matter was still unsettled as of July 2004. This was an election year for the county commissioners. Of the sitting Commissioners, three of five were against the sale of the Law Enforcement Center. One of the 3 was leaving office voluntarily. The other two would face eight challengers in the Republican primary. Two of those eight challengers, Bill Kopp and David Walters, believed the church had a valid contract with the county. Either one of these candidates would give the church the majority they needed among the commissioners. Bill Kopp was elected.

Early in 2005, the City of Wilmington started to consider using the county's Law Enforcement Center as the city police headquarters again. A local architect estimated that it would save Wilmington taxpayers up to 12-million dollars if they bought the Law Enforcement Center.[82] By mid-year, however, the First Baptist Church purchased it from the taxpayers for 1 million dollars.

Now recall Reverend Everette's description of those events:

24

...a few disgruntled members of the community created chaos by claiming the deteriorating building was worth much more money than what the church offered and that the building should be made available for public auction.[83]

Reverend Everette refers to people as "disgruntled members of the community" who "created chaos." I view them as good people working to serve their constituents. Mistakes were made, and I don't believe the New Hanover County taxpayers had a strong voice in the sale of their property. Some may chalk this up to the competency of the County Commissioners. I think it is naïve to ignore how influential a church can be in all matters, including financial and legal matters.

......

Some plotlines in Reverend Everette's book are described with greater detail than others. In his book, Reverend Everette also recalls a member of the congregation who left a large sum of money to the church:

Dr. Jimmy Smith died in February of 2005, at the age of ninety-eight. He had been a member of First Baptist Church for eighty-eight years; longer than anyone ever had. Dr. Smith executed a Last Will and Testament, in September of 2002, when he was ninety-five-years-old. First Baptist Church was named as the primary beneficiary of his estate because Dr. Smith's wife of better than 50 years, Iris, had died in December of 2001 and the couple's only child, James A. Smith, had died in April of 2002 leaving Dr. Smith as the lasting survivor of his immediate family. Extended family members of Dr. Smith challenged his will by filing a caveat contesting its validity on the grounds that Dr. Smith was incapable of executing a will at age ninety-seven because he was not of sound mind.[9] However, in April of 2006, after weeks of testimony from dozens of witnesses in a court of law, an agreement was made between First Baptist Church, family members of Dr. Smith and care givers of the elderly dentist. The portion of Dr. Smith's estate that was realized by

---

[9] Uncle Jimmy was actually 95 at the time he signed the will and the family's primary claim about the will was that it was procured by undue influence, not because Uncle Jimmy lacked competency.

25

the church was in excess of four million dollars after all property was sold and liquidated into cash. This is the largest gift ever made to First Baptist Church. The majority of the assets the church received from the estate were used toward the expansion and renovation of the Activities Center.[84]

The Dr. Jimmy Smith that Reverend Everette refers to is my Uncle Jimmy. It frustrates me to see Reverend Everette write "First Baptist Church was named as the primary beneficiary of his estate because Dr. Smith's wife of better than 50 years, Iris, had died in December of 2001 and the couple's only child, James A. Smith, had died in April of 2002 leaving Dr. Smith as the lasting survivor of his immediate family." This frustrates me for two reasons: 1) It does not acknowledge the bond I and other family members had with Uncle Jimmy throughout our lives, and 2) it presumes a dead man's reason for changing his will when he can't speak for himself.

I'm impressed with the great detail Reverend Everette writes about the church social events in his book. I am unimpressed, and offended, by the shallow depth and departure from facts when it comes to the Law Enforcement Center purchase and my uncle's estate. In his book Reverend Everette wrote, "Good historians do not preselect the evidence according to their point of view."[85] Is Reverend Everette a good historian?

I set out to write this book in order to research and better understand the painful facts about Uncle Jimmy's case. I have been pained for years by the published conclusion Reverend Everette provides in "A Heritage of Hope." The members of that church, and the rest of the world, deserve to know the truth.

7. Two Deaths and a Detective

Dr. James H. Smith went by a lot of different names. I've heard people call him Dr. Smith, and others call him Dr. Jimmy. His wife Iris called him Jimmy, and his son, James A. Smith, called him Dad. I have always known him as Uncle Jimmy, and this is how I will refer to him throughout the book.

Uncle Jimmy and his wife, Aunt Iris, lived in Wilmington. Their son lived about 8 miles away in Wrightsville Beach, N.C. By the year 2000, Uncle Jimmy was 93 years old, and Aunt Iris was not well. Uncle Jimmy needed help taking care of her as well as his other day-to-day affairs. His son, whom we knew as Little Jimmy, was very involved in his parents' care. By 2001, Aunt Iris needed around-the-clock care. Uncle Jimmy was fortunate enough to have the financial means to hire Certified Nursing Assistants (CNA) to care for Iris in his own home. His son, Little Jimmy, did the legwork for his father and hired CNAs from Herring Associates Inc. to care for his mother. Among the CNAs hired through Herring Associations Inc. for Aunt Iris was Patricia Jenkins (Pat).

Aunt Iris Died on December 5, 2001. Her graveside service was held at Oakdale Cemetery. Reverend Mike Queen, of the First Baptist Church, conducted the service. Little Jimmy sat next to his father during his mother's service. Uncle Jimmy's next closest living relatives were his nephews and nieces, including my father, his brothers, and their cousins. Those close relatives who could attend were seated around Uncle Jimmy and his son. Pat Jenkins and some of his other nurses were in attendance as well.

Although Pat Jenkins was hired to care for my Aunt Iris, after Iris' death, Pat stayed on and continued to assist Uncle Jimmy. She continued working directly for Uncle Jimmy with no institutional oversight from Herring. It is important to note that a CNA cannot legally use that title unless working under the supervision of a nursing agency or medical facility. CNAs assist individuals with healthcare needs, activities of daily life, and bedside care, including basic nursing procedures, under the supervision of a Registered Nurse or Licensed Practical Nurse. A CNA working in a hospital, or employed by an agency, is not even allowed to give so much as an enema without a doctor's order. If the CNA is employed directly by the family, and the family (or someone with power of attorney) makes the request for an enema, a physician's order may not be required.[86]

In January 2002, 41 days after Iris' death, Carroll Herring sent Iris' and Jimmy's son, James A. Smith (Little Jimmy), the following letter:

> Mr. James A. Smith
> [Address Deleted]
>
> Re: Smith Service Contract
>
> Dear Mr. Smith:
>
> It has come to my attention that Patricia Jenkins, employee of Herring Associates, Inc., has been hired to provide private duty nursing services for Dr. James H. Smith. Under the contract signed by yourself for services for Mrs. Iris Smith, there is a clause regulating any transaction of this type between a client and a company employee. I have included a copy of that particular contract and urge you to read its contents.
>
> Ms. Jenkins also has a signed contract between herself and Eldercare prohibiting her from working privately with a client with whom she was placed or associated with through her Eldercare employment.
>
> This action is a breach of both contracts and compensation is due our agency in one of two manners. If you wish to override the one year hire abstention clause, you may either pay the agency a 20% registry fee on the gross wages paid to that employee from the onset of her inappropriate employment with you, until such time as to the termination of that employment, or, you may pay a onetime finder's fee of $2700.00 to the agency for said employee.
>
> I am frankly disappointed in the manner of disregard in which you have treated our business contract. I can only hope that your future actions and the manner in which you resolve this

issue, will enable us to mend this rift in our business relationship.

If there is anything that you wish to discuss with me regarding this matter, please feel free to contact me at any of the above listed numbers. I welcome any input that would resolve this issue amicably.

Sincerely,
[signed]
Carroll N. Herring
Director of Services
CNH/cc[87]

Herring sent this letter to young Jim six weeks after he buried his mother. The letter is a straightforward assertion of contract rights; while it expresses Herring's disappointment that Little Jimmy (or Uncle Jimmy) had violated the contract, it did not address his mother's recent death, nor did it caution him about the possible perils of hiring an unqualified nursing assistant without oversight. A Medicare fraud investigator notes that in 100 percent of the cases he investigated, it was the person or people in charge of the elder's care that participated in the abuse.[88] In my opinion, oversight is sorely needed in this industry. You might expect that such oversight would be provided by an organization like Eldercare. No such concern was conveyed in the letter. Just the bottom line: $2700 to "mend this rift".

I assume that Herring Associates did not know the situation at Uncle Jimmy's house. Like the rest of us at that time, they probably could not have imagined what was going on inside Uncle Jimmy's home. But, professionals in the elder care industry should be better informed about pitfalls of unsupervised care than the rest of us. I would have hoped for more in her letter; they were simply attempting to enforce a contract.

.....

I know that Iris' death was crushing for her son. Little Jimmy had a bond with his mother that every son should wish for. Her death was not the only emotional struggle Little Jimmy faced in his life.

29

Little Jimmy was homosexual, and he kept much of his life secret from most people. He might have felt at times that he had no one to turn to. Up until December 5, 2001, he had the unconditional love of his mother. After December 5 that year, he was soaked in depression.

Little Jimmy loved dogs. He had a black Labrador Retriever named Caesar. When Caesar passed on, he adopted another elderly black lab from the local grocer in Wrightsville Beach after that owner died. He used to joke that this dog, named Pedro, had a trust fund. The dog was accustomed to eating butcher's scraps from his owner's grocery, and this trust fund, Little Jimmy joked, was entitlement to those scraps for life.

He owned a Chevrolet Corvette with a rainbow sticker on the bumper, but he often drove his father's Buick Roadmaster. This vehicle may not have fit his personality as well as the Corvette, but it was more practical for the day-to-day assistance he offered his parents, often driving them to their errands around town. Little Jimmy was a friend of mine. He came to my college graduation. He went to my brothers' weddings. We rented light single engine aircraft on several occasions and flew up and down the East and West Coasts. Little Jimmy was a Republican who eventually developed a cocaine habit. He was a complex person.

Uncle Jimmy loved his son. After his wife's December 2001 death, he wrote a new will leaving his entire estate to his son. That February will did not leave anything to his caregivers, and it did not leave anything to his church.[89]

I don't know how long Little Jimmy had been using illegal drugs. I don't believe he had been using them for long, but if he was, he was certainly able to clean himself up for family occasions. I never knew about his drug use until after his death. I suspect that after his mother's death his depression and drug use spiked, and he went into a downward spiral toward his grave.

On April 15, 2002, Little Jimmy was found dead in his house. A little over four months after his mother died, he died of an apparent heart attack. The heart attack was probably caused by cocaine. Some of my cousins and I cleaned up his house after his body was removed. There were signs of a wild party. Alcohol and drug paraphernalia were scattered throughout the house. It crushes me to think that in his last hours, my cousin Jim was surrounded by people that didn't care enough for him to dial 911 as he lay dying on the floor. Family members heard that a friend of Little Jimmy's stole the Buick Roadmaster and left.

The Wrightsville Beach Police Department notified Reverend Mike Queen, of the First Baptist Church, that Little Jimmy was dead. Mike Queen and his Associate, Reverend Jim Everette, went together to notify Uncle Jimmy of his son's death. Uncle Jimmy asked the Reverends to call his nephew, Billy Smith.[90] The next day, April 16, 2002, Uncle Jimmy made Billy Smith his power of attorney.[91] Billy, his brothers, and his cousins were Uncle Jimmy's closest living relatives. Billy lived a mile away from Uncle Jimmy and saw him the most frequently. At the time of his son's death, Uncle Jimmy trusted Billy to take care of his affairs. Billy spoke with Reverend Queen on the day he became Uncle Jimmy's power of attorney. In that discussion, Billy remembers Reverend Queen advising him that a member of the First Baptist congregation said Uncle Jimmy was withdrawing very large sums of money from his bank account on a regular basis. Reverend Queen said that he could not disclose the name of the person who reported it because of confidentiality. Queen also warned Billy that Pat Jenkins was said to have engaged in misconduct in client's homes before.[92]

Reverend Mike Queen conducted the funeral service for Little Jimmy. For the second time in a half year Uncle Jimmy was sitting on the front row of a funeral service for a member of his nuclear family. This time, something different had happened. Pat Jenkins sat right next to Uncle Jimmy during the service. Blood relatives felt as though they were being boxed out. Curiously, Pat's daughter, Theresa Mozingo, was there, too, and seated on Uncle Jimmy's other side. At the time, family members did not know who she was. I spoke to Theresa briefly at a reception held at my parent's house. She spoke highly of my Uncle Jimmy. I thought she must have visited him several times since her mother, Pat, had been hired to assist Uncle Jimmy. She also spoke to me about how she lived in Las Vegas, Nevada recently, but had since moved to Charlotte, North Carolina with a new husband, a Charlotte Police Officer, and was currently pursuing a business venture selling cellulite removal cream.

.....

31

Some things seemed out of the ordinary. In his capacity as power of attorney, Billy's involvement in Uncle Jimmy's financial life increased. Billy noticed that Uncle Jimmy's house was filthy.[93] He started to notice one odd thing after another going on in the household. One of Billy's first acts as power of attorney was to hire a private detective to investigate the situation.

8. The First Detective

Billy Smith hired Ken Johnson, a private detective and president of American Detective Services, Inc., from Zebulon, North Carolina, to investigate Uncle Jimmy's case. Mr. Johnson interviewed Pat Jenkins; her daughter, Theresa; and three other caregivers who were working in the home. As cover, he told them he was investigating oddities in Little Jimmy's death.

Billy informed Detective Johnson that he had discovered that the caretakers had been driving Uncle Jimmy to the bank almost every day it was open since December 2001. Each business day, $9,000.00 was withdrawn from his account. In a 54-page report, Detective Johnson summarized the findings of his investigation. He concluded:

> Initially this investigator interviewed Dr. James H Smith on April 25, 2002. Pursuant to that interviews were conducted with Carol S. Tucker, Linda Davis Phillips, Patricia C. Jenkins, Theresa Mozingo (daughter of Patricia Jenkins) and Betty Braye Parker. (See enclosed transcribed interviews.[Not included in their entirety in this book]) In this investigator's opinion based on these interviews I feel that there is a clear case of exploitation on the part of the four (4) caretakers employed by Dr. Smith and conspiracy to exploit Dr. Smith by these employees as well as the daughter of Patricia C. Jenkins, Theresa Mozingo. Refer to the General Statutes of NC 122C-66.
>
> The initial intent of this investigator was to first interview the caretakers involved in this matter and lock their statements in. Then conduct a follow-up investigation regarding the discrepancies in the interviews. This investigator understands that the matter has been turned over to the Wilmington Police Department for a follow-up investigation.[94]

.....

Excerpts of the detective's interviews:

Pat Jenkins

Based on the detective's transcript, Pat Jenkins appeared to speak freely to him. She went into the details of her responsibilities:

> ...On Monday and Tuesday I work 13 hours because Betty cannot stay she has to drive a school bus at the school. ... So I have to come in at 6 to make sure that Mr./Dr. Smith is not left alone. ... I was always cautious about that because I didn't want anyone to see her [Betty] leaving and come in behind her and break-in and kill him or hurt him. You know things happen. Dr. Smith had told me that the house across the road had been broke in twice. ... I said gee I've got to be careful here somebody could see Betty leave come in hide and kill him and leave before I could even get there. So I've got to be there on time. That's the way it was set-up when I went on this case. See I'm state operated. ... I was working for an agency when I went to work with Iris.[95]

At this point in the interview, Detective Johnson had only explained to Pat that he was investigating the death of young Jim, and he had only asked Pat about the people she worked with and her hours. Everything she said about Uncle Jimmy being killed by an intruder, she volunteered on her own. Detective Johnson then asked if she was a licensed nurse, to which she replied that she was a licensed CNA. Next, he asked her about tape that was on the deadbolt lock on the front door, and Pat replied:

> That's always been there and the reason they did was that Jimmy would not give anyone a key to his house. ... Jimmy was always concerned about the sterling and the silver and all. When I left with Mrs. Iris from the nursing home. Jimmy had a lot of Hypertension there and the nurses looked at him like he was crazy. I was really feared of [Young] Jim's attitude. He would say you all better get my mother straightened out before I kill her. He would holler and I would say oh my god this man has a problem. Somebody is going to get him straight here.

They did put Iris on Zoloft 'cause she had some dementia. I thought to myself this is ridiculous and I've nursed 21 years. I took her to therapy and all and they come out to see her. When Dr. Smith would leave she would cry, "Don't leave me, don't leave me." I would cry with her I felt so sorry for that woman. I thought they want her home and I'll work hard and get this woman home. And I did. … We got her home and Jimmy didn't come around a lot when I was there.[96]

The detective asks her about tape on a lock, and she replies with a tale about Little Jimmy. After Pat explained that "Jimmy didn't come around a lot," the detective noted that "Dr. Smith has been taking a lot of money out of the bank," and then he asked how often Little Jimmy came over.[97] The conversation continued as follows:

Pat Jenkins: He came over and the doctor did take large amounts out.

Ken Johnson: I want you to understand this I'm not trying to… I know he gave his caretakers gifts and whatever. I'm not trying to imply that there is anything wrong with that. I just want the facts in this matter. We are tracking down how much money went where so that we'll know basically how much money Brent Webber has embezzled.

Pat: Have you found him yet?

Ken: I think I have, yes.

Pat: Is he locked up?

Ken: Not yet. He will be.

Pat: I'm glad.

Ken: How often did Jimmy come over?

Pat: Jimmy came over once I got Iris home to her house. He came over approximately on Sunday and he came over on Monday sometimes. A lot of time if he missed Monday he would come over on Tuesday. The other two girls, three girls said he would come over

35

while they were there, and Linda went to his house frequently at night and had boiled shrimp. Jimmy didn't invite me over in the evenings to his house or during the day. He would go out with us to buy groceries at Sam's.[98]

In this section of the interview, Pat swung from her story about Little Jimmy "not coming around a lot" to stating that he came to visit his mother almost every day of the week, while also cooking meals for his father at his own home. One might view a son who was on the scene regularly as a more believable option to explain how $9000.00 a day disappears. The detective's interview continued:

Ken: Did you ever see Dr. Smith give Jimmy large quantities of money?

Pat: Yes, more than once.

Ken: Give me some examples.

Pat: He would say like on Tuesday before they found him dead. I was walking Dr. Smith down the steps and he come squealing around... he come in there with that Roadmaster like a bat out of heaven. He would holler where are you all going. I'd say we are going to walk around in the driveway. We had Dr. Smith in therapy for exercise. They got out of the car, him and Brent. I just started seeing this Brent show up around the last month. We had seen Brent once or twice during the summer last year.

Ken: He dropped out of sight and then reappeared, I understand.

Pat: Right, and I hadn't seen him at all until about a month ago. I asked Jimmy... He came around there one morning about 8:30 am banging on the door. I was back there putting clothes in the washer and dryer 'cause I take Dr. Smith to Sunday School on Sunday morning. I come back in and Dr. Smith said someone is banging at the back door. I looked up and Jimmy was up there just banging so I opened the door and said Jimmy what's wrong. He said I forget and left my key at home. This was twice he had said that in the last two (2) weeks, he rushed over and forget his key and left it at home. I said well I'm sorry I was back there putting clothes in the dryer. He come on in and said Dad,

36

do you need me to take you to Sam's today? Dr. Smith said no I don't think I'm going to go today. He said well do you need any food from the store. Dr. Smith said I need some milk. He looked in the refrigerator. I need some money daddy. He would ask him for money, he knew his daddy would just give him hands of money.

Ken: Where would he have the money? Would he have it one [sic] him?

Pat: No he had large amounts in fact Jimmy had mentioned to us that is was dangerous for my daddy to go to Family Dollar and it's dangerous for my daddy to go here. I said Jimmy you are correct and I'm very concerned about my life and someone knocking him over and hurting him and hurting me.

Ken: Right.

Pat: But this man Dr. Smith was determined to do it his way.

Ken: Who would take him to the bank? I believe it was Carol.

Pat: Carol took him to the bank on Wednesday, Thursday and Friday. He would have me to take him on Monday and Tuesday.

Ken: I believe he invested some stock for his caretakers.

Pat: I don't know.

Ken: Stock in Family dollar?

Pat: I don't know what he did. He talked about Family Dollar a lot to his nurses, about getting it and all, but as far as what they have done I don't know.

Ken: Were you familiar with the amount of money he was taking out of the bank?

Pat: Yes, I was familiar on the two (2) days that I was with him. He told me that he went to the bank every day and Jack [Jack Richardson:

Uncle Jimmy's banker] had told me at the bank that he was coming by every day.

Ken: Did you talk with Carol or Linda?

Pat: Personally about the money?

Ken: Yes.

Pat: Linda and I... Linda says I don't know what he's doing with all this money and I said I don't either. I said I know Jimmy is coming by when I'm here three (3) days. I don't know what he's doing when he is with you all. I don't have any idea. She said well I don't know what he's doing with it either.

Ken: Let's talk about any gifts he gave you. I know that he gave gifts to everybody. Tell me about any gifts that he gave you, any amounts of money or whatever.

Pat: (pause) Well occasionally he did give me a couple extra hundred dollars.

Ken: Like a tip on your pay.

Pat: He would give me say $600.00 a week cause I was the head nurse. He would say you are the head nurse and you are licensed and I feel like you ought to get paid a little more. He would give me an extra $300.00 or so.

Ken: I understand. Any larger sums? He did that with all of his nurses?

Pat: Yeah. $500.00 at a time or something like that occasionally.

Ken: How often did he do that? Did he do that at payday or just periodically?

Pat: Once or twice a week.

Ken: Okay. For what period of time, I'm trying to come up with...

Pat: We understand cause you want to know what Brent had.

Ken: Yeah.

Pat: I've been with Dr. Smith since Christmas and he was doing it before Iris passed. He gave me extra gas money.

Ken: Right.

Pat: I would save it.

Ken: Any other large sums, I know like Carol's situation he helped her buy a car. Any of those type gifts?

Pat: No sir I wish I had a new car.

Ken: I believe that your daughter, Theresa, frequented the house over there too. Dr. Smith said that he helped her with her house, to purchase her house.

Pat: He helped her... he said he wanted to help her with her house.

Ken: He said he adopted her, but not legally.

Pat: Yeah, he always said he never had a girl and he wanted to adopt her.

Ken: That's what he told me.

Pat: I told him it won't necessary, but you know. I talked with my marriage counselor concerning that. I have a counselor, a Presbyterian counselor I talk with. I've been seeing her for three years. I talked with her about all of this. She said that he was competent and if he wanted to spend his money he could do it any way he wanted to. When he offered to help my daughter I said well Dr. what is this for? He said I want to help you get a place to live.

Ken: How much money was involved in that?

Pat: About $4000.00.

Ken: $4000.00

Pat: Yes Sir.

Ken: OK.

Pat: That I know of.

Ken: I believe she is married to a gentleman...

Pat: Ten year police officer, Todd Mozingo, in Charlotte.

Ken: He's with the Charlotte Police Department?

Pat: Yes sir. He's been there ten years. He trains officers.

Ken: Do they live at [address deleted]?

Pat: Sir, I've been there, they just got married in December, and I've been to their house, his apartment one time. I'm sorry it's not an apartment it's a house that he bought, but they are not living there at this time.

Ken: They are not living there?

Pat: No sir.

Ken: Where are they living now?

Pat: They are living in his house that they had before they bought the house. They have to fix it up.

Ken: Have you got her number?

Pat: Her telephone number?

Ken: Yes.

Pat: Yes sir I do.

Ken: Could I get it please?

Pat: [number deleted]

Ken: How much money would you think he has given you over your employment?

Pat: Over my employment?

Ken: Over the total period of your employment as a gift.

Pat: At least $12,000.00.

Ken: And your daughter, all you know of is $4000.00?

Pat: All I know is I came from the wash room one day when she was there talking with him. She does his pedicures.

Ken: Right, he said she did his toenails.

Pat: She does his pedicures. She's licensed. He likes for her to do them. He'll ask when is Theresa, when is my daughter coming back to help do my toes. I tell him I'll talk with her and see when she can come. He handed her an envelope that's all I know. My daughter, I don't get into her business. Last year when I worked for the state agency, I made $14,000.00 last year. That's not counting what he had given me, I want you to understand that.

Ken: I understand. You worked with the state where?

Pat: I worked for Eldercare for 11 years.

Ken: You are not through an agency with him?

Pat: No sir, I'm not and they have tried to pull suit against the estate. I told Elder Associates when Little Jimmy died, she called me, she wanted to know which one died and I told her. She said well they owe me some money. They are contracted with you. She said yes I am I got him down as the other person. I said no ma'am you do not. She said the contract is at the house. I told her I had not seen it; I'll look at it. She said well blah, blah, blah so I got copies of all of it. And Dr. Smith is not on the contract I read over it well. Everybody is trying to get money out of this poor man and they shouldn't be doing that.[99]

Ken: Has Carol or Linda talked with you about the gifts that he gave them?

Pat: No, they never have much to say. I never worked with them before. I've worked with Betty on several cases 'cause we worked for an agency.

Ken: Has Betty talked with you about gifts?

Pat: No she hasn't. The Dr. talked with me about some things and I guess he told you.

Ken: What did he say?

Pat: He just said he gave Betty a couple of hundred. He gave her some money. [S]he seemed to be pretty competent.

Ken: How about Linda?

Pat: Linda. Yes?

Ken: What did he say about Linda?

Pat: He said that he had given her money.

Ken: Did he mention any particular amounts?

Pat: No sir.

Ken: How about Carol?

Pat: Carol, well he said he had give them all money.

Ken: Right. Do you know whether or not he helped your daughter?

Pat: He said they worked hard and they deserved it and he was going to give it to them.

Ken: Do you know whether or not he helped your daughter buy her car?

Pat: No sir.

Ken: Let me ask you this, I just want to get this straight. Were you formerly Patricia Reams on [address deleted].

Pat: Yes sir.

Ken: I believe you had some minor charges in '86, '87 and '90? Communicating a Threat, 1st degree trespassing, simple assault and simple assault? Were those domestic related?

Pat: They were discharged, correct?

Ken: Voluntarily dismissed.

Pat: Exactly.

Ken: Would you like to know why? I'm assuming it was a domestic thing.

Pat: It was domestic.

Ken: That's all I need to know.

Pat: That's why I still have my license, nursing license, it was a relationship I was in and I was breaking up with the guy cause he was a violent type person and I discovered that and got out of the

43

relationship. Being a loving caring nurse for many years as a child on up I got involved with the wrong person and I told him I wasn't going to see him any more and he swang and hit me.

Ken: Was that Jerry Hardy?

Pat: That was Jerry Hardy.

Ken: How about Charles Powell and Johnnie Reams?

Pat: Johnnie Reams was my husband for 12 years, he was an alcoholic and he took up with my mother. He dropped dead and I did not know my mother, she left me as a child and they got together.

Ken: How about Charles Powell?

Pat: Charles Powell I don't know Charles right off.

Ken: That was an assault, Charles Powell in New Hanover on 4-26-87.

Pat: I don't know Charles Powell, it don't come to my mind.

Ken: Okay.

Pat: Oh Charles Powell, excuse me. Yes, I'll tell you why. He took an assault charge on me and they dropped it. I was going to send him to the road for trying to make a pass at my daughter when she was 15. He was next door and he was married to Hass Ellington's daughter, Charlotte. They like racing and my daughter likes racing, her daddy did when I was married to him. We would go to races. He was kissing her and I caught him. I said something to Charlotte, your husband is kissing on my daughter and I'm not going to tolerate this kind of doing. She said you just don't want your daughter to have no friends. I said yes I do, but I'm not going to tolerate such. She is underage and you and your husband are married. I'm not going to tolerate this behavior. She said something to me and I said something back and she swang and hit me and I was fighting her and her husband came over after me. He run down there and took assault charges out on me.[100]

44

Ken: I see, that was a long time ago.

Pat: That was a while back.

Ken: Did Dr. Smith pay by check or cash or some of both?

Pat: He paid by cash. The first year I was with him I got paid by check through Eldercare.

Ken: Right.

Pat: I was the only one that got paid by cash. The other two got paid by check, that's the way Jimmy wanted it 'cause they were from the outside, except for the bonus.

Ken: He would pay the bonus in cash?

Pat: Yes.

Ken: Is your daughter available this morning? Do you think?

Pat: Well yes, unless she's out working. She travels on her job occasionally.

Ken: I was just wondering if it was a good time to call her.

Pat: I gave you her cell number didn't I?

Ken: You gave me...

Pat: That's her cell.

Ken: I ought to be able to get up with her, [number deleted]

Pat: Okay, just a minute and I'll give you their home phone number.

Ken: Okay.

Pat: I'm pretty much embarrassed with those assault warrants.

Ken: That's alright.

Pat: It's [number deleted].

Ken: Who do you have the least confidence in?

Pat: Carol. I like Carol as a person. I have had some trouble with Carol and her attitude. We are professional and like I said when this ordeal happened, when Jimmy died I called her and I said Carol look, Billy Smith has been made the Power of Attorney and she said he can have anybody he wants. I thought I can't believe she said this. I said Carol no, that's not the way it is it has to go to the next of kin. That's a standard, we know and are professional, that's a standard routine, there are not if's and's or but's about it. I hated that she said that that's all she was interested in was money.

Ken: Has Linda made any comments along that line?

Pat: No, Nothing bad. Neither one of them actually said anything it's just I don't feel that way.

Ken: Patricia, there is still going to be a lot of money unaccounted for that I'm going to have to account for. I'm going to give you my number.

Pat: Okay.

Ken: It's [number deleted]

Pat: Let me get a pen.

Ken: Okay.

Pat: 1-919...

Ken: [number deleted]. My name is Ken Johnson and I'm a retired Police Major with the Raleigh Police Department and I have a private detective business.

Pat: Yes sir, I was hoping to hear from somebody.

Ken: I understand that the people who work with Dr. Smith are a little skeptical about revealing how much money he gave them and how I know it's more than they have told me. The issue is we are going to have to account for that money, that doesn't mean anybody is in trouble. It just has to be accounted for because this with some other issues that I'm working on concerning his son and some of his associates and some of the things that were going on there and with withdrawing the amount of money he has. This is likely to be turned over to the District Attorney. If it gets into the court system it's going to be a mess. We don't want it to go there. That's not what we are interested in.

Pat: I understand.

Ken: These people are going to have to tell me the truth about the money that they have received and if it was for investment purposes or whatever. The entire truth or else it is going to be turned over to the District Attorney's office and then everybody's going to be subject to scrutiny and I don't want to do that and the family don't want to do that.

Pat: Do what you have to do.

Ken: That's true. If you think of anything else or any other funds he may have disbursed give me a call.

Pat: He gives to people out in the world, you know like where he goes.

Ken: Right, I understand the [that] he gives the Hooter's girls $200.00.

Pat: He goes there and gives them money. He went with Linda and Carol a couple of times.

Ken: I'm particularly interested in his caretakers at this point because I know that Carol nor Linda have been straight up with me. I don't know why they are doing this that way.

Pat: Right.

Ken: If you want to talk with me any further, give me a call.

Pat: I'll try to think about it, Jimmy came by a lot, but I don't know how much he got.[101]

During these pages of the interview, Johnson obtained at least seven key pieces of information. First, Pat confirmed that the caretakers, not any member of Uncle Jimmy's family, were the people taking him to the bank for daily withdrawals. Second, she confirmed that she was on a first-name basis with Uncle Jimmy's banker, Jack Richardson. Third, she called herself a "nurse" and noted that she was licensed, although she was not operating under the supervision of any higher-level provider in her capacity as a private caregiver to Uncle Jimmy. Fourth, she accused other caregivers of caring only about money, and she stated that she herself felt people should not be trying to get money out of "poor" Uncle Jimmy. Fifth, she acknowledged that Uncle Jimmy had been introduced to her daughter, and Uncle Jimmy was helping her daughter financially in significant ways. Sixth, she stated that she discussed the ethics of accepting gifts and of connecting her daughter with Uncle Jimmy with her own, personal, Presbyterian counselor. Finally, she shifted from stating that Young Jimmy did not come around a lot, at the beginning of the interview, to claiming that he "came by a lot," at the end of the interview. I believe this was an attempt to imply that Young Jim got the money, not the caregivers.

Before the end of Pat's first interview with detective Johnson, she made one last unsolicited comment:

> The thing of it is I'm glad the Dr. I [sic] didn't come between them [sic] I've always been advised by my agency not to come between anybody in the family. I was advised when I went on that job and I'm so glad I didn't come between them if I had I could have been killed. Every time Jimmy come around the Dr. looked at me and I said don't look at me, it's your son. You do what you think is best and he would give him a handful.[102]

The following day, Pat called the detective to correct some information she had given him. She notified him of $36,000.00 that she had in bank and brokerage accounts.[103]

48

All of her references to killing disturb me. In her phone interview with the detective she notes that it would have been "easier for Jimmy to have gotten rid of his mother quicker and his daddy without me."[104] In my decades with this close-knit family, no member has ever witnessed Little Jimmy demonstrating ill will for his parents or being driven by a desire to obtain money from his parents.

Theresa Mozingo (Pat Jenkins' Daughter)

Detective Johnson interviewed Pat's daughter, Theresa Mozingo. Of her relationship with Uncle Jimmy, Theresa said to detective Johnson:

> … you know I do his pedicure and manicure when I take care of him… I tried not to take it [money] from him I do it 'cause I love him. You know that. I just … I'm his little girl is what he calls me. I do feel partial to him. I said you don't need to give me nothing. I don't want it and if I don't take it he'll get mad at me… He gave me a couple of hundred dollars for doing that, which we [Theresa and her husband] used when we went to Vegas. I'm a licensed manicurist. I knew that he wanted me to do that for him.[105]

Some of the elderly people that I know and care about very much are four hours from my house. I certainly would want to assure that they were receiving proper footcare, but I'm not going to drive all that way to cut their toenails for them. Maybe that makes me cold.

Theresa had only known him for a few months when she made the following statements in response to detective Johnson's questions about the missing money:

> When we got back [from Las Vegas]… I don't know where to go from there. I do know that I was in total shock… I came down this past Thursday and we… the funeral [Young Jim's funeral] was on Friday. We got there and Carol was there and I was in total shock. I come by to see him and he said how's my little girl doing and we talked. I looked at him and I said how are you doing? Me and Todd [Theresa's Husband] were getting ready to leave and he said you go… he always gave

Todd a bottle of Scotch. He likes to give me some and we don't even drink. We don't drink period. He gets mad if we don't take his liquor so we took it. He said I got something for my little girl and I said what is that? I'm still thinking about Jimmy and what has happened. I'm still in shock. He handed me an envelope and I was like what is this? I have witnesses that were all there. There was Carol, my mom… I don't know if mom saw it, but I think Todd saw it… he did see it was there. He said here I want you to have this. I said what are you doing? He goes I want my little girl to have some money. I said what in the world, I don't need this. Well, I want you and Todd to have this for your house.[10] I said okay. He was having a fit at me. The first thing that came to my mind was the family is… something ain't right here. Something didn't seem right it didn't feel right when I went in the house. I took the money… It was $2,000.00. On the envelope, it said $9,000.00. You could tell where there had been some more money in there. There was $2,000.00 in there and that's what he gave us. Now… other than that he had to write me a check when I did his toenails the past week. He was so mad about it he said I can't believe I have to write a check for this. He always pays me in cash $100.00 to do it. He goes well I don't even want the check in fact I haven't cashed it 'cause I never wanted it. I told him thank you and I just let it go.[106]

It's refreshing to know that there are still people in the world who will drive four hours to clip an old man's toenails for free. I wonder if there are any nice old men in the Charlotte area whose toenails she cuts for free. I wonder if there are any nice old men who aren't rich whose toenails she cuts for free.

Detective Johnson's interview continued:

Ken Johnson: Are there any other monies that he has given you other than what you charge for the manicures and pedicures?

---

[10] Theresa's husband at the time, Todd Mozingo, would deny receiving any of Uncle Jimmy's money for a down-payment on a house in a future interview with another detective

50

Theresa Mozingo: I don't charge him anything.

Ken: I understand.

Theresa: I want you to know one thing right now is that man means a lot to me.

Ken: I understand:

Theresa: It's not from him giving me money for doing services for me.

Ken: right.

Theresa: He's 95 years old and let me tell you something he remembers more than I do.[107]

Theresa's interview with the detective occurred a day after her mother's. She volunteered information implying that she loved Uncle Jimmy. She also implied that his mind was sharp. If a 95-year-old man was to initiate a legal document, like the writing of a will, or adopting an adult daughter, it would be critical to show mental competence at the time of signing the document, particularly if the will had suspicious beneficiaries. As this interview progressed, Theresa admitted that she had accepted more monies than just the $2,000.00 she first admitted (which contradicts the $4000.00 that her mother, Pat, estimated Uncle Jimmy had given her for the house). The new number she admits to is "...less than $10,000.00."[108] Something was drawing Theresa from Charlotte to Uncle Jimmy's Wilmington home, and I don't think it was his toenails.

When detective Johnson asked Theresa if she visited Uncle Jimmy every weekend she said, "No sir. I've been there probably less than 10 times." She hadn't even seen the man ten times in her life and she was calling herself his daughter and taking home thousands of dollars of his money. In one of Theresa's last comments to the detective she stated:

I'm trying to think if there is any more. I'm sincerely trying to remember if there is any more money. I don't want to tell a lie that's for sure. I don't... If it comes up later I'll give you a call.[109]

If someone gave me thousands of dollars a few months ago, I would remember it.

Carol Tucker

Carol Tucker also admitted to accepting tips in the range from $40.00 to $200.00.[110] She admitted to accepting Family Dollar Stock. She also admitted that she accepted thousands of dollars to help pay for her car and that her daughter accepted a $4,000.00 gift from Uncle Jimmy.[111] When Detective Johnson asked Carol if Brent Webber had ever asked Uncle Jimmy for money, Carol Tucker replied, "Ask Pat that." To this, Johnson replied, "Okay, does she have any more authority than you do?" Carol paused and said, "I don't know. I think she might."[112]

Carol's answers resemble what Uncle Jimmy told the detective. Carol also seems remarkably aware of Uncle Jimmy's financial matters. Carol told the detective that Uncle Jimmy gave his son the house he was living in, and "50% of the farm and 50% of the beach house." When she was asked who owned the other half, she whispered, "Probably Pat."[113]

Linda Phillips

Linda Phillips declined to have her interview recorded. The detective's report notes that Linda admitted to accepting $500.00 in tips and said that Uncle Jimmy suggested that she buy Family Dollar Stock with it. She also accused "the family" of pushing Uncle Jimmy into writing a will.[114] I'm not sure who in the family would push my uncle into writing a will. My father and his cousins were the closest living relatives. His biological relatives would inherit the entire estate under North Carolina law if there was no will written. There would be little financial incentive for anyone in his family to rush him into writing a will.

52

Betty Parker

In her interview with Detective Johnson, Betty Parker admitted to accepting about $40.00 in tips.[115] There are a couple of things about Betty that are different than the other nursing assistants. For one, she is black. The other caretakers involved to this point are white. In a perfect world this would not matter, but nothing in this scenario suggests perfection. I don't believe Uncle Jimmy would have treated her differently because of the color of her skin, but others might have. I'll address the role that racial discrimination may have played in this case later. I haven't seen any evidence that Betty Parker engaged in any serious misconduct.

Uncle Jimmy

In his interview with detective Johnson, my Uncle Jimmy claimed to be giving $5,000.00 per month to his son, $500.00 at a time.[116] [That is small compared to nearly $200,000.00 per month bleeding out of the bank account.] Uncle Jimmy claimed to have given all his caretakers 100 shares each of Family Dollar Stock. Uncle Jimmy also claimed to have given Theresa Mozingo $15,000.00 for a down payment on her house. At one point, Uncle Jimmy said he gave Linda Phillips $72,000.00 to buy Family Dollar Stock and Bank of America stock. At another point in the interview he said he gave Linda "$70,000.00 and then enough to help them with their retirement." He claimed to have given Carol Tucker's daughter some money and doubled her payroll. He said he paid Betty Parker $350 per week and had given her tips as large as $300.00.

As for Pat Jenkins, Uncle Jimmy says, "I've given her the largest amount since she looks after everything in the house. I had been giving her $90,000.00 to put in her lockbox. I told her to take it to his banker [sic], [Uncle Jimmy's banker, Jack Richardson] and deposit it in her name and she did."[117]

The detective asked Uncle Jimmy about Pat Jenkins, "This is Patricia Jenkins. Her former name was Patricia Reams. These are criminal charges on her; communicating threats in 1990 in New Hanover, then a 1st degree trespassing charge in 1990. A simple assault and another simple assault. In her previous marriages when she was using the name Patricia Reams she lived at [address deleted] and she

53

was charged four (4) times with these criminal charges. I didn't know if you knew that and I wanted you to know that. Did you know that?

"No." Uncle Jimmy answered.[118]

I wonder what Eldercare knew about Pat Jenkins past before Pat was placed, by them, into Uncle Jimmy's home.

.....

While Billy Smith was the power of attorney for Uncle Jimmy, Jack Richardson told Billy that Uncle Jimmy had taken extraordinarily large quantities of money out of his account.[119] When asked where the money was going, Uncle Jimmy said, "I was putting it in my account."[120] The money certainly wasn't going *into* any of his accounts. There was much legal debate about Uncle Jimmy's mental competence in his later years. It is hard to tell how well Uncle Jimmy really understood his financial situation. The interviewees contradict one another. Was Uncle Jimmy unable to comprehend the facts at the time? Was someone lying?

These were Uncle Jimmy's final years. In December 2001, he lost his wife. Four months later, in April 2002, he lost his only child. On April 16th, 2002, he gave Billy Smith, his closest living relative, his power of attorney. Ten days later, Ken Johnson, hired by Billy, finished with his investigation.

Billy and his wife were on their way to a friend's house on Wrightsville Beach that evening when Detective Johnson called them and told them that Uncle Jimmy was in danger.[121] They turned their car around and went home to pack a bag. Billy and his wife carried their over-night bags to Uncle Jimmy's house. They planned to excuse the caretakers and sit with him through the night until they could find caretakers to replace them. Linda Phillips was on duty that night. They told her that her services weren't needed any more. She said she would leave but would like to go upstairs and say goodbye to Uncle Jimmy first. When they got upstairs she woke Uncle Jimmy and Billy noticed that he was startled, confused, and disoriented. They realized that they were not properly trained to handle eldercare in the event of an emergency, so they decided to leave Linda on duty and handle the situation as soon as possible.

.....

On April 30, Billy was surprised with notification that his designation as power of attorney was revoked. Otto Pridgen, a lawyer, and member of the First Baptist Church, drew up the paperwork to revoke Billy's power of attorney and assign himself those duties. The revocation and new power of attorney were notarized by Otto Pridgen's legal secretary, who was also his wife, Jan Pridgen.[122]

9. Looking for Help

April of 2002 was a whirlwind. Uncle Jimmy asked Billy Smith to accept his power of attorney the day after Reverend Mike Queen notified Billy of Little Jimmy's, death. Billy knew Uncle Jimmy was at an extremely depressing time in his life and would need a lot of help from friends and family. Billy invited Reverend Queen to talk about how to best care for Uncle Jimmy. Reverend Queen gave Billy a warning about Pat. Billy remembered Reverend Queen saying that Pat Jenkins "got into his (Uncle Jimmy's) head." Billy recalls Reverend Queen saying that Pat Jenkins had done something similar to another member of his congregation. Billy asked him who it was, but, as Billy recalls, Reverend Queen declined to tell due to confidentiality.[123] Billy hired detective Johnson, who confirmed his fears. It's difficult to criticize my father on his actions as power of attorney. He was afraid for his Uncle's health, and I don't think he could have foreseen the consequences of going into Uncle Jimmy's house at night without health care professionals at his side. However, if this scenario is considered a battle to be won or lost, the night Billy and his wife got a call from Detective Ken Johnson was the critical point. They had enough information at that point to know that action would be required to protect Uncle Jimmy, but what action? Already emotional about the events that had occurred up to this point, they rushed to Uncle Jimmy's side with the best intentions, but no real plan for how to care for him. This would give the caregivers time to react. Caregivers already knew that Billy was investigating missing money and other actions surrounding Uncle Jimmy. By the 30th of that month Otto Pridgen was the new power of attorney.

Billy and the rest of Uncle Jimmy's family did not know it yet, but by April 30th, they had become outsiders in Uncle Jimmy's life. Pat Jenkins would remain with Uncle Jimmy for the final years of his life, and the tragic drama would continue with the family frequently excluded from Uncle Jimmy's daily activities. There is evidence that suggests Otto Pridgen himself tried to remove Pat from the house at one time, but it seems to me that Pat had such a firm grasp on Uncle Jimmy's mind that no one could convince him he could live without her.[124]

Otto Pridgen didn't waste any time with his own efforts to manage Uncle Jimmy's affairs. Recall that Linda Phillips, a caregiver, told Detective Johnson that the family was pushing Uncle Jimmy to write a will. On May 1st, the day after Otto Pridgen gained the power of attorney, he took Uncle Jimmy to Dewey Bridger, M.D., for a Mini-Mental State exam.[125] Why might he need an exam? The primary individual beneficiaries of the suspicious will were to be the three white caregivers (Pat Jenkins, Carol Tucker, and Linda Phillips), and Otto Pridgen's wife, Jan.

Billy Smith and his family knew nothing of the mental exam at the time. Billy and the rest of his family were being kept in the dark on many issues related to Uncle Jimmy. Billy continued to look out for what he felt were Uncle Jimmy's best interests. Billy was not trying to hide anything from anyone. He shared information about Uncle Jimmy's situation with the ministers at the First Baptist Church. He went to Jack Richardson and David Whaley, Uncle Jimmy's banker and accountant. He shared his concerns with them to try to protect Uncle Jimmy financially. He went to a friend and attorney, Bob Johnson, to seek advice and asked some questions about the new lawyer on the scene, Otto K. Pridgen. Bob's office was only a few doors down from Otto Pridgen's on Market St. in Wilmington, just a few blocks from Otto's church, the First Baptist Church. Without knowing much about this new attorney, the family was temporarily comforted by the fact that an attorney would be helping Uncle Jimmy with his affairs.

Despite the temporary calm in the Smith family's relationship with Otto Pridgen, there were little dramas that kept popping up. Little Jimmy owned the house that his father was living in. When Little Jimmy died, he left that house to his first cousin's children. This included me, my two brothers, and 11 of our cousins.[11] The 14 of us became intertwined in the situation. We honored Uncle Jimmy's life estate in the house.

---

[11] Little Jimmy also made gifts in his will to Oakridge Military Academy, The Salvation Army, and one of his close friends. Little Jimmy also owned half of the family farm on the Cape Fear River. According to Little Jimmy's will, Uncle Jimmy would inherit this from his son, but in the event Uncle Jimmy died within 30 days of his son's death, that half of the farm would have gone to Billy's son Bill, one of Little Jimmy's 14 cousins/heirs.

Billy and his wife Jodie were determined to keep Uncle Jimmy's spirits up. Jodie knew how important it would be for him to maintain contact with his friends. She wrote the following letter to his Men's Sunday school class to thank them for a tray of food they sent to him for his son's funeral reception:

> May 30, 2002
> Dear Sunday School Class,
>   The sandwich tray you sent Uncle Jimmy was lovely and delicious. He shared it with us and it was especially enjoyed by the out of town family who travelled to the funeral.
>   In addition, the family appreciates all the visits you have made to Uncle Jimmy. It is not unusual for him to add "He's in my Sunday School Class" when he's telling us who has visited.
>   We know he needs all our support now and I thank you for yours.
>
> Sincerely,
>   Jodie
> For the Smith Family[126]

Billy and Jodie already felt certain that an alienation of Uncle Jimmy's lifelong affection for his family members was taking place and wanted to be sure that Uncle Jimmy was surrounded by friends and family as often as possible. Rumors started to fly around the small town about Uncle Jimmy's situation. Billy Smith wrote the following e-mail to family members and Bob Johnson's law office to summarize the family's perceptions on July 9, 2002:

> I probably had the best day today since LJ [Little Jimmy] died. I talked to Mike Queen first. I opened by lightly criticizing him for the lack of communication he has allowed me since I was fired [as power of attorney]. His answer was that he [Rev. Queen] was in the same boat with me. He said that the only time he has visited with UJ [Uncle Jimmy] since the blow-up[12] was awful. He said that UJ folded his arms, looked at him and said nothing. Being stonewalled by UJ is pretty bad, as much

---

[12] The "blow-up" happened when Billy and Rev. Queen suggested to Uncle Jimmy that he dismiss Pat and the other caretakers.

58

as he likes to talk. He said he stayed a few minutes, said a prayer, then left. He said that Jim Everette (associate pastor) was not on the shit list and still had a good relationship with UJ. We talked for about an hour. The bottom line is that Mike [Queen] is out of the loop and unable to contribute much to the cause. I asked about the farm being in a trust for the church [a rumor] and he said if it was he didn't know anything about it. He said he thought it had been put into a foundation of some kind at the bank.

I'm sure this was depressing for Billy and other family members to hear this rumor. This was his Grandfather's farm. He and his family had spent summers there and of course every Thanksgiving. Uncle Jimmy and Little Jimmy had both made multiple, specific statements to family members that they viewed the farm as a "family farm," consistent with statements of Uncle Jimmy's father, and they intended for the farm to stay in the Family. Back to Billy's e-mail:

I put in a call to David Whaley (accountant). He is out until tomorrow.
I then called Jack Richardson (banker) and asked if bank regulations and the law would allow him to talk to me about UJ. He laughed and said, "Yes, if you'll promise not to take me to court." He offered a wealth of information and I wished as I talked to him that I could have recorded everything he said for you all. I asked if the money was still flowing and he said that after he and I stopped it (on my watch [as power of attorney]) that UJ slipped in a couple of times to get the regular $9,000. When he learned of it he went to UJ's house and was able to convince him that to continue that would get UJ into big trouble as well as the girls. UJ conceded, went into the kitchen cabinet and retrieved $24,000 and gave it to Jack to put back into the bank.

Note that large sums of money were flowing out of Uncle Jimmy's bank account, even after his son died. Back to Billy's e-mail:

Speaking of the girls, he [Jack Richardson, the banker] said that Pat was the most capable and competent of all [I wonder who told him that] and that [in Richardson's perception] Linda Phillips was the trouble maker. I had heard that UJ gave one of them a check for two million dollars. Jack confirmed that Linda was the one. Linda took the check home, but Jan Pridgen learned of it and demanded that she give it back to her. She did and the check was destroyed. I asked him about the farm being in a foundation and his answer was "That will never happen." He said that he was hoping that they could muster enough cash at UJ's death to pay the death taxes so the farm could remain in the family. UJ told him that he sincerely wanted the farm to remain in the family. UJ told the same thing to Mike Queen. I told Jack that in my opinion UJ was not worth near the money he is reputed to be. Jack said, "Oh, yes he is!" I said I hope you know where it is. He said he did. He also said that UJ owned timber land in Pender County with a sizeable timber crop yet to be harvested. The last thing he said was that the most important thing for UJ to do was to reconcile with his family before he dies. I was impressed, that kind of talk coming from a banker. He said that UJ's greatest fear was that his family was going to sell his house out from under him. I was shocked that someone would stoop so low as to convince him of that.

I then went straight to UJ's house. Pat was still there. I told her that I wanted to talk to him and I wanted her to hear what I wanted to say. By then he was in the hall (he looked GREAT). I told him that I was upset to learn that he was fearful of us trying to kick him out of his own home. He said, "who in the goddam hell told you that!" I said it didn't matter who said it but I wanted him to hear it from me that his family would NEVER do any such. I told him that we would ALL sleep in the street before we would allow that. I told him that his family loved him and cared for him and that we would be there for him right to the end and that he would stay in that house until his dying day. I told him that although he had given up on me I would never give up on him. I think he understood the sincerity. As I left Pat told me that Linda had been terminated. I made no reply and tried to conceal my shock.

I then called Jan Pridgen. Jack Richardson had told me that she was getting the situation under control and had convinced the girls that they were employees, not heirs. She was very cordial and forthright with me. She has also terminated Betty Parker.[13] She said that they kept UJ stirred up, and the only one that could really keep him calm was Pat. I mentioned Pat's daughter, and she agreed that that was unethical and that she was out of the picture. The new sitters are coming in from a new agency. It looks like they might be getting into place what we tried to get into place three months ago. I hope so. Jan said that UJ seemed to be happier now than he had been.

I feel a lot better about the situation than I did yesterday.

Keep praying for him,

Dad/Billy[127]

I can only guess why Jack Richardson thought Pat was the most competent and Linda was the troublemaker. Family e-mails from that time-frame indicate that family members believed that Linda was not acting badly, but the family was highly suspicious of Pat.[128] I believe that Pat and the Pridgens started planting seeds in the banker's head to convince him that Pat was the most competent "head nurse" and that Linda was a troublemaker. Linda had recently accepted a check from Uncle Jimmy for two million dollars. I suspect that when Uncle Jimmy gave Linda a check for two million dollars it was a kick in the seat to Pat and the Pridgens, since the Pridgens took Linda's check away from her.[129] Perhaps they thought Uncle Jimmy was not competent enough at the time to decide whether he could give such a gift or not. Billy recalls Linda Phillips calling him and saying to him that she finally understood why he and Jodie showed up in the middle of the night to remove the nurses, and that she would never work with Pat Jenkins again.[130]

I think the Pridgens and Pat Jenkins must have made the decision to take Linda's two million dollar check away from her without consulting Uncle Jimmy, because Uncle Jimmy wouldn't have fired her right after giving her a 2-million-dollar check. This contributes to my belief that Uncle Jimmy was not calling the shots in his personal affairs.

---

[13] Betty Parker was one of the black caregivers. The family has seen little to no evidence that she participated in misconduct. She was not mentioned in the will, but her employment was terminated.

Emails between family members at the time capture the family's exhausting frustration. The family felt that something terrible was happening to Uncle Jimmy, but they didn't have enough information to take action. The family continually struggled with the decision to ask for help from Adult Protective Services.[131] They were cautioned that Adult Protective Services would check to see that Uncle Jimmy's health and physical needs were being taken care of but would have a limited ability to investigate anything under the surface. If Adult Protective Services were called in, the family feared they would find no smoking gun to prosecute, and that would add fuel to Pat Jenkins' fire as she tried to convince Uncle Jimmy that we were trying to have him declared incompetent and take his money. Hindsight shows plenty of evidence that might have been used against the caretakers, but the family was still on the outside and wouldn't learn many of the facts until after Uncle Jimmy's death.

In early April 2002, Uncle Jimmy trusted Billy with his personal affairs and gave him his power of attorney. By July that year, Billy was an outsider, and couldn't even piece together enough information from all available sources to determine the truth about his Uncle's health and well-being.

…..

The May 1st mental exam that Dr. Bridger administered implied competence. I don't know if Dr. Bridger didn't have confidence in the exam he issued, or if he guessed there was a storm brewing that would require more than a Mini-Mental state exam, but he referred Uncle Jimmy to Dr. Christy Jones with Coastal Neuropsychological Services for a more thorough examination. Uncle Jimmy had appointments with Dr. Jones' practice on July 29th and August 13th with a follow up on September 4th.[132] All of this was unknown to Billy and the rest of the Smith family. On September 25th, Jan Pridgen requested that Billy write an obituary for Uncle Jimmy.[133] Billy thought it was odd, to say the least, to write an obituary for a man who was still alive, no matter what his physical condition. Billy smelled a rat. He thought that Otto and Jan Pridgen might take the obituary to Uncle Jimmy and tell Uncle Jimmy that Billy was planning for his death. Billy declined to assist them with their request.[134] The next day, September 26th, a new will was signed by Uncle Jimmy.[135] The existence of this new will remained unknown to family members.

Years later the family would see evidence suggesting that the Pridgens, Attorney Bob O'Quinn, Jack Richardson, and Reverend Everette all had some involvement in his estate planning and/or the drafting of a new will. No one from the family was asked to contribute anything to this effort, nor were family members informed that the drafting was underway. During the trial evidence surfaced that Uncle Jimmy may have started losing his mental faculties, and possibly couldn't remember family members names at the time this will was drafted. [136] Could there be a connection between Uncle Jimmy forgetting family members names and the Pridgen's request for Billy to write an obituary? Consider these parts of the new will:

For an estate valued at approximately 5 million, the new will:
Paid all debts out of the principal of the estate
Paid all taxes out of the residuary of the estate
Gave the ~650 acre farm on the Cape Fear River to the First Baptist Church
(With a provision for Billy's oldest son, Bill, to buy – not receive as a beneficiary – only the house itself and 5 acres)
Gave ~80 acres in Brunswick County to the First Baptist Church
Gave Billy Smith (Nephew) $1,000.00
Gave Jack Smith (Nephew (one of Billy's brothers)) $1,000.00
Gave Lisa Shelhart(Grandniece) $5,000.00
Gave Erin Shelhart (Grandniece) $5,000.00
Gave Linda Shelhart (Niece) $1,000.00

This new will left out close relatives. This gave 100% of Uncle Jimmy's real property to the First Baptist Church. Most of the non-real property assets would therefore pass in the residuary of the will.

This makes the remaining changes to the original will more striking-
"to my faithful care givers…":
Gave Jan Pridgen (Otto's wife) 10% of the residual estate
Gave Pat Jenkins 10% of the residual estate
Gave Carol Tucker 10% of the residual estate
Gave Linda Phillips (whose employment was terminated two months prior to writing will) 10% of the residual estate
Gave the First Baptist Church the remaining 60% of the residual estate

Directed that $100,000.00 of the Church's share be placed in a fund established at the First Baptist Church for the benefit of Roy Piner (handicapped man)

Appoints Otto Pridgen as executor.[137]

There are some quirky things about this will. Not just the obvious things I have addressed already. If you weren't a member of our family, you would miss one of the major quirks about this will. A family tree will help explain:

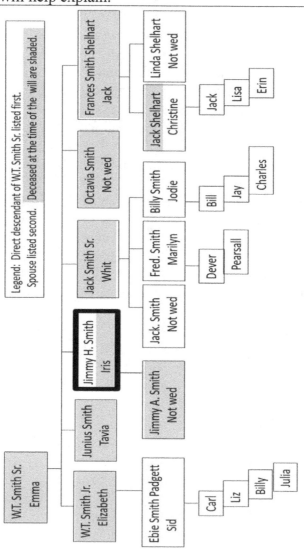

Those names that are shaded here predeceased the signing of the will. Notice that one of Billy's brothers (Fred) was left out of the will. Two of Uncle Jimmy's sister Frances' grandchildren were remembered (Lisa and Erin), but a third (Jack) was not. Uncle Jimmy's brother Bill's family (W.T. Smith Jr.) was ignored completely. Did Uncle Jimmy intentionally leave out Ebie, Fred, and Jack? What could explain this?

I believe that Uncle Jimmy did not write this will. I believe that Otto and members of the church leadership wrote the will, and they only included the family members that they knew about. If I'm right, they only had 5 months to write the will from the time that Otto and Jan entered the scene to the time that the will was signed. Fred wouldn't have visited in this time frame. He lived in Georgia and was tending to his terminally-ill wife. Ebie wouldn't have visited in that time frame either. She was tending to her husband who had recently suffered a stroke. Lisa and Erin's brother Jack was a Rhode Island State Trooper with three kids. He comes to town about every other Thanksgiving but didn't visit in these five months. His sisters did visit, and they were beneficiaries of the new will.

It is also quirky that only 5 acres of a 600+ acre farm were offered to a family member, particularly since the house and 5 acres would be in the middle of the land. That would require an awkward easement through the remaining land. Uncle Jimmy had known this land his whole life, and I don't think this fact would have escaped him when his mind was strong.

It was no surprise to see my brother Bill's name in the will in relation to the farmhouse. I had heard that Uncle Jimmy thought that Bill, a cardiologist, would be the only family member who could afford to pay property taxes on the farm. This specific reference to Bill also consistent with Little Jimmy's last will. The taxes on a 600+ acre farm might have put a burden on some of us, but any one of us could have afforded to pay taxes on 5 acres and a ~200-year-old farmhouse in the Columbus county low lands next to a paper mill on the Cape Fear River. Something doesn't add up here.

There is some more unusual verbiage in that paragraph of the will: "The purchase price William T. Smith, IV [Bill] is to pay First Baptist Church for this property shall be determined by an appraisal conducted by a licensed real estate appraiser selected by my personal representative."[138] Who is "my personal representative" and when was

65

Uncle Jimmy going to choose this representative? Was he going to choose the appraiser when the appraisal was needed... from the grave?

In Uncle Jimmy's previous will, he left everything to his son. After any debts were paid, the previous will held: "I give and bequeath all of the residue and remainder of my property and estate, whether real or personal and whosoever situate, including all property which I may acquire or to which I may become entitled after the execution of this Will, to my son, JAMES A. SMITH, absolutely, in fee simple, forever."[139] Why would he write, "to my faithful care givers" in his new will? The first of these two wills was signed in February 2002. Was Uncle Jimmy taking romantic poetry classes in the seven months between the time that will was signed and the new will was signed? This new will, of course, gave approximately a half-million dollars each to three "faithful care givers" and one legal secretary who he had known for approximately five months. People who know Uncle Jimmy well are highly suspicious that this is not his voice.

I'll lay out a timeline for clarity:

Apr 30   Otto Pridgen instated as power of attorney.
May 1   Mini-Mental state exam with Dr. Bridger... referred to Dr. Christy Jones.
Aug 13   Dr. Christy L. Jones Ph.D. 1st evaluation.
Aug 15   Dr. Christy L. Jones Ph.D. 2nd evaluation.
Sep 4   Coastal Neuropsychological Services follow up.
Sep 25   Letter from Billy to Otto stating that he'll write obituary another time.
Sep 26   New will signed.

In the summer of 2002, Billy and the rest of the family were in the dark about Uncle Jimmy's affairs. They didn't know about the psychological evaluations. They didn't know a will was being written. They didn't know who to turn to for help, but still believed that the leadership of the First Baptist Church would help. They believed head pastor, Reverend Queen was "on the outs" with Uncle Jimmy, but Reverend Everette was still on the inside. The family didn't know that Reverend Everette was directly involved in discussion about the will, prior to its drafting. On 6 August 2002, about 7 weeks before the will was written, Billy sent this e-mail to his son Bill and Reverend Everette:

Bill,
It occurred to me today that we should be including Mike Queen and Jim Everette in the correspondence of this most awful situation in our family. Jim's e-mail address is [address deleted]. Please include him in future mailings. He will share all with Mike [Reverend Mike Queen].
Dad[140]

10. Timber

A lot of e-mails flowed throughout the family during these years. Reverend Jim Everette was carbon copied on many. There were common themes. The family couldn't decide whether they should call in Adult Protective Services or not. The consensus was always that the risk didn't outweigh the possible benefits since, at that time, the care takers (as far as the family knew) were keeping Uncle Jimmy in good health, and investigators were unlikely to find a smoking gun. Other e-mails noted how Uncle Jimmy looked. Some days he looked good, and other days he looked unwell.

In August of 2002 a volley of e-mails started to circulate around the family with a new subject. Billy found out that the trees on Uncle Jimmy's farmland were being clear cut by a man named John Newton. He had reason to believe that the harvest was being sold far below market value. Billy reached out to an acquaintance in the timber business, Buddy Tate, who agreed that Uncle Jimmy could have gotten more for the timber. Billy sought advice from Bob Johnson writing "Buddy says that there is little we can do short of going to court. I asked him about stopping the cutting long enough to have it surveyed and he said that would be hard to do, and if they suspected that we were trying to do that, they would put extra logging crews in to speed up the harvest. I might add that O.K. never called yesterday (as he said he would) to give me John Newton's number. I'm sure he has warned Newton of the family's concern. As far as I am concerned, O.K. Pridgen has put his cards on the table. I will let him know my sentiments the next time I see him face to face.[141]

Bob Johnson did some research for Billy and estimated that Uncle Jimmy was being paid for approximately 3,000bf per acre. Buddy estimated that most of the acreage being cut should produce 10,000bf per acre and some as much as 20,000bf. Bob noted, "If after hearing this he [Otto] does not take action we need to reconsider incompetency proceedings."

Otto Pridgen did take these concerns to John Newton. Mr. Newton drafted a letter dated August 6th describing the low density of the trees per acre on Uncle Jimmy's land. He also noted that the trees there were smaller than the average land in the area. He noted that a lot of the trees had reached their "growth climax" and were "producing no positive growth. This simply means that the trees there are rotting on the inside and are starting to die." In that same letter, a response to a request to consider delaying the harvest until a later time he noted, "The timber on this tract as a whole is mature and overdue to be harvested."[142] I'm no timberman, but I can't understand why these "mature" trees that are ripe for harvest are smaller than the other trees in the area. One way to determine the value of the trees would have been to get a second estimate. Otto Pridgen didn't. Uncle Jimmy might not have been aware of this.

Another e-mail from Billy to Bob Johnson on August 8th highlights the urgency of the situation:

> I'm sure Buddy Tate realizes the urgency of the matter. The chain saws are running hard and fast. I hope they can set up a meeting asap. Also remember that Pridgen told you and me that he knew nothing about timber, and that Richardson and Whaley were driving the timber sale. They have both denied any such. Thank you for everything,
> Billy[143]

Why wouldn't Otto Pridgen's story align with the banker's and the accountant's? Billy and his family had no knowledge of the will at that time. Billy was still trying to ensure that Uncle Jimmy's affairs were being handled the way Uncle Jimmy would want. Billy made one last attempt to stop the harvest and on August 9th he wrote to Bob Johnson to tell him Buddy Tate spoke with John Newton face to face and "put the fear of God" in him. Billy told Bob to expect a visit from John Newton.[144]

Otto Pridgen defended John Newton in a letter on August 9th.[145] The timber harvest went forward to completion. After Timber is harvested it is usually replanted. In addition to his timber land Uncle Jimmy had a plowed field, an irrigated garden and a field that the family called "the dove field" since that is where they would hunt dove with Uncle Jimmy. Uncle Jimmy would lease the plowed field to a neighboring farmer and close friend named Larry Fowler. Larry is a country boy. He has worked the land his entire life. He lived next to Uncle Jimmy's farm and worked at the paper mill on the other side of the land. He farmed and hunted Uncle Jimmy's land and knew it as well or better than Uncle Jimmy, himself. He had sold timber in his time and knew quite a bit about its value.

Larry would look after Uncle Jimmy's land on a day to day basis since Uncle Jimmy lived 40 minutes away in Wilmington. He would notify him of farm house break-ins, run off vandals and trespassers, and remove fallen trees from access roads and more. Larry was Uncle Jimmy's single point of contact for anyone that wanted to hunt on his land. For safety purposes, Uncle Jimmy required anyone who wanted to hunt on his land to check in with Larry. Larry never asked for much in return. A friendship like the one between Larry and Uncle Jimmy is worth its weight in gold. Larry must have felt it was a slap in the face when he found out that Otto had ordered the entire tract, including the plowed field, the garden and the dove field to be planted with trees.

Legally, it could be more than just a slap in the face. A general power of attorney gives authority to act on behalf of someone in legal matters. The person with the power is required to act as the client would, not to act as he or she would in their own affairs. In other words, if you gave me a power of attorney to spend your money on a red convertible, I can't go out and buy you a green pick-up truck. I don't know if Uncle Jimmy wanted the timber harvested, but after that occurred Billy spoke to him personally about the planting of trees. Uncle Jimmy told Billy that he wanted the plowed field and the garden to remain in the current state. Billy wrote a letter concerning this to Otto on October 1st, to stop the planting outside the timber tract.[146]

In another example of abuse of power of attorney, Larry Fowler spoke to Uncle Jimmy early in 2003 and agreed on a price for renting the plowed field and hunting rights. Larry notified Otto of the agreement and Otto said, "I'll think about that for a few days and let you know."[147]

Daily events slowly eroded the family's trust and confidence in the Pridgen law team. Billy and other family members started taking detailed notes about everything they saw that struck them as odd or unethical. Larry Fowler called Billy one day to tell him that he had been checking on the farm house and noticed that it had been broken into. The alarm had been pulled off the wall and the wires were snipped. Earlier in 2003 Billy arranged for the alarm to send a distress signal via phone line to the police and Larry Fowler in the event of a break in. After Billy took the phone call from Larry, he called Jan Pridgen to see why the alarm didn't call anyone. In his personal notes from March 4, 2004 Billy remarks:

> ...I told her [Jan Pridgen] that there was no phone service, and her reply was that they were paying the phone bill every month. She acted like the alarm having been disconnected from Larry's house was news to her. (The alarm [now] only gives an audible alarm, but goes to no one's telephone at this time.) [What good is that to a house isolated in 600 acres?] She said that Dr. Smith was probably the one to terminate the alarm service to Larry's house. They always attribute the decision to him when their actions are questioned. They also credit his input when they make decisions. A recent example of this is planting the dove field in pines. I can almost assure you that Uncle Jimmy will nod in agreement to about anything you ask him.[148]

Note that: Uncle Jimmy would "nod in agreement to about anything you ask." Back to Billy's memoirs:

> When I got there [to the farm], the first thing I noticed was that the gate was closed, but there was no lock on it. Larry met me at the house, and when we went in, we realized that the alarm had not been torn off the wall, but it appeared to have been carefully cut very cleanly with snips. I saw no apparent theft or vandalism in the house. The lights were on in the hall, which indicated to me that whoever did it was there at night. I also found the smokehouse door open. I did not go upstairs, but Larry did.
>
> I went to the hardware store and bought a new lock for the gate and also hasps and padlocks for the back-hall door, the dining room door and the kitchen door. I installed all of these on the exterior.
>
> This is the strange part. Kip Pridgen [Otto's son] was up there the day before Larry found the trouble. The reason we know he was there was that he got stuck and called Larry to pull him out. Kip was actually on Larry's Aunt's land when he got stuck. After they pulled him out, he said nothing of the problems at the house. Larry called Kip while I was there to tell him about the break-in and ask if he knew anything about it. Kip's reply

71

was that the gate was open and he just assumed that one of us was there. He also told Larry that he did not go in the general vicinity of the house before getting stuck. After getting pulled out, Kip went by the house and saw lights on and thought someone was staying there so he did not stop. He said he meant to tell his father all of this, but it slipped his mind.

It would be OK with me if Pridgen wanted his son to go by the place to do a security check, but in my opinion, this is proof that security is not Kip's reason for being there.[149]

Billy continued to try to press the Pridgen's to care for that farm and farmhouse the way he thought Uncle Jimmy would have when he was still capable. Uncle Jimmy would not have wanted the ~200-year-old farm house that he inherited from his father to fall into disrepair. Billy continued his memoir describing a conversation with Otto Pridgen:

I then brought up the condition of the house, saying that it was rapidly falling into a state of disrepair. I reminded him that it was over two hundred years old and a piece of history, and that I would hate to be the one responsible for allowing it to go to ruin. He smiled and nodded in agreement but did not voice anything. We then discussed the roof and also the front porch columns which appear to be rotten to the point of possible collapse. He said that he would look it over also. We also mentioned to him that Uncle Jimmy had instructed Little Jimmy to put a new roof on the house, so the man was/is aware that it is in need of a new roof. My fear is that if Pridgen makes any repairs they will be slip-shod and half-assed.[150]

Repairs were not made while Otto Pridgen held Uncle Jimmy's power of attorney. Uncle Jimmy would not have wanted this historical farm house, for which he had been the custodian for the last half-century, to fall into disrepair. He was certainly financially capable of repairing the house. I don't think he was mentally capable of making those decisions at that time.

On June 14th, 2004 Otto wrote Larry Fowler a letter and stated, "...I do not feel comfortable in leasing hunting rights on Dr. Smith's farm for the 2004-05 hunting season due to the fact that Dr. Smith is

72

ninety-seven (97) years of age."[151] I don't see the connection between a birthday and hunting rights. To me it just seems like Otto Pridgen was taking over Uncle Jimmy's decision making.

11. Nurse or Not?

In late November, 2002, after the family Thanksgiving celebration, Billy's son Bill was visiting Uncle Jimmy with his wife and 19-month-old daughter. Uncle Jimmy asked Bill to "call him later". Pat Jenkins became "hysterical" and shouted, "You can't do business here!"[152] Pat called the police, reporting Bill for talking to his Uncle Jimmy and threatened to get a restraining order against him. I haven't seen any evidence suggesting that Bill has ever done anything offensive to Pat or Uncle Jimmy. When the police arrived, Uncle Jimmy told the officer to arrest "'the woman in the white dress' (referring to Pat)."[153] Bill's feeling that Pat was not an appropriate caregiver compelled him to write a letter to Otto detailing his concerns. In his letter, he noted Pat's behavior, and his opinion that she was isolating Uncle Jimmy from his friends and family as well as instructions she claims she got from Otto himself to keep Uncle Jimmy from participating in family functions.[154] I wonder if Uncle Jimmy had such a good time at the annual Thanksgiving party with his family that year that Otto and Pat thought they might be losing control of him. Bill wrote another letter to O.K. Pridgen noting how badly he felt the family was being treated and expressing details about his perceptions of her misconduct.[155]

Uncle Jimmy was invited to a New Year's Day party at Billy's house that year. Otto wrote a letter on December 30th to Billy notifying him that Uncle Jimmy would be accompanied by Pat and Carol at the party. In Otto's letter, he writes, "I hope the family can put personalities aside and appreciate the good job these ladies are doing taking care of Dr. Smith." [156]

To this letter Billy replied:

> We will be delighted to have Pat accompany Dr. Smith to our home on New Year's Day. We certainly would not want to jeopardize the degree of care that he requires by limiting his staff.
> I only hope that this does not make Carol feel that her competence is being challenged or questioned.
> [signed][157]

Bill wrote another letter to Otto on December 2nd notifying him that he had called and reported Pat to the North Carolina Board of

Nursing. He notified Otto that "legal recourse for a wronged individual is severely hampered if a nurse aid is hired as an individual contractor and not through an agency or institution."[158]

Bill's letter to the North Carolina Board of Nursing included signed statements by himself (a Cardiologist) and his wife (a Registered Nurse) stating that Pat is using the title "nurse". He also included applicable pieces of detective Johnson's transcript in which she claims the title "nurse".

On February 11th, 2003, the following letter was sent to Pat Jenkins from the North Carolina Board of Nursing:

Dear Ms. Jenkins:

The North Carolina Board of Nursing has received information that indicates you have identified yourself as a "head nurse" while you were delivering care to James H. Smith on numerous occasions. We understand you have referred to yourself as both "nurse" as well as "head nurse". Our records indicate that you do not now hold nor have you ever held a license to practice nursing in North Carolina. Therefore, **YOU MUST IMMEDIATELY CEASE AND DESIST FROM IDENTIFYING YOUSELF AS A LICENSED NURSE.**

North Carolina Statute 90-171.43 states:

No person shall practice or offer to practice as, or use any card, title or abbreviation to indicate that such person is a registered nurse or licensed practical nurse unless that person is currently licensed as provided by this Article."

Nurse is a protected title and may only be used by those individuals that are appropriately licensed to practice nursing in North Carolina. Again, **you must immediately cease and desist from identifying yourself as a licensed nurse.** Should you persist in misinterpreting yourself, then this matter will be reported to the District Attorney in your area for whatever action is deemed appropriate. If you have any questions, please do not hesitate to call me.

Sincerely,

[signed]

Donna H. Mooney, RN, MBA, Director of Discipline[159]

12. The Best Advice Money Can Buy

Throughout 2003 and 2004 e-mails kept flowing throughout the family. Bob Johnson and Reverend Everette often landed in the "To" or "CC" line. Conversations with Otto and Pat continued to make family and friends feel like Uncle Jimmy was being hidden from the outside world. In one instance, Billy borrowed a key to Uncle Jimmy's farm house. Otto called Billy and asked him for the key. Billy told Otto he would return it to Uncle Jimmy personally. Shortly thereafter, Pat showed up at Billy's place of business asking for the keys. In another instance, Pat Jenkins quizzed Uncle Jimmy's friend Bill Gentry about what he wanted to discuss with Uncle Jimmy before she allowed him in the house.[160]

There were also family e-mail discussions about how family members thought Pridgen was handling affairs differently than Uncle Jimmy would have wanted. Marvin Brown is a black man who lives on a farm near Uncle Jimmy's land. Marvin Brown was a friend and neighbor of Uncle Jimmy's. Access to some of Marvin's land is through Uncle Jimmy's land. At one point family members heard that Otto tried to deny Marvin use of Uncle Jimmy's road.[161] This showed the Pridgen's ignorance of the land, and ignorance of Uncle Jimmy's bond with his friends and neighbors.

The list of these events go on through the last years of Uncle Jimmy's life. Again, family members raised the question of whether the family should request an investigation by adult protective services came up. Uncle Jimmy's niece Ebie summarized a common concern in an e-mail on May 11, 2003:

> I don't know if APS would find any problems since his situation would look good to an outsider. i.e. clean house, his condition, and of course the sitters and OK would put on a real show for them. I think the APS would take the side of the sitters and OK.[162]

Bob Johnson replied:

> I have just read the e-mails from Billy, Pearsall [one of Uncle Jimmy's grand nephews] and Ebie. I believe that Ebie is right. An outsider would believe that Uncle Jimmy is well taken care

of. You should not make an issue of that as you would probably loose [sic] on it. The issue that you should address with Pridgen is the lack of access of the family, friends at the club, and church. Explain that even at his age and condition he needs to have social intercourse with those people who have been near and dear to him for a long time.

If what we all suspect is going on is, then it will be good ammunition that the people in charge are keeping him under their control and secluded from family and friends. That is necessary if they are to control him...[163]

I realize that Bob was probably right about everything that he said in his e-mail, but there is one thing that is terribly frustrating to me. Nothing in his e-mail suggests that he sees a way to remove bad influences from Uncle Jimmy's life. When could that "good ammunition" be used? Not until after Uncle Jimmy's death.

In another e-mail dated January 11, 2005 Billy again wrote to Bob Johnson. This time Billy was asked by his cousin Ebie to consider hiring another attorney for a second opinion. The e-mail follows:

Bob: Since Thanksgiving [2004] the Smith family has become even more frustrated and dissatisfied with Mr. Pridgen's style of management and his lack of respect for his client's family. My cousin, Ebie Padgett, has discussed the situation with an estate attorney in the High Point area and he has recommended that we present our case to Mr. Matthew Dill and ask him for his opinion. You have been abreast of the whole thing since the very beginning and we want your assistance in making this decision. Mr. Dill may very well tell us the same thing that you have all along, and if that is the case, we feel that a second opinion from an estate specialist might help us put our frustrations aside and watch a poor situation worsen.

We also want to raise the question of alienation/exploitation again and determine if it is advisable at this time to blow the whistle on those that took advantage of him three years ago.

Lastly, I won't go into detail now, but I will say that I suspect that my uncle's wealth is nowhere near what it has been perceived to be. He has always had an obsession with money and in his later years that obsession became hallucinogenic. However, it is his money and there is certainly no better way to spend it than to ensure his care and comfort in his last days. Dr. Smith could live a long time yet and we fear that if his affairs are not being prudently handled there might not be enough to see him through to the end. Hence we are seeking a way to oversee or police Mr. Pridgen's management... [164]

Bob Johnson replied:

Matt Dill is a good lawyer. His expertise is in estate planning and probate. I would certainly encourage you to get a second opinion. I think that what you are going to hear is that your only option now is as it has been to have the social services department intervene if you believe the caretakers are taking advantage of him. As you know this has always been an option which the family has not been willing to pursue.[165]

Billy began to pursue a legal guardianship for Uncle Jimmy. Billy met with Christopher Leonard, another lawyer in Wilmington with estate expertise. Mr. Leonard was primarily concerned with two hurdles that Billy and his family would have to get over to have a legal guardian installed. First there would be a proceeding to determine incompetence. An adult is incompetent in the eyes of North Carolina law if that person "lacks sufficient capacity to manage his own affairs or to make or communicate important decisions concerning his person, family or property..."[166] As it is described to me: A person needs slightly more competence than a vegetable to be considered competent.

If the family could get over that hurdle, the second hurdle would be to appoint a guardian. The Clerk of Superior Court would appoint a guardian. The law does not give any priority to family members in this matter. In fact, the Clerk would have to consider appointing Otto Pridgen as guardian since Uncle Jimmy signed a power of attorney appointing Otto. Hindsight shows tangible evidence to show why Otto should not have been appointed guardian, but despite the family's suspicions at the time, family members, still on the outside, had little concrete evidence in hand.

78

The last and most difficult factor in the family's decision making is wondering how Uncle Jimmy would feel if his family asked strangers to come into his house and determine his competency. How would any of us feel in that circumstance? As hard as it was for the family to recognize the first signs of dementia in a family member, imagine how hard it would be to recognize those signs in yourself. Imagine how hard it would be to admit to yourself that someone else will be making all your personal decisions for you for the rest of your life.

Perhaps the family would have received different advice from a lawyer specializing in Elder Abuse instead of estate planning, but even a lawyer highly trained in elder abuse would have limitations. Lawyers can't bring Uncle Jimmy back to life. Lawyers couldn't convince Uncle Jimmy that his family loved him. Lawyers can only sue and/or seek a settlement. A settlement might include financial restitution, but it can't rebuild a man's relationship with his family. This was the real battle the family was fighting, and lawyers weren't much help.

In an e-mail from a grand-niece-in-law of Uncle Jimmy's to the family captured the family's feelings of desperation. She wrote, "When this craziness started, I believed the only way to a positive result was legal action. Now I think the best – and only – thing we can do is to spend time with Jimmy. ... I believe that all of the conversations with the banker, preacher, accountant and the others that have given us 'friendly' advice have only bred alarm." [167] The decision to contact Adult Protective Services was not an easy one.

13. Home Sweet Home

Billy Smith was born in Wilmington, North Carolina and lived there his entire life. Most of his friends and family are there. Wilmington is not a large city. Word travels fast through a small town. By mid-2004 Billy started to suspect that elements in the First Baptist Church were involved in the alienation of him and his family. He started to fear that Otto, and possibly others were spreading misinformation about him to discredit him. Specifically, Billy believed that people were saying that he had done something awful to his uncle and that is why he had been fired as power of attorney. He wrote this note to Reverend Mike Queen:

> Mike:
> If you have no objections and church policy will allow, please make the attached letter available to your membership either through bulletin boards, adult Sunday School classrooms or however you would consider the best distribution.
> Thank you,
> Billy

The attached letter:

> To: The members of First Baptist Church
>   Wilmington, NC
> From: William T. Smith III
>   [address deleted]
> It has come to my attention recently that there is a rumor circulating among your congregation that I must have done a terrible injustice to my uncle, Dr. James Henry Smith, giving him reason to terminate me as his power of attorney back in the spring of 2002.
>
> I wish to make it clear to all of you that there has been no wrongdoing of any kind on my part toward him or any other member of my family. I have lived in this community my entire life and have enjoyed the reputation of being an upright and

80

honorable person. All that know me well can and will attest to this fact.

I also wish to make it clear that I will not stoop so low as to engage in mud-slinging gossip with those who would attempt to destroy my reputation.

If any of you wish to discuss the unfortunate situation that has surrounded my uncle during the last three years I will be happy to meet with you. I would also suggest that you contact your pastor, Dr. Michael Queen. He is familiar with the situation entirely and can explain the truth of the matter. I am also confident that he can and will support my integrity.

My Telephone number is [number deleted]. Please feel free to call any time.
Sincerely,
[signed]
William T. Smith III
June 14, 2004[168]

Billy still trusted Reverend Queen. He still had no idea that a new will was written. He still didn't know that Reverend Everette had participated in planning meetings about the will. Reverend Queen might have distributed Billy's letter to his congregation. If he did, no one took up Billy's offer to call. The First Baptist Church was making Billy Smith uncomfortable in his own hometown.

Uncle Jimmy's comfort was deteriorating also. By April 20th, 2004 Uncle Jimmy's dementia was apparent. That day Billy wrote in his memoirs:

I went to visit Uncle Jimmy yesterday about 1:00 PM. He was up and sitting at the kitchen table. He looked better than he did last week. They had picked up his lunch plate and taken it back to the kitchen. He had declined it all, but was drinking his milkshake/ensure. Pat said that he had eaten breakfast of scrambled egg and grits. Last month I mentioned that he seemed to be in a demented state when I visited. He has not been that way on the last few visits, but seems to be tired and weary.

Recently he has almost quit using his speaking device. Not only when I visit but Carol has said that he just mouths what he wants to say. But shortly into his visit he reached for his device. Pat helped get it in place, then he said to me, "I don't need anything... where is your wife?" I told him that she had gone to Atlanta to visit her family. He then smiled and said something that was unintelligible.[169]

When Uncle Jimmy said, "I don't need anything.", Billy felt like he was saying, "I don't need you anymore." Billy told this to Pat and Carol and he recalls that the two women chuckled. On his way out the door Billy congratulated Pat and Carol telling them both that "...they had succeeded in destroying a lifelong relationship."[170]

Terribly hurt, Billy continued to try to look out for Uncle Jimmy's best interests. Billy's cousin Ebie would also not give up the good fight. In her January 3rd, 2005 e-mail to Otto Pridgen she wrote:

Mr. Pridgen,
Several of us in the Smith family who sent Christmas cards to our Uncle Jimmy had them returned. They were stamped undeliverable because a forwarding order has expired. The forwarding address had been to your office.
I do not appreciate your screening who in the family can maintain contact with another member of our family. My father was William Thomas Smith, the oldest brother of Uncle Jimmy. I am very close to my Uncle as I was to Aunt Iris and their son, Jimmy. All of the Smith Family has always maintained a tight bond and nothing you do can break it.
Sincerely,
Elizabeth Smith Padgett[171]

If Otto didn't know that Uncle Jimmy's niece Ebie existed when the will was written he certainly knew about her after that. By the end of 2004 Uncle Jimmy's dementia was near total and his physical health was weak. He was sleeping in a hospital bed in the first floor of his two-story house. On January 13th, 2005 Billy's son Bill met with Otto Pridgen to discuss this and some of the family's other concerns about Uncle Jimmy and his affairs. In an e-mail dated 14 January he described his meeting to the family:

>...He [Otto Pridgen] spent a few minutes remarking on his surprise that UJ had "lasted this long" and complimented his tenacity. He then mentioned that it had become quite hard/impossible to understand use of his voicebox, and that all communication was through mouthing and gestures. About this time, his wife/secretary arrived and he said she could understand him better. He [Otto Pridgen] made some glowing remarks about "those women" who are taking care of him, and commented that "they're not late for work, and they don't call in sick..."[172]

When I read Bill's e-mail I imagine Otto talking to Bill about Uncle Jimmy's "faithful caregivers." The e-mail continues and relates more about Jan Pridgen's description of Uncle Jimmy's healthy eating habits declining and how she had given instructions to the care givers to rotate Uncle Jimmy in bed to avoid ulcers and to change his diaper several times nightly so that he would not sleep in urine.[173] Why a professional care giver would need these instructions from a legal secretary is beyond me.

The e-mail then discusses maintenance of the farm house. Billy and the rest of Uncle Jimmy's family were taking personal time and energy to keep the farmhouse from falling into disrepair. Otto would oversee the projects that Billy and his family undertook, and would pay for out-of-pocket expenses from Uncle Jimmy's account. The e-mail then relates how Bill's conversation with Otto and Jan Pridgen turned to Uncle Jimmy's boastfulness about his wealth. Bill related that Otto and Jan said, "When he came home from the rehabilitation facility [and was sleeping in a hospital bed on his ground floor], I was told that he cursed ("Goddamnit") at the caregivers and wanted to sleep in his upstairs bed 'because I have billions of dollars.'"[174]

I am familiar with this side of my Uncle Jimmy. My entire adult life I remember him bragging about his financial successes in his life and offering advice on investments. I also remember him bragging about the value of his farm. In the last decade of his life he told family members it was worth between 6 million and 600 million. The family knew better. When Uncle Jimmy died, the most recent appraised value of the land was under $350 thousand.[175] Was Uncle Jimmy boasting, or was he delusional about the value of his land?

By 2004 there was no doubt about Uncle Jimmy's lack of mental capacity. On walks, he would say take me to 1725. This was his house number. He would sometimes say this while he was standing in his front yard. He would sometimes say this while lying in the bed in the den inside his own home. How lonely might Uncle Jimmy have felt, lying in a bed in his own house asking his sitters to take him home. What is the difference between a house and a home?

By January 19th, 2005 the family decided to pursue legal action to have a guardian appointed for Uncle Jimmy, no matter what the personal consequences.[176] It was too late. On February 22nd, 2005 Uncle Jimmy died in his house.[177]

14. The Funeral

February 22, 2005 was a Tuesday. On Friday, February 25th Reverend Mike Queen conducted his funeral service. I was deployed when My Uncle Jimmy died, and I was not able to attend the funeral. One of my brothers asked me to send an e-mail to Reverend Queen relating family stories to be noted in the funeral ceremony.[178] At the time, I was happy to hear that Reverend Queen used my e-mail extensively in his oration.

Billy Smith made the funeral arrangements. There would be a service in the First Baptist church and another at the graveside. Pat Jenkins and Jan Pridgen sat behind a friend of the family at the church service. That friend of the family, Joan Teer, remembers Pat Jenkins and Jan Pridgen sitting behind her and "yapping with each other literally during the entire service."[179] It's interesting to me that these two women, who didn't know each other a few years earlier, would sit next to each other at the man's funeral and talk throughout. It's not just the fact that they would chat irreverently during his funeral that bothers me. It also bothers me to wonder how these two bonded in the previous years.

For the graveside service, Billy Smith specifically asked that there be no tent and no chairs. He didn't tell anyone why at the time. The reason he wanted no chairs was he didn't want Pat Jenkins to be able to grab a seat on the front row. No caregivers and no one from Otto Pridgen's law office showed up at the graveside service.[180]

While no nurses showed up at the graveside service there were more at the church service than just Pat Jenkins. Wanda Day and Alicia Bethea were two black nurses who were hired late in Uncle Jimmy's life. The color of their skin shouldn't matter, but somehow, in this case it seems to. Like Betty Parker, they didn't seem to be in the inner circle of caregivers who appeared to be acting badly toward the family. They worked on the night shift. They were not mentioned in his will. Wanda and Alicia presented Billy with a condolence card at the funeral reception after the church service. Inside the card was a business card with their contact information.[181]

Prior to the funeral Billy's son Jay called the attorney that wrote Little Jimmy's will. Jay, like the rest of Uncle Jimmy's family, was suspicious of Otto Pridgen's intentions. He told Little Jimmy's attorney, Bob O'Quinn, that he was concerned about the contents of the will, and Bob O'Quinn let Jay know that he knew about the will and the family would not be happy about the contents.[182] On the Monday after the funeral Billy went to Otto Pridgen's law office and asked for a copy of the will. The next day, March 1st, 2005, Billy went to Reverend Queen's office to speak about it.[183] Billy notified Reverend Queen that he intended to contest the will. At that time, Billy still saw Mike Queen as the man who first warned him that Pat Jenkins might be dangerous. He still saw Mike Queen as the man who told him that Uncle Jimmy wanted the farm on the Cape Fear River to stay in the family. He still hoped that Mike Queen could help lead this horrible situation to justice.

On March 2nd, 2005, recognizing that the church was the heir-apparent to the farm Billy sent an e-mail with the following recommendations to Reverend Queen:

Mike: This will confirm our conversation yesterday regarding the farm and also I wish to add a few thoughts that we didn't discuss.

1– I hope you will establish a relationship with Larry Fowler to ensure security of the property.
2- I think that you should change the locks on the two gates. Kip Pridgen has in the past used the land as if it was his own and he is improperly using the Heath family's land also.[14]
3- You should inventory the contents of the house and/or take photographs. We fear that Pridgen is going to rape that property after he gets through with Dr. Smith's residence. The interior of that house looks exactly as it did when I was a child, and needless to say, it is sacred to the family. There is only heirloom value to the contents.
4- Ask Pridgen for the keys. If he will give them up that will be a sign that he is not interested in the property. The key to the front door is an antique and cannot be copied. The security code to the burglar alarm is [code deleted], the same as [code deleted].
5- Turning the water on and off is complex. I would have to show someone how to do that.

---

[14] The Heath family land was neighboring land to Uncle Jimmy's

6- I won't overload you with anything else. I know you have a lot on your plate. I have taken the liberty to copy this to Jim [Reverend Everette]. Maybe you can dump it all on him!
Billy[184]

Billy left a copy of the will on Reverend Queen's desk as he prepared to leave. At the end of the conversation Billy remembers Reverend Queen telling him not to forget his copy of the will. Billy told the Reverend that he made that copy for him. Reverend Queen told Billy that he already had a copy.[185]

Reverend Queen wrote the following reply:

Thanks Billy,
We will be in touch with you as soon as we can convene our trustees.
Mike Q.[186]

. . . . .

Billy started to seek evidence to take to court. Billy took the envelope with the condolence note and business card that the two nurses from the night shift had given him. It seemed like a bit of a long-shot that they would provide information that would be helpful in Billy's case to contest the will, but at that time he didn't have much concrete evidence to go forward with. When he called and asked if they would be willing to talk about events that transpired in Uncle Jimmy's house Wanda said, "We've been wanting to talk."[187]

15. Three Enemas

With a legal battle looming the Smith family started to compile evidence that supported their case that Uncle Jimmy was unduly influenced and possibly otherwise abused late in his life. The family's expectation was that Otto Pridgen and his team would try to project an image of the Uncle Jimmy's family as a group of people who cared nothing for the man other than his money. E-mails started to zip back and forth between family members recalling good times spent with Uncle Jimmy. The family also noted times when they felt Uncle Jimmy was being isolated from his family and friends. The following e-mail, dated March 3, 2005, from Uncle Jimmy's grand-nephew, Jay, is a fair representative of many family members:

> I thought of more experiences this morning.
> First – Shortly after Little Jimmy died, the family tried to fill that space the best we could. One weekend, Alicia [Jay's wife] and I drove Jimmy to the farm with Bill and Amy [Jay's brother and sister-in-law]. We took pictures (which I can produce), rode and looked at the farm, saw about 8 turkeys and sat on the front porch and talked. It was probably one of my fondest memories of Jimmy. He talked about growing up at the farm, hunting, farming, etc. We even stopped at the produce stand on the way out of town (on the county line) to get tomatoes. He knew the lady behind the counter. All in all – an incredible trip.
> A day later – we were told Jimmy was no longer allowed to ride in anyone's car except a nurse's.
> Second – On MANY occasions Alicia and I would schedule time to visit Jimmy. A significant majority, they would tell us to come at a certain time and they wouldn't be there. One time we were 15 minutes late – no one was there. We called later in the day and were accosted by Pat that we stood Jimmy up. I'm sure this is what she told Jimmy as well.[188]

Very little of the family's memories would be useful as evidence in court. The court would see this as hearsay. This he-said-she-said evidence isn't meaningful coming from a person whose family stands to gain in court. Billy Smith sought concrete evidence and witnesses who did not stand to gain personally.

Billy sent the following letter to Uncle Jimmy's accountant, David Whaley on March 3, 2005:

> If you will recall back in May or June of 2002 you and OK Pridgen went to Dr. Smith's home to sort out and make sense of the pile of paperwork in his home office.
>
> During the time that I was POA there was a recent will of Dr. Smith's that was on the floor with some other bills, etc. My question is; did you and Pridgen find that will, and if so what was done with it. I don't need it immediately but I would like to know if you witnessed it being removed from the house by Mr. Pridgen, or even if you are confident that Mr. Pridgen took it to his office. In other words, I just need to know where it is in case the authorities should ask for it.
>
> Thanks a lot.
>
> [Signed][189]

Billy remembered seeing the older will while he was Uncle Jimmy's power of attorney. The will Billy remembered seeing left nothing to the First Baptist Church, the nurses or the Pridgens. Billy hoped that will would show a jury that Uncle Jimmy had no intention of leaving the farm to the First Baptist Church before the church leadership started to exert their influence on him. Billy didn't know if he would be able to find the previous will to prove his point.

The family requested a record of 911 calls from Uncle Jimmy's residence. He knew Pat Jenkins called the police once when his son was visiting and wondered if there were any other similar calls. There were no calls noted in the report prior to Little Jimmy's death. There were 8 calls made from November 29, 2002 to February 10, 2005. The nature of the incidents were listed as "Breaking and entering," "Property Damage," "Larceny," and "Domestic Disturbance."[190] It seems to me that the environment Pat Jenkins and the rest of Uncle Jimmy's staff brought into his home was not as serene as one would hope.

.....

Billy and his son, Bill, made an appointment to visit Wanda Day and Alicia Bethea. They were eager to hear what the night nurses wanted to talk about. Billy offered to drive to Wanda's house but Wanda told them that she had seen Otto Pridgen riding past her house. She was afraid that she was being watched and she was afraid to meet Billy in anyone's home. Billy made arrangements to meet at St. Andrews Covenant Presbyterian Church in Wilmington.

The interview with Wanda and Alicia confirmed many of Billy's worst fears. Wanda and Alicia told them that they were extremely suspicious of the behavior they saw in the house, particularly that of Pat and the Pridgens. They said that Pat told Uncle Jimmy "all the time" that if she ever left he would die. They said Pat would threaten to quit if she didn't get her way and that Pat could convince Uncle Jimmy to say things he wouldn't have otherwise. They said that Pat would flirt with Uncle Jimmy and was probably making sexual advances toward him. In the interview, Billy recalls seeing Jan rub her breasts on Uncle Jimmy and Alicia said that she saw Pat do the same thing. Alicia relates Pat saying, "oh, you know how to keep a man, right? ... only thing you got to do is put a little bit of your pee in his drink, and you see how much Dr. Smith love me."

Wanda and Alicia told the Smiths that Dr. Bridger (the same doctor that administered the "mini-mental-state-exam") would prescribe anything that Pat diagnosed and Jan Pridgen read to him over the phone. [191, 15, 192] According to Alicia Dr. Bridger prescribed medication after a phone conversation. They said that when Pat would get angry with Otto Pridgen she would say things like "I got rid of Billy" and "I can get rid of OK." Wanda and Alicia felt they had to do things Pat's way or no way at all. Pat's way reportedly included following family and friends around the house and tape record his conversations with them. According to Wanda and Alicia, Jan Pridgen was involved in the tape recording as well. Wanda said to Billy and Bill, "She [Jan] taped us, you, anybody who came in there at first." They said that Pat and the Pridgens would speak badly of the Smith family. Then they dropped the bombshell. Imagine what Billy and Bill must have been thinking while sitting there talking to these two women who had been caring for their uncle when they heard:

---

[15] Dr. Bridger admitted to prescribing medication over the phone based on caregiver reporting.

Alicia: To me, she hurt him. Just like that day, when, Sunday she gave him three enemas.

Wanda: <feigning Pat> "Don't tell nobody, don't tell nobody."

Alicia: She was scared.

Wanda: Scared to death! When I came on at three o'clock. I came on at three o'clock. Now you got to write down everything. When I came on at three o'clock she was giving him enemas. I say now, why was she giving him enemas?

Alicia: She called me at like two o'clock . . . Is you coming tonight?

Wanda: Enemas, Enemas, Why you giving him enemas?

Alicia: Yeah.

Wanda: <feigning Pat> "Well, he got to use the, he's impacted, he's impacted." And she.

Alicia: And he was already using the bathroom 'cause I could tell he was bleeding out of his rectum.

Wanda: And he bled.

Bill: Oh my God.

16. The Best Trial Lawyer in North Carolina

When Pilate saw that he was getting nowhere, but that instead an uproar was starting, he took water and washed his hands in front of the crowd. "I am innocent of this man's blood," he said. "It is your responsibility!" Matthew 27-24

Put yourself in Billy's shoes. Would you sit back and say, "Oh, well. Win some, lose some," or would you fight? Billy decided to fight. He asked Bob Johnson how to go forward legally. Bob Johnson recommended hiring the law firm Maxwell Freeman and Bowman out of Durham, NC. Bob described Jim Maxwell, to family members, as the best trial lawyer in North Carolina. Billy prepared a 6-page summary of the events surrounding Uncle Jimmy's last years for Jim Maxwell. In it he noted the family's 3 goals:

> To bring justice to those who have exploited and manipulated our late uncle, including criminal, civil, professional society rebukes or IRS punishment, as applicable
> To eliminate the exploiters above from any type of inheritance from our uncle's estate
> To ensure that the family farm in Columbus County, NC. Remains in the family, which was Dr. Smith's lifelong verbalized intention[193]

Note that none of the family's stated goals were to take the entire estate. When it came to Uncle Jimmy's material possessions the family was primarily interested in the farm land. Out of a 5-million-dollar estate the family was asking for a farm with a tax value of under $350,000. To my knowledge, Uncle Jimmy never told any surviving member his family that he intended to leave any of his financial wealth, other than the farm, to his family. However, Uncle Jimmy did tell family members that he wanted the farm to stay in the family. He also told this to Reverend Mike Queen and the banker, Jack Richardson. It's hard to guess what Uncle Jimmy's intentions for the rest of his estate would have been after his son's death if he had not been influenced by his caregivers, his law team, and his church.

As Billy pressed forward he got some of Uncle Jimmy's medical records. He found some disturbing administrative notes. He forwarded this information to Reverend Mike Queen and Reverend Jim Everette in an e-mail dated March 5, 2005:

> Please recall Oct/Nov of 2003 when Dr. Smith was hospitalized for an appendectomy. Also recall that his minister and his family were not allowed to visit. We got his medical records last Friday. In the personal information area of his chart was this statement:
> *RETIRED DENTIST – ESTRANGED FROM FAMILY*
> Is it becoming clear now?
> Billy[194]

Billy felt he was building a rock-solid case and that all he needed was help from the leadership of the church. He wrote Reverend Queen, and included Reverend Everette, since Reverend Queen was with the group that made Uncle Jimmy angry the day they confronted him about Pat Jenkins. Billy thought the church leaders were as naïve of the facts as he was and felt that if they were made aware of the truth they would stand up for what is right. Billy wanted to work together with the church and was prepared to give the church almost everything in the estate other than the farm if those who alienated him from his uncle got nothing.

Billy received a letter from Carlton Fisher, a realtor, and the chairman of trustees at the First Baptist Church, dated March 7, 2005:

> Dear Mr. Smith:
> This letter is in response to your conversation with Mike Queen, Pastor of First Baptist Church- Wilmington.
> The Board of Trustees has met concerning your comments and the will of the late Dr. James H. Smith. The Board of Trustees is not going to question the validity of Dr. James H. Smith's will because it is outside our scope of authority.
> Any further communication with First Baptist Church should be through me as chairman of the Trustees. Thank you for your cooperation.
> Sincerely,
> [Signed]
> Carlton Fisher[195]

Who in a church has the authority to question the validity of a will? How would Billy ever find out who has that authority if he is not allowed to talk to anyone in the church other than Carlton Fisher. I can't help noticing that Mr. Fisher did not say he would not question the validity of the will because he believed the will was valid.

.....

The family drama with the Pridgens continued. Otto Pridgen scheduled an estate sale to liquidate the personal property in Uncle Jimmy's house into cash. Uncle Jimmy's family wanted to stop the sale until they could prove that Otto Pridgen had abused his authority as power of attorney and remove him as executor. The estate sale was an auction scheduled for March 12, 2005. Among the questions the family would ask Jim Maxwell was, "Can immediate action be taken to halt liquidation of the estate?"[196]

On March 7, 2005, Billy and some other family members met with Jim Maxwell and asked their first round of questions. That evening Jim Maxwell sent a fax to Bob Johnson:

> Bob:
> I met this morning with a number of the family of Dr. James H. Smith. I have spent some time since that meeting in reviewing a large volume of information that they left with me, but it is far too much for me to have assimilated at this point. However, it does appear clear that a Caveat is warranted – at least, as to the caregivers, POA and wife of POA who are beneficiaries under the proposed will. Enclosed you will please find a letter that I am attempting to Fax to Mr. Pridgen which sets forth where we are at the present time. I will have a Caveat drafted by Wednesday and hope that I might be able to call on your office for some assistance in getting it filed on Thursday in order to block this sale of personal property that is now scheduled for Saturday. I will be back in touch with you.[197]

The same day Jim Maxwell sent the following by fax and express delivery to Otto Pridgen:

Dear Mr. Pridgen,

I have been retained by the family and legal heirs of James Henry Smith in regard to his Estate and the events surrounding the execution of a document that I understand has now been offered for probate as his Last Will and Testament which bears an execution date of the 26th day of September 2002.

This letter is to advise you that it is our intention to file a Caveat to this Will and to do so no later than this Thursday, March 10, 2005. Pursuant to the provisions of N.C.G.S. §31-36, once this caveat is filed and the statutory bond posted, all further proceedings in relation to the Estate must be suspended except the preservation of the property and the collection of debts of the Estate. I mention this item specifically because it is my understanding from the family that there is presently scheduled to be some type of "Estate Sale" of personal property this Saturday, March 12, 2005. My clients have received notice that if they wanted to "claim" any of the "275" items to be sold, that they would have to do so by today. My clients will not be picking up any items and none should have been disposed of in any manner since the date of Dr. Smith's death. All items of personal property of Dr. Smith must be preserved as mandated by statute until the caveat is resolved.

In addition, with the death of Dr. Smith, title to the real estate at [address deleted] passed to a number of my clients pursuant to title documents and the Last Will and Testament of Dr. Smith's son, James Aiken Smith. Effective with the filing of the Caveat, it would be their intention to secure that property and to remove anyone else who may still be in Dr. Smith's home. We would be willing for the furniture and personal property presently located within that home to remain there (under proper security) until such time as the Caveat is resolved. The alternative would be to have this personal property moved to some storage unit during the pendency of this action and that would seem to be an unnecessary depletion of the assets of the Estate. It is my understanding that they [sic] may have been an inventory taken for the purpose of the proposed sale this Saturday and that would certainly be helpful in identifying the items that are presently in the house which comprise a portion of Dr. Smith's estate.

Understandably, we have just been retained in this matter and our investigation of the relevant facts has just begun. There is a substantial body of material to be reviewed as well as banking, financial and medical records to be obtained.

I will be back in touch with you as this matter progresses, but was anxious to get this information to you as it appears that events involving Dr. Smith's Estate are moving at a rapid pace; particularly, those related to the disposal of personal assets. With best wishes, I am

> Yours very truly,
> [Signed]
> James B. Maxwell[198]

This was the beginning of the formal legal battle. Informally, it was the beginning of a legal education for the Smith family. The family's objectives were refined as the ordeal progressed. There is a lot more to winning a court case than convincing a jury that you are on the moral high ground. A very specific avenue within the boundaries of the written law would have to be used to contest the well. Jay Smith sent out an e-mail that evening summarizing a meeting with Jim Maxwell for all the family members unable to attend:

Family –
We had a good meeting with the attorney this morning. The attorney took a moment to explain wills and the process of contesting them. It was a crash course in Will Contestation 101. There are two primary takeaways. One, Jimmy's type of will is one of the most common and is the strongest. Two – there are two allowable reasons to contest. First – if Jimmy was incapable of writing it. Second – if there was undue influence. Next, we tried to give him a crash course in Who's-Who in the Smith family, all the aliases of UJ, LJ, Jim, Jimmy, Dr. Smith etc. We also tried to explain the connections with the church, OKP and John Newton. We told him about Theresa Mozingo and any others with some connection (Dr. Bridger, Jack

96

Richardson, Bob O'Quinn). We tried to keep everything as concise as possible knowing we wanted to get through out stated objectives. So with the brief summary, we handed him binders full of all our e-mails, transcripts, wills, 911 calls, and other docs. I expect his para-legal has some reading to do.

Bill then gave him our objectives (I've summarized Bill's list):

Prosecute those who wronged Jimmy
contest the will
Protect Woodford [nick name for the farm]
Advice for handling [address of Uncle Jimmy's house deleted]
Protect Wilmington family[16]

The attorney responded in reverse order:

5. Protect Wilmington Family: He didn't believe he was able to do anything for us here. This is more of something we would need to take up with local law enforcement.

4., 3. Advice for handling [address of Uncle Jimmy's house deleted] and Protecting Woodford: Basically – he said both of these would be handled with the answer of #2.

2. Contest the will: There is a simple mechanism for contesting a will. You need to file a caveat with the clerk of court. This caveat will do two things – first the executor cannot 'dispose' of any property until the caveat is settled (this will stop Saturday's Red Tag Sale). Two – one element of the caveat will be to disqualify OKP as the executor. The court will probably appoint a new third-party executor. This will occur before Wednesday of this week.[17] On Thursday, Bill and Dad will go to the home with a locksmith and police escort to evict Carol and lock the house up tight.[18]

After this has occurred the attorney will initiate a discovery procedure to start collecting financial, medical, depositions and other 'facts'. These docs will also play into objective #1.

---

[16] The family began to fear that Pat Jenkins or one of the others involved might do something to harm the family members.

[17] The caveat would be filed, but the executor would not be appointed by "Wednesday of this week."

[18] The family was wrong about how swiftly things would move. Carol was not "evicted" that Thursday.

97

We talked a little about how to handle the church aside from the other inheritors. While we don't believe the latest will was inked by Jimmy, I think we all believe he wanted to give money to the church (even though his last will did not mention them).[19] What the attorney said would happen is this... When our case is presented to the four 'sitters', their attorney will more than likely recommend they settle to keep from loosing [sic] everything including their shirt in attorney fees. The church may settle for some agreed on $$ or we may choose not to contest that piece of the will (this can be determined later). However, if the will's stated inheritors want to challenge our complaint without settling the case it will go to a jury trial.

1. Prosecute those who wronged Jimmy: First- we will not forget that this item is **Number 1** on our objective list. Neither will our attorney. Through the discovery process, he believes that appropriate authorities will investigate and prosecute any criminal wrongdoing.

Next - it is noteworthy to state that we should not talk about Pat's guilt or anyone else's guilt at this time. We all have a gut feeling that they are guilty but want fact to speak for itself. If we write or state something that can't be substantiated, we may be guilty of libel or slander. Generally, we should communicate suspicions with family only. We can begin talking about this case as it becomes legal record. i.e. Thursday we can state that we have filed a caveat to the will and have removed the tenant.

Important point – Any contestation case in NC with merit will be paid out of the estate. The attorney took our case without a retainer confident it has merit. There are some reimbursable hard costs he will encounter. He will ask the family to front those funds.

Jay[199]

Hindsight shows a naïve enthusiasm in the family at that time. It seemed like an open and shut case. The family, however, misunderstood how the position of the church would complicate

---

[19] The entire family was not convinced that Uncle Jimmy would have given money to the church in his will if there was no undue influence.

matters. As the discovery period progressed the family would find out exactly what they were up against.

The following day, Bill's wife was in the neighborhood of Uncle Jimmy's house and noticed a vehicle parked in front loaded with boxes. She called Bill and he drove to the house with a camera and found Carol Tucker, an antique salesman, an adult woman and a boy who appeared to Bill to be 10-12 years old. In an e-mail to Jim Maxwell dated March 8, 2005 Bill recalls:

> ... They were all talking on cell phones, and the adult was talking on her cell phone about "getting an injunction", and "suing the estate for 25% of the worth of the contents of the house". I presume she is with the antique dealer, and I am sorry that they have invested their time and will get caught in the middle, but they should have smelled a rat. She told me while on the phone that she hears I am a doctor, and then asked what kind. She then stated, "not a very good one, I bet". I didn't say a word except to announce my entering the house and to say, "Hey Buddy" to the boy so he wouldn't feel threatened. ...[200]

After the meeting with Wanda and Alicia the Smiths were convinced that the Pridgens and the sitters were taking Uncle Jimmy's personal possessions out of the house. The Pridgens seemed to think that if they gave up control of the house the Smiths would take the valuables out of the house. Jay was concerned about someone suing him for slander or libel. I can't help wondering who was telling the Antique Salesman's assistant about Bill's medical profession. I get the impression that whoever described Bill to the antique salesman wasn't very flattering to him.

I'll take a moment to brag about Dr. Bill Smith. He attended New Hanover County public schools from Kindergarten through 10th grade. He spent his Jr. and Sr. years of High School at the North Carolina School of Science and Math in Durham, NC. He went on to Duke University where he graduated with honors as a Chemistry major. He was accepted into Medical School at the University of North Carolina at Chapel Hill. After medical school, he was given his first choice of residency hospitals. He chose Massachusetts General in Boston. He went back to Duke University to complete a fellowship in

Cardiology prior to returning to Wilmington to practice. He is an outstanding Cardiologist.

When I wonder who might have said these unflattering remarks about Bill Smith my imagination doesn't wonder very far. I suspect that any time Pat Jenkins and the Pridgens discussed the situation with anyone outside the family they did their best to project an image of an awful family that cared nothing for a man other than his money. The church rumors, Wanda, Alicia, and the antique salesman made it clear to the family that someone was saying bad things about them behind their backs. This and other evidence suggests the family was being slandered, not the other way around.

17. The Whole Ball of Wax

Otto Pridgen hired his old friend, Lonnie Williams, from the Wake Forest Law School class of '53 to take the case for the propounders.[20] Lonnie Williams notified Jim Maxwell by fax on March 17, 2005 that he would be representing the propounders. In the last sentence of that fax Lonnie Williams wrote to Maxwell, "Although Mr. Smith is bitter, I am hopeful that as to necessary steps which do not place the Estate at risk, we can cooperate to get them done."[201] At that time, Williams did not know much about the Smith family that his clients didn't tell him. I think it would be fair to call Billy Smith "angry" at that time. How would you feel if you just heard that someone gave your uncle enemas causing him to bleed through his rectum? The term "bitter" is just insulting.

Lonnie Williams called Reverend Queen on March 18, 2005 to speak about the case. Mike Queen told Lonnie Williams that the First Baptist Church was seeking counsel elsewhere.[202] Lonnie Williams is no stranger to the First Baptist Church. At one time, he was a member. In 1996 his family helped the First Baptist Church purchase the Wilmington Light Infantry building next door to the sanctuary. The team that worked with him on that purchase included Carlton Fisher (future chairman of the church trustees), Dr. Bertram Williams and Reverend Queen.[203] In 1999 Lonnie Williams, Sr. was awarded the title of Deacon Emeritus at the First Baptist Church.[204] Sometime before March 18, 2005 Lonnie Williams left the First Baptist Church. There were signs of a shaky relationship between the propounders.

.....

Billy wrote Bob Johnson an e-mail and asked him his opinion of Lonnie Williams entering on behalf of the Pridgens and the caretakers. Bob replied, "Not a surprise. He is or was a member of 1st Baptist and finished law school with OKP. Lonnie Jr. is very active in 1st Baptist. That is one reason I did not recommend him. He is a very good lawyer and is highly ethical. When he sees the facts of this case. He won't like what his clients did."[205] I believe Bob Johnson is a great

---

[20] Propounders wish the will to stand as is. Caveators wish the will to be invalidated.

101

man with the best of intentions, but, like the rest of us, he was wrong again.

.....

Wilmington was a small town. When word started to travel around town that Billy was getting embroiled in a legal action against Otto Pridgen people started to call him and tell him stories, they had heard. People told him stories about Otto Pridgen and how little he was respected professionally. One person told him that in Lonnie William's law firm, Marshall, Williams & Gorham, all the lawyers are Lonnie's "yes men" and Lonnie had a reputation for being one of the harshest lawyers in Wilmington.[206] As if this case wasn't complex enough, the "Gorham" in Marshall, Williams & Gorham was a close friend of Billy Smith's. Dumay Gorham was a member of St. Andrews Covenant Presbyterian Church... the same church Billy Smith has been a member of his entire life. Dumay Gorham was my basketball coach in the church youth league that played games at the First Baptist Church Activities Center. Small town.

Dumay Gorham knows a lot more about the Smith family than our childhood basketball skills. Dumay Gorham wrote Billy's father's will. When Billy's father died, it was revealed that he left his estate to his three sons. The gift to one of the three sons, who had no children of his own, was withheld, and reserved for his grandchildren. The grandchildren (myself included) voluntarily took legal action to overturn that will and give our uncle his inheritance back. Does that sound like a greedy family?

One of Billy Smith's Aunts used Dumay Gorham for her legal counsel. Billy's Aunt Tavia needed help in her elder years and she chose Billy as her power of attorney. Billy helped her through her daily routine and when she needed around-the-clock care Billy took her and her dog, Matilda, into his own house. One day, about two weeks after she moved into Billy's house Aunt Tavia asked Billy for her attorney's phone number. Billy gave her the number and sat and listened as she called Dumay Gorham. She asked Dumay to amend her will so that she could leave everything to Billy. Billy had seen signs of dementia in his Aunt Tavia. His experience with Uncle Jimmy taught him how vulnerable an elderly person can be when it comes to these matters. After Tavia got off the phone Billy called Dumay and told him not to change her last will. Does that sound like greedy a family?

102

Aunt Tavia's will remained intact until she died in her bed in Billy's house with Matilda at her side. Billy and 47 other family members were beneficiaries. Dumay knew exactly what kind of person Billy Smith was. When it became evident that Uncle Jimmy's case would go to trial Billy asked Dumay if he would testify in court for him. Dumay said that he would ask his law partner, Lonnie Williams, before he committed. Dumay declined to testify on Billy's behalf.[207]

The facts of Uncle Jimmy's case were complex, but the community that the facts existed in were more-so. Many social ills played a part in Uncle Jimmy's life, but there was one more not-so-subtle layer of complexity that would be added with the introduction of a third law firm. Most cases have two clearly defined teams. When this case found the court room, there would be one law team representing the caveators (the family) and two separate law teams representing the propounders. Lonnie Williams represented the Pridgen's and the caregivers. The First Baptist Church hired Bob Hunter, from Greensboro, NC.[21]

I can imagine many reasons why the church would want to put distance between themselves and the other propounders. For one, the family was making discoveries that made them believe the Pridgens and the caregivers engaged in undue influence. Another subtler reason is that the will left specific dollar amounts and other specific gifts to everyone except Pat Jenkins, Carol Tucker, Linda Phillips, Jan Pridgen and the First Baptist Church. The will gave those 5 entities each a percentage of the residuary. In other words, after all bills were paid, and the other specific gifts were distributed those 5 parties would get their share of the remainder. If any party in the will were proven to have exercised undue influence against Uncle Jimmy, they would lose their share. That share would be redistributed to the rest of those receiving gifts in the residuary. For example, if Billy Smith could successfully show that the Pridgens and the three caregivers noted in the will were afoul, then the church would get the entire residuary. Instead of 60% of a five-million-dollar estate, the church stood to get the whole ball of wax.

---

[21] Roy Piner would also be represented by Bob Hunter.

18. Drama

The background drama continued non-stop as Jim Maxwell prepared for trial. An agreement was reached on the estate sale. The antique salesman held a private showing for the family prior to the public auction. One of Uncle Jimmy's Grand-Nephews, Jack Shelhart, was a Rhode Island State Trooper, and was unable to attend either of the auctions. He sent Billy an e-mail stating, "If possible, I would like to bid in "absentee", I am interested in some heirloom to remember Uncle Jimmy and Aunt Iris by. Something appropriate for a fireplace mantel. I was thinking some type of clock, if available, I would trust you to bid on my behalf..." [208] I think Jack's e-mail is a fair representation of how most family members felt about Iris and Jimmy's personal possessions. No one felt they needed anything in the house, but everyone wanted something to keep in their memory.

On April 27, 2005 Jim Maxwell drove to Wilmington to get to know the people and the community better. During that visit, he and Billy went to the First Baptist Church and started discussions for a possible settlement. In attendance were Dr. Mike Queen, Carlton Fisher, Bob Hunter, Billy Smith and Jim Maxwell. Neither Lonnie Williams nor any of his clients were present at that meeting. Jim Maxwell presented the Smith family's perspective to the First Baptist Church. The family believed that the Pridgens, Pat Jenkins, Carol Tucker and Linda Phillips all received their shares through undue influence. The family had not yet seen any of the evidence that suggests that church leadership may have been involved in undue influence. The family felt that, even though his last will offered nothing to the church, it was not unlike Uncle Jimmy to include the church in his charitable giving. Billy's family felt confident that Uncle Jimmy intended for the farm to stay in the family and would have made this clear in his will in the absence of undue influence. The solution to the problem that Jim Maxwell was seeking was for the family and the church to work together to prove that there was undue influence on the part of the Pridgens and the caregivers. Once proven, the 40% of the residuary left to those parties would go to intestate heirs, or blood relatives.

If you have been paying close attention to the details, you might have noticed that the best trial lawyer in North Carolina made a mistake. The church and each of the 4 women were to receive a portion of the residuary under the will. Under North Carolina Law if any of those individuals were proven to have exerted undue influence their share would be distributed to the remaining parties in the residuary (in this case, the church, not the family). Never-the-less, in late April 2005 the family's (naïve) intentions were to remove the Pridgens and the caregivers from the will and use their 40% to buy the farm from the church. The family would pursue the "undue influence" route to invalidate the will. The incapacity route seemed harder to prove. Some family members believed that he had the minimum mental capacity required to write a will. All family members agreed that he was highly susceptible to undue influence.

With the family's cards on the table the meeting progressed in hopes of reaching some common ground on which the foundation of a settlement could be built. On behalf of his clients, Hunter indicated that the church felt like they were just caught in the middle of the two sides. Jim Maxwell had the impression after that meeting that Reverend Mike Queen knew that the family was right about the awful things that were occurring inside Uncle Jimmy's house during his life. Maxwell was led to believe that many members of the church "were totally in sympathy with the family and believed that this whole thing was a 'terrible' injustice." By the end of that meeting it was Jim Maxwell's belief "that the family and Church were all going to end up on the same side." Jim Maxwell felt that the Smith family was setting up a "no-lose" situation for the church. If the Caveat failed, the will would stand. If the Caveat was successful, the family still intended to give the church 60% of the estate and would purchase the farm.[209] By the time the depositions were taken under oath the reverends would give the family a different impression. While Jim Maxwell recalls Reverend Queen being supportive of the family at that meeting he remembers the realtor, and chairman of trustees, Carlton Fisher, saying "little or nothing". Reverend Jim Everette, was not present at that meeting.[210],[22]

---

[22] Jim Maxwell left that meeting with the feeling that he had built a strong foundation for an agreement between the family and the church. He expected that the family would be able to buy the farm from the church at a fair price. He hoped that the price would be a slight discount to the family since there would be no realtor's fee. He may not have known that Carlton Fisher was a realtor. Jim Maxwell was learning the facts of the case rapidly, but he still had more to learn about the community that the facts existed in.

There was more drama during the legal discovery phase. Lonnie Williams sent a message to the family via Jim Maxwell letting them know that the furniture contents of the farmhouse could be bought for $6,000. This e-mail from Lonnie William's account was signed, "Regards, Algonquin J. Calhoun."[211] I had never heard of Algonquin J. Calhoun, but Wikipedia tells me he is "a somewhat crooked lawyer" from the Amos "n" Andy radio and television sitcom set in Harlem.[212] Why would Lonnie Williams sign off with the pseudonym Algonquin J. Calhoun?

.....

Lonnie Williams was handling the furniture in the farmhouse for the estate. He notified the family's lawyer that the furniture was worth $6000. Maxwell sent a reply offering $6000 for the furniture on behalf of the family.[213] In a subsequent message from Williams the price went up to $8,000.[214] The best way I can describe the farmhouse furniture is old country furniture with tattered upholstery. I couldn't see anyone spending $8,000 dollars for the lot. It's even hard to imagine spending $6,000 on it. There is a piano in the farmhouse that might have minimal value. The keys are all stained yellow and the wood finish is significantly deteriorated. It has spent its entire long life in an old farmhouse without climate control. It might have some antique value, but as an instrument, it would be a tuner's nightmare. Lonnie Williams wrote Jim Maxwell an e-mail on 27 April to let the family know that someone had put a $1,000 bid on the piano. The family was pressed for time to purchase the piano, but no one in the family was willing to pay that price. No one ever showed up to take it. I suspect the cost to move the piano out of that old farm house exceeds the value of the piano itself.[215] On June 21 Jim Maxwell notified the family that "the 'buyer' did back out because there were some 'repairs' that might be necessary. Williams advised Bob Hunter (the church's attorney) that the Executor [Otto Pridgen] had decided to leave the piano in the house for whomever ultimately got that or wanted the piano."[216]

19. The Plan

These nagging issues kept popping up, but Jim Maxwell continued his research on the case. Among other things Jim Maxwell sought "1) all bank records for Dr. Smith from Wachovia for his checking, CAP Account, money market account etc. from approximately 2000 forward; 2) tax returns prepared by Dr. Smith's CPA from approximately 1999 forward; and, 3) all records of Mr. Pridgen during the period he was serving as power of attorney for Dr. Smith, which began in the Spring of 2002."[217] While Billy and his family had done their best amateur detective work, the real discovery was about to begin.

In a letter to Billy with the bold capitalized letters **"PRIVILEGED COMMUNICATION"** across the top Jim Maxwell laid out his strategy to pursue the caveat. There were seven elements of undue influence that were established in the case of *"IN RE: The Will of Campbell*, 155 N.C. 441, 573 S.E.2d 550 (2002)". That case would provide the precedent that would guide Jim Maxwell throughout the trial. The seven elements were:

1) Old age and physical and mental weakness of the person executing the instrument.
2) That the person signing the paper is in the home of the beneficiary and subject to his constant supervision.
3) That others have little or no opportunity to see him.
4) That the instrument is different and revokes and prior instrument.
5) That it is made in favor of one with whom there are no ties of blood.
6) That is disinherits the natural objects of his bounty [disinherits family].
7) That the beneficiary has procured its execution.[218]

While it would not be necessary to prove all seven elements, to the family (still naïve) it seemed like they would be able to hit a home run and prove all seven without too much difficulty. On the 12th of May, the Superior Court of North Carolina commanded Uncle Jimmy's CPA and banker, David Whaley and Jack Richardson, to produce tax records from 1995 to 2004 and bank records from 1995 through April 2005. The court also commanded Otto Pridgen to produce "Complete documentation in regard to your position as power of attorney for Dr.

James Henry Smith, including but not limited to, copies of all correspondence, including e-mails and telephone messages/notes; copies of all contracts, agreements and/or legal documents signed by you as power of attorney for Dr. James Henry Smith (including any and all documents in connection with the clearing and sale of timber on the 'Smith farm' in Columbus County, North Carolina); copies of all financial records pertaining to attorney fees, expenses/costs, fees paid to care providers or any other expenses/costs charged to Dr. James Henry Smith and/or paid as power of attorney for James Henry Smith; and any and all letters, notes, drafts or communications in relation to the preparation of the paper writing dated September 26, 2002 and designated as the Last Will and Testament of James H. Smith." The court also commanded Pat Jenkins, Linda Phillips and Carol Tucker to produce their "complete tax returns (including income and gift), copies of contracts with Uncle Jimmy and copies of notes, cards, memos and letters to Uncle Jimmy."[219]

Bob Hunter was also hard at work on his side the case for his client, the First Baptist Church. Among his efforts were Requests for Admissions. This was a list of 12 items that the propounders wanted the caveators to admit. The 12 requests had major errors that had to be corrected before the Smiths could even respond. Among the errors were: 1) The church's law team misnamed the deceased "William" instead of "James" and 2) In one request the church asked the family to admit that 9 family members were "all the heirs at law and next of kin" to Uncle Jimmy.[220] Jim Maxwell sent corrections to Bob Hunter with a Smith family tree that showed 11 family members were "heirs at law" to keep the case moving forward. Apparently, the leadership of the First Baptist Church didn't know Uncle Jimmy's family tree any better than the people who wrote the will. I wonder if they were one in the same.

The three law teams had a conference to discuss how to go forward with the litigation. Hunter invited the attorneys together because he wanted to reach a speedy settlement. His clients stood to gain 60% of 5 million dollars in assets plus two pieces of real estate. The Church could net over 4 million dollars. Jim Maxwell described Hunter's agenda and Lonnie Williams reaction at the meeting in an e-mail to the family on June 14th, 2005:

... he [Hunter] wanted to discuss when a mediation could occur; what the discovery schedule would or should look like, what information would be "voluntarily" shared (without the need for substantial discovery) and, when a trial date could be set. To say that Mr. Williams was caught a bit off guard and was not too receptive to such a discussion would probably be a bit of an understatement. After getting over the initial shock of Mr. Hunter's fairly aggressive approach to seeking a resolution, Mr. Williams' indication was that he saw absolutely no reason for his clients (Jenkins, Phillips, Tucker, Ms. Pridgen and Mr. Pridgen) to try to settle anything as they were not going to "willingly" contribute anything financially to a settlement.[221]

Though Williams indicated that his clients would not settle the case Hunter pressed forward with his agenda at the meeting. He suggested that there were legal risks to all parties except the church in this matter. He noted that the facts of the case don't pass the "smell test" and suggested that the three care takers and Otto's wife could lose their bequests completely. Bob Hunter had also found a legal trump card for his clients that might defend them against the family's suit. Hunter discovered Jim Maxwell's mistake. Hunter notified Maxwell of his legal opinion that if the family convinced a jury that the Pridgens and the caretakers had exerted undue influence it would benefit only the church and not the family. After "additional research" Jim Maxwell replied to Hunter "that he may be correct on that point."[222] To this date, the family still had no idea how the Reverend Everette was involved in the planning of the will, so this looked like it could be a show stopper.

It was obvious that Bob Hunter was well prepared to represent his clients. When the trial started it hit the front page of the Wilmington Star News. A prominent church being involved in a lawsuit seemed to send a minor tremor through the small city. An anonymous caller called Billy after seeing that Bob Hunter was representing the church. The caller warned Billy that Bob Hunter "Gets what his client wants."[223]

The law teams were in place. The "best trial lawyer in North Carolina" was representing the family, the lawyer who "gets what his client wants" was representing the church, and Lonnie Williams was representing the Pridgens and the caretakers.

Lonnie Williams brought one of his partners, Charles Meier, onto the case. Maxwell recalled that Meier came to the hearing with no brief or notes except what he prepared as he sat in court waiting for the hearing to start.[224] The attorneys met after this hearing. Maxwell and Hunter noted the people they might want to depose. Lonnie Williams "indicated that he did not know if he wanted to take any depositions." Per Maxwell's notes, Williams stated that it was his preferred practice to not give witnesses an opportunity to "rehearse" their testimony, but to catch them "cold" in his examination at trial."[225]

．．．．．

Judge Alford was assigned the case. Maxwell would ask Judge Alford to allow the legal action to move forward with assertions of incapacity, and undue influence. The family half expected the judge to deny the incapacity but hoped he would allow them to proceed with the claim of undue influence. Maxwell informed the family that the judge could theoretically deny both. Hunter's trump card could end the suit.

This hit the family like a ton of bricks. The churches lawyer said that the facts of the case don't pass the "smell test". At one point in the meeting Lonnie Williams even said that Uncle Jimmy thought he was worth $10 million, but he was only worth a little over 5 million (another indicator of incapacity to manage his own funds). Even after the family made it clear that they would try to protect the gift to the church, there was no indication that the church would make it easy for the family to claim their ancestor's land. The family perceived that, despite the evidence of misconduct, the church would not help pursue criminal or ethical misconduct action against their congregation members, the Pridgen's, or the caretakers. From his first meeting with Bob Hunter and Carlton Fisher, Jim Maxwell understood that the Church's "primary obligation is to be certain that it protects and preserves the fiduciary obligation that it has to its membership."[226] At that point family members started to perceive that the First Baptist Church of Wilmington, NC prioritized fund raising over morality. The family waited on pins and needles for a ruling from Judge Alford.

20. A Search for Witnesses

Preparation for trial continued. During his April 27, 2005 visit to Wilmington, Jim Maxwell interviewed friends of Uncle Jimmy, Henry VonOesen and Margaret Banck. These two were longtime friends of Uncle Jimmy and his family. In his personal notes Jim Maxwell described Henry VonOesen as "a very distinguished, very upright, healthy-appearing male. He was very articulate and should make a good witness." Henry VonOesen noted that the family's relationship with Uncle Jimmy was very good, but changed noticeably "after the caretakers (specifically Pat Jenkins) came on the scene." VonOesen recalled a time when he went to visit Uncle Jimmy and was "put off" when almost immediately after they sat down one of the caregivers came in and sat down and listened to everything they said. VonOesen felt it was highly inappropriate for this third party felt it necessary to listen to the conversation. VonOesen also recalled talking to his friends Harold and Margaret Alexis who told him that they stopped visiting Uncle Jimmy because the caretakers made them feel uncomfortable."[227]

In his personal notes Jim Maxwell describes Margaret Banck as "a very close friend to Dr. Smith's [Uncle Jimmy's] sister..." who "...was a fairly frequent visitor in the home..." Margaret Bank visited Uncle Jimmy one time and took him a cake she had baked. She recalled sitting in his kitchen visiting with him when a young woman came in without acknowledging her presence and "plopped herself down in Dr. Smith's lap and became exceedingly familiar with him immediately." Banck recalls that as this younger woman was conducting this "extremely inappropriate" behavior Pat Jenkins walked in and introduced the younger woman as her daughter. During another visit Banck recalled taking some Silver Queen Corn to Uncle Jimmy's house and Pat Jenkins, answered the door. Pat told her that Dr. Smith could not eat it, did not want it and shut the door.[228]

These witnesses spoke kindly of the Smith family, and harshly of those in Uncle Jimmy's house in his final years. The family would need more than that, however. The next thing Jim Maxwell needed, was for the propounders to formally state their positions for the court. They would do so in interrogatories.

21. Interrogatory Number Nine

Before Judge Alford would make a ruling on the merit of the caveator's claims he would make a ruling on the propounders motion to Quash the subpoenas vs. the caveator's motion to compel. That first ruling was made early in July, but Judge Alford's paperwork didn't make it to the interested parties for over a month. As the Smith family waited for the Judge's ruling Jim Maxwell's investigation started to turn up some very enlightening information. On July 5, 2005, Jim Maxwell wrote a letter to Billy, his son Bill and his daughter-in-law Anna. He included Anna because of her knowledge of the law and Smith family dynamics. Attached to the letter was a copy of the Pridgen's final billing statement to Uncle Jimmy. Lonnie Williams had sent the final bill to Maxwell with a request that he "advise whether the statement may be paid or whether I will need to petition the clerk for a hearing."[229]   Jim Maxwell's letter to family members read:

> Dear Billy Bill and Anna,
>   I would really like you to closely look at the bill that is enclosed herewith. The problems with this are striking and noteworthy. Jan Pridgen shows that, for the month of February, she "normally" had 4 calls every day, 7 days a week with Pat. My recollection (and I have not gone back to look) is that Pat only worked 3 days a week and then generally only until 3:00 in the afternoon. There are a couple of calls, as Dr. Smith was dying, to Wanda and one to Carol.
>   I will look to talk to you after you have had a chance to look at this.
> Yours very truly,
> [signed]
> James B. Maxwell[230]

The bill covered the time period from February 1, 2005 to February 22, 2005. These days were the last 22 days of Uncle Jimmy's life. The amount billed by the Pridgen's was $13,065.00. That is close to $600.00 per day, seven days a week. It is interesting to look through Otto and Jan Pridgen's bill to see what kind of legal work they did to earn $13,065.00. They didn't write a will for him in that time period (that was already done). They didn't buy or sell stocks for him. They

112

didn't handle any litigation in the court system for him. Otto Pridgen did log a phone call with John Newton. John Newton was the timber man who had clear cut the Columbus County farmland. The timber was cut almost three years earlier, so it is curious that Otto billed Uncle Jimmy $60.00 for a phone call with Newton then. The itemized bill is not extremely detailed, but it appears that they billed him nearly $2,000.00 for "bookwork" and tax preparation. One of the most outrageous items on the bill is the $450.00 that Otto Pridgen charged Uncle Jimmy to go to his birthday party.[231]

There are many entries regarding calls between Jan Pridgen and Pat Jenkins. Some had additional notes about the subject of the phone call. For example, on February 1st:

Call to Pat; morning report; bp 97/50
$37.50

Call from Pat; Allene Croom wants to visit
$15.00

Call from Pat; she has birthday decorations
$15.00

Call from Pat; noon report; bp low; Allene came by
$37.50

Call from Pat; he said he didn't need anything to help him swallow
$15.00

Call from Pat; afternoon report; low bp
$37.50

Call from Pat; evening report
$37.50[232]

February 1st was also the day Otto took the call from John Newton. In addition to those bills on that day Jan billed Uncle Jimmy $97.50 for "mail, etc." and Otto billed him $225.00 for "from home to Dr. Smith's to office". The total came to $667.50 for February 1st. In those 22 days, there were at least a dozen entries similar to Otto's "from home to Dr. Smith's to office" on the 1st. There were also over eighty-five calls made between Jan Pridgen and Pat Jenkins from February 1st to February 20th. Jan's last phone entry with a call from Pat on the 20th read, "call from Pat; xxxlgbm."[233] Jan Pridgen describes this as an "An extra large BM."[234]. BM is the abbreviation for bowel movement.[235] There was not a single call logged to or from Wanda on the bill up to that point. On the evening of the 20th there were two calls to Wanda

113

(not from Wanda). One was from Jan and the other from Otto. They both read, "call to Wanda; he's going down."[236] What did Jan and Otto know that night that made them break their normal habit pattern and call Wanda on the night shift twice? Why didn't anyone take him to the hospital?

Reviewing this bill has led me to some sickening conclusions about Uncle Jimmy's final days, but there is more about the bill that doesn't pass the "smell test". Pat often made morning, noon, afternoon and evening reports to Jan Pridgen, but she would also call any time someone wanted to visit (Allene Croom for example). Some such notes recorded in the Pridgen's last bill are as follows:

February 3rd between the afternoon and evening report
Call from Pat; Billy and Jodie came by
February 5th between the noon and afternoon report
Call from Pat; Dr. Bill and Thomas are there
February 9th between the morning and noon report
Call from Pat; Billy came and brought a bday card from Ebie Padgett
February 13th between the morning and noon report
Call from Pat; Jane Davis is coming by
Call from Pat; Jane Davis brought flowers; he was sleeping[237]

This bill reinforces my suspicion that the Pridgens and Pat Jenkins were running an information control operation in that house. Pat increased her presence to seven days a week from three, and Jan Pridgen seemed to be running the headquarters.

.....

The Pridgen's billing statement was a good piece of evidence for the Smith family, but they continued to hope for a settlement. Part of an agreement suitable to the family would include the transfer of the Columbus County farmland at a fair price. After Uncle Jimmy's son died, the farm property was appraised at $344,500.00.[238] The family expected that during the real estate boom of that time period the property might fetch a little more than that, but they were completely unprepared for the news that Hunter brought from the church. An appraisal of the farmland was completed for Carlton Fisher, realtor, and head of trustees for First Baptist Church. His appraiser valued the land at $1,493,000.00.[239] How did a half million-dollar piece of property

114

turn into a 1.5-Million-dollar piece of property in three years? The family's trust in the First Baptist leadership eroded further.

.....

Jim Maxwell produced "interrogatories", or questions, for the propounders to answer as well as requests for production of documents. Among the 12 interrogatories Maxwell produced for Otto Pridgen to answer was:

> "Interrogatory No. 9: On September 26, 2002, James Henry Smith signed a paper-writing purporting to be his Last Will and Testament. The document was apparently prepared by Wilmington attorney, Robert O'Quinn, was witnessed by Dr. Frank R. Reynolds and Edward A. Rusher, Jr., and was notarized by Tammie B. Anderson. Please indicate:
> Were you or your wife present when Dr. Smith signed this document on September 26, 2002.
> Answer: No

> Where (physical location) was the document signed by Dr. Smith?
> Answer: On information and belief, at Dr. Smith's residence: [address deleted]

> Did you provide any information to Mr. O'Quinn, either orally or in written form, prior to Dr. Smith's signing the document on September 26th, 2002?
> Answer: Yes.

> If the answer to 9(c) immediately preceding is "yes", please describe the information you provided Mr. O'Quinn.
> Answer: I told Mr. O'Quinn earlier that Dr. Smith wanted to make a will.

> Did you or your office assist, in any manner, in securing the attendance of Dr. Reynolds and/or Mr. Rusher as witnesses to Dr. Smith's signature on that document?
> Answer: I have no recollection of this other than I am sure that I told Mr. O'Quinn that Dr. Smith frequently played

115

cards with Dr. Reynolds and Mr. Rusher and that they had known him for many years and would be glad to go to his home to witness the execution of his Will as Mr. O'Quinn's office was not handicapped accessible and Dr. Smith could not climb the stairs to get there.

When did you first learn that you were to be named or had been named as Executor of James Henry Smith's estate in the document he signed on September 26, 2002?

     Answer: September 26, 2002, after he had executed his Will.[240]

While I believe that much more of Otto Pridgen's testimony is false, Interrogatory No. 9 provides testimony for which there is strong evidence that Otto is not honestly cooperating. As you continue reading, keep in mind that Otto claims that he offered no oral or written information to O'Quinn other than to tell him that Uncle Jimmy wanted to write a will. Keep in mind that Otto claims that he did not know that he would be named executor until after the will was executed.

Jim Maxwell wrote his assessment of the interrogatories in a memorandum to family members on August 8, 2005:

     As a follow up to the various discovery responses that we have mailed to you, I am enclosing a copy of some "partial" (and I would suggest "selected") medical records that Mr. Williams has provided to us in response to our discovery request. As you will see, he describes these records as "limited but powerful" and that is because he believes that they clearly establish that Dr. Smith had mental capacity at the time the will was executed in September 2002.

     We have requested additional records other than these but, I find these records more curious than "powerful." First of all, you will note in the responses to our discovery that I have sent you, that Mr. Pridgen has denied that he had "anything" to do with the execution of Dr. Smith's Will, other than to make arrangements with Mr. O'Quinn (the attorney who drafted the Will) in order to accommodate Dr. Smith's infirmities and inability to go upstairs to Mr. O'Quinn's office. Yet, as early as May 2002 (approximately one month after Pridgen was appointed power of attorney),[23] he is taking Dr. Smith to various doctors in an effort to demonstrate that he is "competent" or "has the mental capacity" to execute a new will. Copies of those reports were even sent to Pridgen.

Secondly, in their responses to our discovery and, despite the fact that Ms. Jenkins, Tucker and Phillips all are certified Nurse Assistants (Ms. Jenkins is a NA II), they all denied that they were "caregivers" for Dr. Smith until June 2003. This is a blatant effort to try to establish that they did not have a fiduciary relationship with Dr. Smith at the time the Will was executed. If they did have such a fiduciary relationship, then, as you know from prior discussions, the law will presume that they used undue influence to obtain benefits through the Will. (A person in a fiduciary relationship who receives a r[b]equest in the "ward's" Will is "[p]resumed to have exerted undue influence.") By their answers to the discovery they are trying to distance themselves from that problem. However, the neuropsychologist that they used was apparently not aware of or part of this scheme (other than being duped into doing a mental status exam) and she refers to Ms. Phillips (the one who received the large "payment") as "a nurse." That would be information that would be provided by one of only a few sources: Dr. Smith himself, one of the caregivers, or Mr. Pridgen. Thus, in July 2002, and prior to the time the Will was being redone, Dr. Smith and/or Mr. Pridgen, believed that these women were nurses and not "companions."

Quite frankly, it almost appears to me from this that the "plan" to get Dr. Smith to change his Will began and was orchestrated almost immediately after Mr. Pridgen became the power of attorney. It further appears that Pridgen and others were aware that there was going to be serious questions about this and had Dr. Smith examined by, at least, two physicians to try to bolster their claim that he had the mental capacity to do what he was getting ready to do. The "smell test" gets "fouler" with each passing day.[241]

---

[23] This was a mistake in Maxwell's memo, it was only one day later, not one month.

With his memo was a copy of a Mini Mental State Exam done by Dr. Dewey H. Bridger and a Neuropsychological report conducted by Dr. Christy Jones. He got a perfect score on the Mini Mental State Exam which included questions like, "What is today's date" and "Show the subject a wrist watch and ask him/her what it is. Repeat for a pencil."

On the Neuropsychological exam he did not do as well. He was administered several tests by Dr. Jones' staff. The first was the WAIS III test which gave the following results:

IQ/INDEX	STANDARD SCORE	PERCENTILE RANK
Verbal IQ	86	18
Performance IQ	77	6
Full Scale IQ	80	9
Verbal Comprehension Index	84	14
Perceptual Organization Index	82	12
Working Memory Index	92	30
Processing Speed Index	69	2 [242]

The percentile rank indicates what percentage of the population he did better than. This is not the total population of the world, but is the population of people in his age group who have taken the test. It appears that at the time Uncle Jimmy signed his Will he had a weaker mental performance than 80% of elders who have been tested for mental capacity.[24]

Uncle Jimmy didn't do well on the test. She attributed his poor performance to "language limitations as a result of his voice box... Thus, he was administered the untimed and relatively non-verbal Raven's Coloured Progressive Matrices as a measure of intelligence. Results suggest performance that falls between the 50th and 75th percentile."[243] I get the impression that the first test didn't give her the results she wanted, so she used another test to curve the score up. Even with the curve Uncle Jimmy was below average at the time of the exam.

Her team administered other tests. The Boston Naming Test suggesting "expressive speech that falls within the Average range." The Controlled Word Association Test "suggested mild impairment in terms of verbal fluency. As it was timed and involved verbal responses, results are interpreted to suggest at least average verbal fluency."[244]

---

[24] Except in the working memory index.

Once again I get the impression that Jones curved the score. The Wisconsin Card Sorting Test and the short form of the Category Test suggested "moderate impairment in terms of executive functioning." Trail Making Tests A & B results suggested "performance that was significantly impacted in terms of manual dexterity deficits and speed of processing." The Greek Cross from the Wepman Aphasia Screening Test results suggest borderline constructional dyspraxia.[245]

Jones' staff used the Wechsler Memory Scale-III to examine his memory functioning. Again, the results showed a low percentile:

MEMORY DOMAIN	STANDARD SCORE	PERCENTILE
Auditory Immediate	77	6
Visual Immediate	88	21
Immediate Memory	78	7
Auditory Delayed	83	13
Visual Delayed	84	14
Auditory Recognition Delayed	90	25
General Memory	82	12
Working Memory	91	27 [246]

Again, she seems to curve the results, in her own words:

> To examine the extent to which speed of processing and overall attention are impacting neurocognition, Mr. Smith was administered the Ruff Two and Seven Selective Attention Test. Results suggest speed that falls below 99% of the population but accuracy that falls within the Average range. The average level of accuracy suggests that the Wisconsin Card Sorting Test and the Short Form of the Category Test may have underestimated Dr. Smith's frontal lobe functioning.[247]

Finally, Uncle Jimmy was administered the MMPI-2 to assess the extent to which psychiatric distress might be contributing to neurocognitive dysfunction. This test suggested no evidence of "psychopathology, including anxiety or depression."[248]

Uncle Jimmy's wife died in December of 2001. His only child died in April of 2002. If what The Pridgens and the caregivers claim was true, then the rest of his family wanted to put him in a nursing home and take his money. By August of 2002 Dr. Christy Jones assessed that he had no anxiety or depression. Jones must have thought the man was hard as nails. I can't help thinking that Christy Jones was a hired gun. Based on my research, I estimate that she only spent about 10 minutes face to face with Uncle Jimmy. Her employees administered the tests. I suspect she spent far more time interfacing with Otto Pridgen, and Pat Jenkins, whom she referred to as Uncle Jimmy's "nurse" in her records. I suspect that Dr. Jones felt a duty to protect Uncle Jimmy from the family that Pridgen and Jenkins described.

One of the legal qualifications used to determine if a person is mentally competent to write a will is the ability to understand his/her financial situation. Christy Jones included five paragraphs of notes on Uncle Jimmy's "background information". The things she included in the background information include his age, education, medical conditions and the fact that he was assisted by his "nurse" Patricia Coston Jenkins. Jones also noted that Uncle Jimmy gave another "nurse" a check for a large sum of money for "saving his life". According to Jones' notes, that "nurse" kept "a family member from putting him in a nursing home."[249] If Jones was aware that that nurse's employment was terminated shortly after the check was written she failed to put it in her report. If Jones knew that there was not enough cash in the checking account to cover the check, she neglected to put that in her report also. She did include in her report that Uncle Jimmy's Attorney, Otto Pridgen, "allows him to spend approximately $1000 per day."[250] She did not make a note of why a man who is competent to handle his own finances was put on an allowance by his lawyer.

Then there is a very interesting note that Jones made in Uncle Jimmy's background information. She writes, "His finances are overlooked by a CPA and an attorney, who took over the finances when his nephew wanted to fire the nurses (by the patient's report)."[251] In a 5-paragraph report, why did this one sentence get the parenthetical with "(by the patient's report)"? How much of the "background information" did not come from the patient? I suspect most of the "background information" was fed to her by Pat Jenkins and Otto Pridgen.

.....

Jim Maxwell's investigation was turning up valuable information, but he still wanted all the information he had requested in his first request for production of documents. The judge ruled that information was relevant and ordered disclosure, but Lonnie Williams would file a Motion for a protective order to prevent his clients from having to divulge the information requested by the caveators. Jim Maxwell would have to gain a Motion to Compel to the propounders to get the information he requested. Once again, the parties would have to wait for a judge's decision. Before the decision would be made the attorneys would take their first round of depositions.

22. Depositions Part I
The Three Legged Stool
August-September 2005

The depositions were taken in the presence of all three law teams. Witnesses were brought in individually, and sworn under oath, and recorded by a court reporter.

Linda David Phillips

If you look at Linda Phillips' deposition independently it looks believable. She said that she was recommended to Uncle Jimmy by his friend Margaret Banck.[252] She said that she and Carol Tucker started working for Uncle Jimmy about the same time.[253] She claimed that she was not hired as a nurse.[254] She did say that Pat Jenkins and Carol Tucker usually wore white (like a nurse), but she said it was just easier for them not to decide what to wear, and did not suggest that they were nurses uniforms.[255] She said that she never saw the family visit Uncle Jimmy until after Little Jimmy died, which may be true since she worked late hours.[256] She admitted that she never visited Uncle Jimmy after her employment was terminated.[257]

There were some things in her deposition that didn't add up. She said that Uncle Jimmy had only given her $500.00 in gifts.[258] This conflicted with the $72,000.00 Uncle Jimmy told the detective that he had given her. She said that the 2-million-dollar check was just a joke and that she had no intention of cashing it.[259] This also conflicts with other data, this time from Dr. Jones' report. She said that when Jan Pridgen asked her to return the check she did so, but claimed that she was not fired by the Pridgen's after the incident with the 2-million-dollar check.[260] She claimed that the Pridgens changed her working hours so she left employment voluntarily.[261] One significant detail that she left out of her testimony was that after she was fired she called Billy and asked him if she could speak with him. Billy recalls that she confided in him that she was fired and that she would never work a job with Pat Jenkins again and said that she could finally understand why Billy and Jodie showed up late that night to remove her and the other nurses.[262]

She continued her deposition and said that Uncle Jimmy wanted to leave his farm to Billy's son Bill, but changed his mind after Bill took Uncle Jimmy to the farm and showed him "what they were going to do with this stuff over here, and ... what they were going to do with this pile of stuff over there."[263]

I'll be the devil's advocate for a second. Let's assume that Uncle Jimmy was irritated with Bill because he was presumptuous about future ownership of the farm. Would this make Uncle Jimmy deny the rest of his family the farm? Would this make him want to carve out 5 acres around the farmhouse to be sold to Bill after his death? This does not sound like Uncle Jimmy to me. I don't think this was a logical way for Uncle Jimmy to act unless his competence was shaken, and/or he was unduly influenced by someone else.

Dr. Frank Russell Reynolds, M.D.

Dr. Frank Reynolds would prove to be a good witness for the propounders. He witnessed Uncle Jimmy sign his will. He was not a beneficiary, and would not benefit, or suffer, no matter which way this trial went. He knew Uncle Jimmy for a long time and understood his attachment to his farmland.[264] He knew he took his bible class to his farm on occasion.[265] He visited and played cards with Uncle Jimmy regularly. He felt that Pat Jenkins and Carol Tucker provided excellent care for Uncle Jimmy.[266] The court reporter's transcript gives me the impression that Dr. Rusher is well spoken. He used proper grammar, and even speech. However, at one point in his interview, the court reporter captured some stammering. Jim Maxwell asked Reynolds if Uncle Jimmy ever referred to his caretakers as nurses and Reynolds replied, "I can't—I don't—I don't recall him—they were his—his helpers, different—I don't—he—he never spoke of them as nurses. They were just there."[267]

He also said that Uncle Jimmy was knowledgeable about his business affairs as of the date the will was signed and that he could not be easily led. When asked if it would surprise him to find out that Uncle Jimmy had been withdrawing $9,000.00 per day for several months Reynolds replied, "I—I don't know enough about his finances to say that it would surprise me, but I'm sure that if he did it, it was for some reason."[268]

Reynolds obviously did not see the side of Pat Jenkins that Billy and his family saw. Perhaps the caregivers were on their best behavior when the card players were visiting. Never-the-less he was a witness that was extremely damaging to the family's case.

Edward Armel Rusher, Jr.

Much like Dr. Reynolds, Ed Rusher would be a good witness for the propounders. He testified that he visited Uncle Jimmy about 1 to 2 times a week until Uncle Jimmy had an appendectomy.[269] He testified that Uncle Jimmy loved his farm.[270] He testified that Uncle Jimmy was good at cards and understood his financial situation.[271] He testified that Uncle Jimmy was not easily led.[272]

Otto Kilgore Pridgen, II

As I read Otto Pridgen's deposition I almost felt sorry for him. He spoke about his Wake Forest education. He said that his classmate, Lonnie Williams, "...was probably one of the better students, sat up close to the front..." About his self he stated, "I sat in the back of the bus."[273] He noted that after graduation he went back to Wilmington to practice law and "...did anything that I could to try to—because I was married and had a small child to try to make a living and just to—just what you could imagine. I did not—I could not specialize in anything, because that was totally impossible. I'm an only child, and my family had never used lawyers. And I didn't even know the names of any lawyers here, so I just had to start from scratch and do whatever I could. I've done everything from soup to nuts."[274] He stated, "The practice of law has deteriorated or degenerated terribly in the past ten years with the advent of advertising... that's really been horrible for the personal injury practice. Of course, the criminal practice has been socialized you know."[275]

When asked if he had ever handled trusts, or estate planning he stated, "My clients, in general, are not too concerned about a tru—they wouldn't even know what the word trust means, and their estates have never been a burden."[276] When asked if he had ever served as a power of attorney he stated, "I'm sure that I probably had to do one or two minor things like sign somebody's name that was going out of the country to a deed or something like that, but nothing of this size or scope."[277] When asked if the North Carolina rules of Professional Conduct would consider a paralegal working under the direction of an attorney to have a fiduciary relationship with the client he stated, "... I have no idea what the rules of professional conduct say about something like this."[278] When asked if he had any "...social or other type relationship with Dr. Smith" he said, "Dr. Smith's social world was far above our family."[279]

I think Otto Pridgen had a grudge against the aristocracy of the First Baptist Church. Otto Pridgen's parents were members of the church when he was born. He spent his entire life in the congregation, but it seems, even with a law degree, he was not accepted into the elite center of this social circle. He would never walk among the giants that brokered the purchase of land for the activities center. He would never have his picture hung on the wall like the one in his Sunday School classroom, the Smith classroom, named after Uncle Jimmy's father.[25] He would never have a building named after him, like the Sidbury house. I wonder how different things might have turned out for Otto Pridgen if he had someone to guide him in the early days of his law practice.

Otto Pridgen stated that until the time that he drafted the papers to revoke Billy's power of attorney he had never done legal work for Uncle Jimmy.[280] Pridgen testified that Uncle Jimmy approached him to be his power of attorney once Uncle Jimmy decided to revoke Billy's power. He testified that Uncle Jimmy called him on the phone after accidentally calling his son first. Otto explained that he has an unlisted number (Why would a law firm have an unlisted number?), so an attempt to find him in the phonebook might lead you to his namesake son.[281] He claimed to have had no knowledge of Uncle Jimmy's personal affairs prior to being hired, and all through my research I wondered how he might have gotten the "intelligence" that would prompt him to establish a professional relationship with Uncle Jimmy. Pridgen testified that a law partner of Bob Johnson's went to visit him right after an "intervention" that Billy Smith had. According to Otto Pridgen, Bob's partner disclosed to him that she had seen a detective's report that indicated caregivers were taking large sums of money out of his bank account.[282] It's curious that Uncle Jimmy had never hired Otto

---

[25] The "Smith classroom" is in the basement of the Sidbury house, and is named after William Thomas Smith, Sr. This is where Uncle Jimmy and Otto Pridgen attended Sunday school.

Pridgen to do any work for him in the past, but Pridgen claims the larynx cancer survivor called him on the phone on this occasion.

Pridgen testified that around the time that Uncle Jimmy first employed him he was given a copy of Detective Johnson's report and was aware of its contents.[283] He states that he did his own investigation into the matter.[284] He described the detective's report as follows: "The report was typical law enforcement work. It was very facile--fascial—childish or however you want to put it."[285] He stated that the money that was flowing out of Uncle Jimmy's bank account did not go to the caretakers.[286] Pridgen testified that the money was going to Uncle Jimmy's son and described the lavish lifestyle Little Jimmy was living. "Now—and on top of that" Pridgen continued "he was a homosexual, and this lifestyle, you can push a lot of money up your nose with cocaine."[287]

When asked about Dr. Christy Jones neuropsychological report in which she wrote Jimmy's lawyer "allows him to spend approximately $1000 per day."[288] Pridgen explained, "No. I'm sure that what he [Uncle Jimmy] told her [Jones]—he should have told her that he was given walking around money, cash, if he wanted it of a thousand dollars. We didn't—we cut off all cash."[289] Pridgen states that taking his money out of his account and giving it to whomever he chooses was Uncle Jimmy's business, and he "never challenges his decisions", then why did he control his cashflow?[290] When Pridgen was asked why he took the $2,000,000.00 check away from Linda Phillips he said, "I wanted it back." After another "Why?" from Jim Maxwell Pridgen said, "I did. My business. I wanted the check back. I told her to give me that check back. Something wrong with that?"[291] Notice that Pridgen was conducting Pridgen's business, not Uncle Jimmy's. If it was truly a joke-gift, why not just cancel the check, and let Linda keep it?

Pridgen even testified that he had a luncheon with Uncle Jimmy's banker at which the banker suggested a charitable trust presumably to protect Uncle Jimmy's assets from the IRS after his death. Uncle Jimmy was not at that meeting. Pridgen decided that a charitable trust was not right "for a man ninety-five years of age..."[292] A foundation would have diminished the amount the executor would dispose of after Uncle Jimmy's death. If Otto Pridgen knew that he would be paid a percentage of the estate as executor, he would know that a foundation could reduce his payment from the estate to near zero.

126

Of course, it would also diminish the 10% of the residuary that his wife would receive.

Otto Pridgen stated in his career he had drafted "a lot of wills" for people.[293] Pridgen also claimed that he did not know the contents of the will until after it was executed.[294] Pridgen had trouble explaining why he referred Uncle Jimmy to Bob O'Quinn to draft his will. The conversation went as follows:

O. Pridgen: I said, "Well, Dr. Smith, I can't do this for you." And you'll—in my opinion, you better get another lawyer, and you can get the same lawyer that drew [Little] Jimmy's will. And that was Bob O'Quinn. He knew you and whatnot and get Dr.—I mean, Bob O'Quinn to draw it.

Maxwell: Okay. And why was it your opinion you could not draw a will for Dr. Smith?

O. Pridgen: I didn't want to draw it for him.

Maxwell: Okay. Why did you not want to draw it for him?

O. Pridgen: I thought it would be stupid.

Maxwell: And why did you think it would be stupid?

O. Pridgen: That was my best judgment.

Maxwell: Did you know that your wife was going to be a beneficiary?

O. Pridgen: No, I did not.

Maxwell: Then what would have been stupid about you drawing a will for a person you were serving as power of attorney for?

O. Pridgen: I just thought it was stupid.[295]

Otto testified about the timber harvested from Uncle Jimmy's Brunswick County Property (not the family farm): "The track of land in Brunswick County, approximately 80 acres, is landlocked. The—

it's inaccessible except crossing other people's property. The other person who has a road down there is a man named George Robins, and he's an old son of a bitch. And he was always friends with Dr. Smith until we asked George Robins to let us use the road to get to the – access to cut timber."[296] It's notable that George Robins seems to have been friends with Uncle Jimmy until Otto Pridgen entered the scene. On September 2nd, a $7500.00 check was written off of Uncle Jimmy's account made payable to Squires Timber Company with the memo, "1/2 of payment to George Robbins for road usage [sic]." O.K. Pridgen signed that check.[297]

As for the family farm, Otto Pridgen testified that he did not take more than one bid for Uncle Jimmy's timber sale to John Newton that occurred in 2002.[298] He said that even though he had "never laid eyes on John Newton before" that taking multiple bids "... ain't my way of doing business."[299]

Pridgen gave testimony about the final bill he submitted to Uncle Jimmy's estate.[300] Recall the phone call that Pridgen made to Newton on his final bill to Uncle Jimmy.[301] When asked why he called Newton years after the timber was cut Otto replied, "...I suppose I was calling him to tell him that you all were going to be calling and wanting to talk to him about this."[302] What made Otto Pridgen think that the family (or the family's attorney, who hadn't even been retained yet) might want to talk to John Newton about the estate three weeks before Uncle Jimmy died? The facts make me wonder if the Pridgen's knew about Uncle Jimmy's demise three weeks before he had and extra, extra, extra, large bowel movement? Is it possible that the call to Newton was to get everyone's story straight before the will would be revealed to the family?

Jim Maxwell asked Otto why there is no record that Otto and Jan Pridgen called a physician after Wanda reported to them that Uncle Jimmy was "going down."[303] The deposition continued as follows:

O. Pridgen: When a man is dying, what can a doctor do?

Maxwell: So it was your determination that he was dying?

O. Pridgen: I think he was.

128

Maxwell: And it wasn't important for you to have some medical practitioner come see him to confirm that?

O. Pridgen: Well, Pat and Carol have seen a number of people die. I've seen a few, and I don't know what more could have been done.

Maxwell: Okay. So you simply decided you didn't need to find out if there was anything else to be done?

O. Pridgen: I knew there was nothing else to be done. There wasn't no finding out. This man was dying slowly. I had called Dr. Bill [Smith]… approximately, three weeks, maybe a month before this and told him that we were losing Dr. Smith….[304]

Jack Richardson

Jack Richardson had been Uncle Jimmy's financial advisor for about 2 years at the time his will was written.[305] He provided bank and securities statements from Uncle Jimmy's account.   A lot of his responses were in line with what the family expected. He testified that he cautioned Uncle Jimmy about withdrawing large sums of money from the bank. He said that he told Uncle Jimmy that this was not the right way to avoid paying estate taxes.[306] He assumed that a lot of the money was going to Uncle Jimmy's son, but also said that Uncle Jimmy told him he was tipping his caregivers.[307] Richardson testified that Uncle Jimmy said some of the caregivers would not "ever have to work again."[308]

When it came to the family's interactions with their uncle, Richardson testified that the family rallied around Uncle Jimmy after his wife Iris' death.[309] He said the transition period (around the time between his wife's death and Otto Pridgen's entrance as power of attorney) was very hard on Uncle Jimmy.[310] This contradicts the neuropsychologists report that he had no depression at that time.[311]

When asked if Uncle Jimmy understood his financial wealth at the time of his death he said that Uncle Jimmy understood his liquid assets well, but overestimated the value of his farmland. He stated that Uncle Jimmy thought his total net worth was around 10 to 15 million dollars.[312] Richardson also testified that he remembers a conversation where Otto Pridgen (who claimed to know nothing of the contents of the will at that time) said that "the church would be taken care of" in the will.[313]

More to the point, Richardson testified that he had several meetings with Otto Pridgen and Reverend Jim Everette in which they discussed financial planning. At many of these meetings Uncle Jimmy was not present. At one meeting, he hand-delivered some information about charitable giving to Otto Pridgen.[314] This information included measures that could reduce the taxes and attorney's fees against the estate. At another meeting Otto Pridgen informed Richardson that Uncle Jimmy would not be using these cost saving measures.[315] When asked if he had spoken with Uncle Jimmy about his "long-term--after his death plans" for the farm he started to stammer a little bit. He answered:

> The initial conversation around the farm was more inclined that—that this would probably be a family asset. And then the second—or later on it—it—it turned from a—becoming a family asset—still thinking family asset, but the conversation was that Dr. Smith's nephew--....--Nephew Billy's son, Dr. William Smith, would be financially able to maintain that farm. And so it was more of a condition that it—that it would be an opportunity for Dr. William Smith to have an opportunity to go after that asset or—if he chose to.[316]

I can't help wondering why this particular question was so tough for Richardson to answer. I wonder who might have talked to him between the time that he spoke to Maxwell privately and the day of the deposition.

During his deposition, the family learned how involved Reverend Jim Everette, of the First Baptist Church, seemed to be in his estate planning. Richardson testified that "...one of my early meetings was with Dr. Smith and a representative from First Baptist Church, [Rev.] Jim Everette...." He testified that he remembered this meeting occurring before Otto Pridgen held Uncle Jimmy's Power of Attorney[26].[317] Note that these meetings with Reverend Everette started before Otto was appointed. This was among the family's first

---

[26] Reverend Everette confirmed that these meetings occurred before Otto held the power of attorney in a 2020 interview.

discoveries that the church leadership might have been involved in the planning of the will.

During the luncheon with Otto Pridgen where Richardson suggested tax saving measures such as a foundation, Richardson said they also discussed "...some things going on with the church at that time. They were looking for some additional property and whether or not to make an acquisition or like a ten-thirty-one exchange[27] and gift it to the church." This was the meeting where Otto notified Richardson that he would not be pursuing tax and attorney fee savings measures, so I'm confident Pridgen did not suggest the real estate gift to the church.[318] This meeting occurred near the time that The First Baptist Church was planning (and perhaps fundraising) to buy the New Hanover County Law Enforcement Center. When asked the amount that Uncle Jimmy was talking about making at that first meeting with Everette, Richardson replied "...a million dollars seems to be a dollar amount that rang out in my—you know, my ear."[319]

Richardson was asked if he ever called Reverend Everette or Reverend Queen to tell them about the disposition of the will. Richardson answered, "I'm fairly certain I did not call Mike Queen. I had—and it seems to me that I may have called Jim Everette to find out where things were, but I do not remember giving information about the will in detail or even—I don't know at what point I knew that the church was included."[320] It is interesting that it was not always apparent to Richardson that the First Baptist Church would have been included in the will at all. It's also interesting that the banker was asking Reverend Everette where things were, as if Everette was on the inside of the planning effort.

At one point Richardson said that he would not speak to a member of the church about Uncle Jimmy's financial affairs outside Uncle Jimmy's presence.[321] At another point in the deposition he was asked why he hand-carried information to Otto Pridgen instead of delivering it directly to Uncle Jimmy. Richardson answered:

---

[27] One tax saving measure Richardson discussed was a 1031 exchange. A 1031 exchange would involve the sale of one piece of real estate (the Woodford farm for example) and the nearly simultaneous purchase of another piece of property (the Law Enforcement Center for example) in such a way that capital gains taxes would be avoided on the sale.

Richardson: O.K. [Pridgen] at that point was the power of attorney—had power of attorney for Dr. Smith's affairs, and at that point I—I was—I felt it was more appropriate to go through the power of attorney with information to—to build some consensus around what direction we wanted to take rather than going directly to Dr. Smith and then trying to go through the power of attorney.

Hunter: Well, was Dr. Smith incapable of understanding these—these vehicles [living trusts]?

Richardson: I wouldn't say that as much as the noise around—the clatter around these kinds of structures for me would have—I thought it would have been an easier path to come through Jim Everette and O.K. Pridgen as a—as a three-legged stool with myself included and Mr. Whaley [the tax accountant] to talk about some of these options...[322]

I think that Jack Richardson did his best to give an honest deposition. I think that there were times when he felt that his professional reputation might be at stake. He said that when Uncle Jimmy was withdrawing $9,000.00 per day, paperwork was filled out to report an unusual transaction to the IRS, but never actually confirmed that the report was submitted.[323] I think he probably surmised that something unethical was going on in the financial planning and was concerned that he might be accused of wrongdoing. I think that he was trying to be honest, but his testimony at times seemed evasive, and I have the perception that he tilted his testimony in favor of the propounders, Jim Everette and Otto Pridgen, the other two legs of the three legged stool.

Robert A. O'Quinn

Bob O'Quinn was the lawyer that drafted the questionable will for Uncle Jimmy. He testified that he bumped into Otto Pridgen on the street one day and was asked to prepare the will.[324] O'Quinn knew the Pridgens, but had little contact with them professionally. He did recall a case he handled "many many years ago" in which Otto was the opposing attorney.[325] As you read the following keep Otto Pridgen's response to Interrogatory number 9 fresh in your mind. Recall that Otto testified that he did not know that he was to be the executor of the will until after it was signed by Uncle Jimmy. Also, recall that Pridgen testified that the only oral or written information he gave O'Quinn was when he let him know that Uncle Jimmy wanted to write a will.[326]

Bob O'Quinn testified that he received a phone call from Otto Pridgen in which Otto briefed O'Quinn on the terms of the will. O'Quinn said that he felt "...horror at the fact that a third party would be calling me and telling me what to put in somebody's will."[327] He felt that it was ethically improper for Otto to do this, and also felt it was inappropriate for Otto's spouse to inherit under the will.[328] Because O'Quinn was suspicious he drafted the will and personally took it to Uncle Jimmy's house. At that meeting some very interesting things transpired. Not all the things that transpired were good for the family's case.

O'Quinn went over each one of the "issues" that he felt needed to be addressed personally. Pat Jenkins and Otto Pridgen were present when O'Quinn went to speak to Uncle Jimmy about the will.[329] Uncle Jimmy told O'Quinn that he wanted to make a $5,000.00 gift to each of his grand-nieces, Lisa and Erin Shelhart in the will.[28] He also changed some language in the will to reflect a gift to the "Roy Piner fund" at the First Baptist Church instead of the "fellowship fund." The fact that he could make decisions like that for his will might be an indicator of competence.[330]

On the other hand, there were some oddities about his correspondence with Uncle Jimmy. O'Quinn testified that after he made the final changes to the will and carried it to his house for signatures Uncle Jimmy told him that Lisa and Erin "never had anything in their life, had only jobs flipping hamburgers, and he wanted them to have a hundred thousand dollars.[331] O'Quinn asked Uncle Jimmy if he wanted to change his will. Uncle Jimmy told O'Quinn not to re-draft the will, but to "Tell Otto to give it [$100,000.00] to them now." Otto Pridgen was not present that day, so O'Quinn wrote him a letter to that effect.[332] Otto Pridgen was asked about this in his deposition, to which Otto responded:

> I've never seen Erin or Lisa. I assume that they live somewhere else, not around here, and I've never heard of these young ladies

---

[28] "Erin" is misspelled "Erwin" in the court reporter's transcript.

before. And Dr. Smith never said anything to me about giving these young ladies any amount of money whatsoever, and he had every opportunity a million times to tell me to give money to anybody he wanted to.[333]

One possible explanation for why Uncle Jimmy wouldn't have followed up on the $100,000 gifts to his nieces is that he may have thought the gifts were delivered. Before I get back to O'Quinn's deposition, take a closer look at Uncle Jimmy's burger-flipping nieces: Uncle Jimmy knew that these two of his grandnieces didn't grow up with the same financial means that most of their cousins did. It was like him to be generous, and these two were likely candidates for his generosity. Why was this gift stifled, when so many others were flowing out of his home?

I can understand why Bob O'Quinn considered this evidence of competence, assuming that Uncle Jimmy understood his nieces' situation. What Bob O'Quinn didn't know is that Lisa was preparing for a master's degree and was employed by the State of Rhode Island, and her sister Erin was preparing for a bachelor's degree in education and would become a school teacher. I don't doubt that Uncle Jimmy would want to give his nieces, who needed financial support for education, such a gift. However, considering them simple burger-flippers, and forgetting their individual achievements is an indicator that he was losing mental capacity.

In light of this testimony and the knowledge about Lisa and Erin's lives, it is interesting that Bob O'Quinn said under oath that he was "Absolutely" satisfied that Uncle Jimmy knew who his nieces and nephews were.[334] I could forgive a single mistake, but there were several other problems. Bob O'Quinn took handwritten notes when Otto presented the terms of the will to him over the phone. In one place his notes said, "Linda and Jack Shelhart".[335] Linda and Jack are Uncle Jimmy's sister's children. Jack had been dead for years, but he had three children... Jack, Lisa and Erin. It is interesting to me that Linda and Jack were grouped together in O'Quinn's notes, as though Uncle Jimmy was talking about giving a gift to the deceased, instead of the next generation. He later remembered Lisa and Erin, of course, but somehow their brother, (the living) Jack Shelhart, never made it from O'Quinn's notes to the will. O'Quinn offered an explanation, "It was either missed or eliminated, or not added back in by Dr. Smith.[336]

134

The familial confusion does not end there. Otto Pridgen told Bob O'Quinn that Uncle Jimmy wanted to leave a gift to his brother Jack's sons.[337] Otto did not know the names of those sons as he relayed this information to O'Quinn over the phone. O'Quinn thinks he got a call back from Otto or Jan with those names.[338] Jack and Billy were included, but Fred was not. At about that time Jan Pridgen called Billy and asked him for an obituary for Uncle Jimmy.[339]

Bob O'Quinn testified, "There was never any issue in my mind about mental competence on the part of Dr. Smith in the brief amount of time I spent with him."[340] This is interesting considering the name juggling and last-minute decision to give $100,000.00 to burger-flippers. O'Quinn did make the point clear that he was basing that on only about 2 hours of face-to-face time with Uncle Jimmy during those visits.[341] He said that he never talked to him on the phone because this was difficult for Uncle Jimmy [due to his voice box].[342] Recall Otto's testimony that his first professional interaction with Uncle Jimmy was by phone. The rest of the interaction O'Quinn had on Uncle Jimmy's behalf was through Otto and Jan Pridgen.

On the subject of undue influence, Bob O'Quinn, Attorney at Law, said, "I can't tell you the legal definition [of undue influence], as I sit here, but, to me it would be something where they take away his will and make it their will, and I did not see that happen."[343] There was the term in O'Quinn's notes relating to the will… "faithful employees". When asked, "Whose word is that?" O'Quinn testified, "It's Otto Pridgen's word."[344] This testimony of Robert O'Quinn, attorney at law, suggests to me that he absolutely does **not** understand the concept of undue influence.

23. Maxwell Smart

Missed it by that much!

Fictional character, Maxwell Smart

The family believed they had a strong case. Despite the evidence, there were legal hurdles that the family would have to get over before the case could go forward. The family had high hopes for Jim Maxwell's law team. Some family members started calling him "Maxwell Smart" after the fictional hero.

I can't capture the facts with the legal precision that Jim Maxwell can, so I include a letter that he wrote the Smith family after the first round of depositions that describes the up-hill legal battle the family faced:

FROM: Jim Maxwell

DATE: September 8, 2005

While it is still fresh in my mind, I wanted to give each of you my impressions of our three days in Wilmington last week and the practical impact those days may have on our Caveat and other issues. The three days were often intense, sometimes informative and, on occasion, beneficial. They were at times contentious. After several days of reflection, some aspects of our case seem clearer.

1. The stated purpose of the trip last week was three fold:
2. To conduct a hearing before the court on our Motion to Compel Mr. Pridgen to produce all his records while serving Dr. Smith as his power of attorney ("POA")
3. To have a hearing before the Clerk of the Superior Court of New Hanover County over the more than $13,000 in fees Mr. Pridgen wanted to pay himself for his service as Dr. Smith's POA for the first 21 days of February, 2005 (to which the Church and we objected as being "unreasonable")

To take a number of depositions of witnesses or interested parties under oath, including:

A. Bob O'Quinn – the attorney who drafted the September 26, 2002 Will;

B. Dr. Frank Reynolds and Ed Rusher – friends of Dr. Smith and respected citizens of Wilmington who witnessed him signing the Will on September 26, 2002);

C. Jack Richardson – Dr. Smith's financial planner/adviser at First Union National Bank who had recommended some sound estate planning;

D. Mr. Pridgen and his wife, Jan;

E. Pat Jenkins, Carol Tucker and Linda Phillips – the three care-givers who (along with Jan Pridgen) were to each receive 10% of Dr. Smith's residuary estate (about $500,000 each).

As it developed, a dispute arose during Mr. Richardson's deposition on Monday afternoon about whether he should be allowed to turn over to us Dr. Smith's CAP Account records from the bank (summary of all his checking, saving and security transactions with the bank). I had subpoenaed those records for the bank and Lonnie Williams objected on the grounds of relevancy. That issue was also heard before Judge Fullwood on Tuesday morning.

Generally speaking, all of the rulings we received from Judge Fullwood or the Clerk of the Superior Court were favorable to us and the information we gleaned from the depositions that were completed should be helpful in allowing us to better evaluate the merits of our Caveat. Unfortunately, we did not have time to take all of the scheduled depositions and, in order to complete them, it would be necessary to come back to Wilmington for the depositions of Pat Jenkins, Carol Tucker and Jan Pridgen (although Ms. Pridgen did testify at the Hearing on the award of fees for February 2005). If we are to complete those depositions, it is the present intention to do so during the latter part of September.

Hearing on Our Motion to Compel:

You will recall that in the discovery we submitted to Mr. Pridgen, we asked that he produce for our inspection all of his records while serving as Dr. Smith's power of attorney from April 30, 2002 until February 21, 2005. These requested records included: all checks that had been paid by or on behalf of Dr. Smith, all bills received and payments made for the care givers; all bills submitted and payments for attorney fees; any and all letters/memos/correspondence of any kind on Dr. Smith's behalf; any and all materials related to any estate planning;

and, information on the contract for "clearing" the timber at Woodford Farm. Mr. Pridgen only produced the latter documents and Lonnie Williams objected to producing any of the other information as being "irrelevant" to our Caveat or a "fishing expedition" on behalf of a "disgruntled nephew" or other "distant" relatives who hoped to benefit from Dr. Smith's estate. I felt that the law was on our side and so argued the court. As has become typical of his "style" Mr. Williams did not argue any "law" to the court, but rather went off on personal attacks of the motives of the family. The Hon. Ernest B. Fullwood, Senior Resident Superior Court Judge for New Hanover County listened patiently to all parties, asked some relevant questions and said he would take some time to consider the issues and let us know later Monday afternoon or Tuesday morning. Since we did not hear from Judge Fullwood's office on Monday, the attorneys went to see him Tuesday morning before he resumed court. At that time, he ruled with us that all of the POA documents in Mr. Pridgen's possession were relevant or could lead to relevant information and he asked that I prepare an Order directing that Mr. Pridgen produce them. I have drafted an Order to that effect and hope to have it signed shortly and the information available prior to resuming any depositions.

On Tuesday morning (when we went back to get the Judge's ruling on the Motion to Compel), I also raised the issue and asked the court to rule on Mr. Williams' objection Monday afternoon to our reviewing the financial records from Dr. Smith's CAP Account at First Union from January 1, 2000 until Dr. Smith's death. Our interest was two-fold: 1) we were interested in learning whether or not the size of the estate had been materially reduced in that time period; and, 2) we were interested in confirming how much total money, and for how long a period of time, had the $9,000/day in cash been withdrawn from Dr. Smith's account. This "hearing" in the hall outside the courtroom where Judge Fullwood was presiding over a jury trial, was extremely contentious as Mr. Williams was "outraged" that we would be allowed this information. Again, Judge Fullwood disagreed with Mr. Williams and determined that we were entitled to that information. He did limit the time for the disclosure from the period that Mr. Pridgen had become POA until Dr. Smith's death (April, 2002 – February, 2005). However, since each month has an accumulation of what has occurred for "year to date," it gave us the information for all of 2002 on the cash withdrawals (which turned out to be nearly $600,000 by the end of

April, 2002). As an aside, this information is particularly "telling" in that Mr. Williams and Mr. Pridgen have consistently maintained that the money Dr. Smith was withdrawing was going down a "bottomless pit" which they called "Jimmy [Uncle Jimmy's son]," It has been their contention that Jimmy [the son] was using these funds to support his life style and for his drug and alleged gambling debts. What we now know from the records is that there was $9,000 taken in cash on April 15, the day Jimmy was *found* dead in his home – meaning he could not have obtained the money that day – and on the next six successive banking days until Billy, Dr. Queen and Jack Richardson stopped the practice in late April. Obviously, that $63,000 could not have gone to the "benefit" of Little Jimmy.

Hearing on Pridgen's Fee Request:

Approximately two months ago, Mr. Williams submitted to the attorney for the Church and myself a copy of Mr. Pridgen's last bill for his services as power of attorney for the month of February 2005. Since Dr. Smith had died during that month, he could not approve that bill. Prior to paying himself, Mr. Pridgen wanted our consent since these funds would be from the Estate account. Both Mr. Hunter, on behalf of the Church, and I, objected to the fees sought as being "unreasonable" fees for services as a POA. Mr. Pridgen's total bill was for a total of $13,065 for 21 days and represented "charges" for every single day in that time period of time (including Saturdays and Sundays). More egregious from my standpoint was some of the "line items" contained in the bill. Mr. Pridgen was charging Dr. Smith $150/hr for his time and $75/hour for the time of his wife/paralegal, Jan. Included in his charges was 3 hours ($450) for going to Dr. Smith's 98th birthday party on February 3 ("Everything I did for Dr. Smith was part of my responsibilities as power of attorney as I was not a 'social friend' of his") and 1.5 hours nearly every day when he stopped by Dr. Smith's house on his way to work to watch him being fed his breakfast, getting his morning shave or shampoo and "observing" the caregivers administering lotion all over his body ("he had the 'skin' of a much younger man because of this attention").

In addition, and in spite of the fact that Dr. Smith had, at least, two care givers for all daylight hours of each day (who were being paid at the rate of $13.50/hour) Ms. Pridgen (who was being paid $75/hour) listed such "chores" or personal services as doing the grocery shopping

139

(grapefruit was delivered to the Elks Club on Fridays and she had to be there to get it "fresh"), going to the drugstore or buying general household or office products to assist Dr. Smith. It would have been assumed that one of the care givers could have taken time to undertake those chores at less than 20% of the charges for Ms. Pridgen. After a five hour hearing in which the Pridgens contended that they "had" to do these "services" for Dr. Smith since none of his family would volunteer to do them, the Clerk reduced the requested fees by 37% and awarded $8,242,50. While that is still a "generous" fee for what appears to be "personal services" as compared to normal legal services performed by a POA, considering that this was the Clerk of Superior Court of New Hanover County and that she deals with Mr. Williams on a regular basis and sees Mr. Pridgen in the courts as well, this was courageous on her part. It is fair to say that the other side appeared extremely disappointed in this outcome. A copy of that signed Order is enclosed [omitted from this book].

Of perhaps greater significance than this ruling is that we learned (from Jan Pridgen) during the Hearing that for the 33 months that preceded February 2005 (beginning in May, 2002 when Mr. and Ms. Pridgen began to render their "services" to Dr. Smith, their fees "averaged" $17,000/month! That is a total of $561,000 in fees for serving in the ministerial capacity as POA! If the Clerk believed that the fees Pridgen wanted to collect for the last month of Dr. Smith's life included 37% of charges that were unnecessary, unreasonable or inappropriate and, if we were to apply that same principle to the preceding 33 months period where the bills totaled $561,000, then the Pridgens could owe back to the Estate $207,570 in excessive or unreasonable fees. This could and, perhaps, should be a subject for review at a later date.

Depositions:

When members of your family met with me in early March, we discussed the issues that most concerned the family over the Will and the last few years of Dr. Smith's life. Simply stated, there was a general feeling that Dr. Smith had historically had a close relationship with his extended family (which was felt to be reciprocated) and that, unless there had been some inappropriate influence exerted upon him, it was unlikely that he would have disinherited his family and/or not retained the Woodford Farm for the family by his Will. These suspicions were

140

further "fueled" when it was learned that he had left 40% of his residuary estate, or approximately, Two Million Dollars ($2,000,000) to four women that he had known for no longer than 20 months (maximum) and one for less than 4 months [Jan Pridgen], but who were around him on a daily basis on a 24/7 schedule from the time of his wife's death until the Will was signed on September 26, 2002. As I once stated to Lonnie Williams when he was (once again as he has done continuously since the caveat was filed) complaining that I had filed a frivolous Caveat that had no merit to it on behalf of a "greedy" family: *"A deaf, dumb and blind man with a 5th grade education, standing on a street corner in downtown Wilmington would have been suspicious of the circumstances leading up to and surrounding the making of this will."*

Understandably, you had strong suspicions that there had been some wrongdoing in the procuring of Dr. Smith's Will, but, at that point in March, you had only your "suspicions." Therefore, the Caveat was filed alleging the two normal grounds for contesting a Will: lack of mental capacity of the testator and the exertion of undue influence on him to cause him to execute this document as his Will. Because we had not had a chance to talk with any of the parties at that point, we could not identify "who" might have exerted the undue influence or what the basis was for our allegations of lack of mental capacity (other than the obvious concerns over a 95 year old gentlemen with the medical history of Dr. Smith who was apparently so in firmed that he needed 24/7 care). The scheduling and taking of depositions (sworn testimony of the intended parties) is the only way to obtain the information necessary for you to be able to learn if there is a valid basis for your suspicions and that was the purpose of these depositions.

Legally, lack of mental capacity and undue influence have been defined by our Supreme Court as requiring proof by the party alleging either of these that:

Lack of mental capacity: Generally stated, our appellate courts have held that one has sufficient mental capacity to make a will if he has the capacity to know the kind, nature and extent of his property, and the natural objects of his bounty, and to understand the legal consequences of the instrument. *In re Will of Shute*, 251 N.C. 697 (1960). Mental capacity to make a will is not the same as mental "competency" to care for one's self and there are cases where individuals who have been declared "incompetent" to manage their

141

own affairs and have various health issues, have been found to have mental "capacity" to make a will. *In re Will of Martin*, 64 N.C. App. 211 (1983).

Undue Influence: Recognizing that it is often difficult to have direct proof of undue influence, our appellate courts have indicated that there are four elements of undue influence which should be established to make out such a claim: 1) the person making the Will is one who is subject to influence; 2) an opportunity to exert influence existed; 3) a disposition of beneficiaries to exert influence; and 4) a result indicating that undue influence was exerted. *In re Will of Dunn*, 129 N.C. App.321, (1998). The Supreme Court of North Carolina has further identified the following factors as being relevant in determining whether a testamentary document was procured as the result of undue influence:

a. Old age and physical and mental weakness of the "victim" (one making a will);
b. That the alleged victim is in the home of the beneficiary and subject to their constant association and supervision;
c. That others have little or no opportunity to see the victim;
d. That the will is different from and revokes a prior will;
e. That it is made in favor of one whom there are no ties of blood;
f. That it disinherits the natural objects of his bounty; and
g. That the beneficiary has procured its execution.

In re Andrews, 299 N.C. 52 (1980).

Of this list and without our taking any depositions, it would appear that: (b) is satisfied in that care givers were constantly in Dr. Smith's home; (d) is met in that this Will is certainly different from his others (although with Little Jimmy's death, he had no "immediate family" left); and (e) is certainly established in that none of the four women are blood related to Dr. Smith. While Dr. Smith was advanced in years at age 95 when the will was signed, (a) would be contested to determine whether he had any "mental weakness". Likewise, the other side will contend (and did so in depositions and testimony before the Clerk) that (c)is not an issue since they allege that the family did not try to see or offer assistance to Dr. Smith after Billy was relieved as power of attorney. In addition, since several members of the family are to receive some amounts (ranging from $1,000 to $5,000), the propounders contend that the Will did not totally "disinherit" the natural objects of Dr. Smith's bounty as required by (f). Most importantly, the women will vehemently contest that they did anything to "procure" the will in which they were beneficiaries as required by (g). Since we know that (a), (c), (f) and (g) will be contested, it was on these issues, that we needed to hear from the parties involved and scheduled depositions.

It is important for you to remember that the time period we are interested in ends with the signing of the Will on September 26, 2002. In order to succeed in having the women disqualified as beneficiaries, or to set aside the entire Will of Dr. Smith on the basis of alleged undue influence, we would need to be able to prove the seven elements listed above existed prior to that date. Unfortunately, some of the evidence from the "disinterested" witnesses last week will create severe problems for us in that regard.

On the issue of mental capacity, Reynolds, Rusher and Richardson would seem to be the most critical for both sides. The first two are longtime friends of Dr. Smith's who are respected citizens of Wilmington and are disinterested witnesses as they are not beneficiaries. In addition, Reynolds and Rusher were playing cards with Dr. Smith two to three times a week during the time we are interested in and were in a good position to observe his mental condition and abilities. Both of them attested to his good "card skills" at gin rummy; indicated that, in their opinion, he clearly knew what his assets were and knew all of his family. In addition, Jack Richardson testified that in his dealings with Dr. Smith he seemed to understand what his assets were (although he was prone to "inflate" the values) and clearly knew who his family was. Standing alone (not counting all the medical reports we have been given as to Dr. Smith's competency), that would probably be sufficient to establish mental capacity. Certainly, Dr. Smith was 95, he was thought to be in need of some level of personal "care" 24 hours a day and he has some physical limitations. However, we have uncovered no evidence that he was not mentally alert, and in fact, all the credible evidence seems to indicate that he was mentally alert. I do not believe we can succeed, or have any basis to succeed, on invalidating Dr. Smith's Will because he lacked mental capacity to execute it on September 26, 2002.

On the issue of undue influence, Mr. Rusher and Dr. Reynolds both indicated that Dr. Smith appeared to be well cared for by his care givers and enjoyed an easy relaxed relationship with them. As Dr. Reynolds put it, many older people have a certain "odor" about them, but that was never the case with Dr. Smith. He was always fresh, well groomed and alert. More importantly, as two of Dr. Smith's oldest and best friends, they were unequivocal in expressing the opinion that no one could impose his/her will on Dr. Smith unless he wanted them to do so. According to both of them, he clearly had "a mind of his own" up to the last times they saw him (prior to the hospitalization in October, 2003 – well after the will was signed). In connection with Woodford Farm, Mr. Richardson testified that initially Dr. Smith had talked about leaving it to "Dr. Bill" (because he appeared to be the most financially responsible member of the family), but that in later discussions Dr. Smith indicated he was interested in preserving the Farm for a youth or church retreat for First Baptist. He did indicate that he wanted Bill to have the "opportunity" to obtain a portion of it (exactly what was done in the Will with the option that has been granted to Bill!). This was the same testimony that Linda Phillips gave.

However, the most important evidence for the propounders on the issue of a *lack* of undue influence came from Bob O'Quinn, the attorney who drafted the Will and assisted Dr. Smith in executing it. Mr. O'Quinn learned from Mr. Pridgen that Dr. Smith wanted a new will and Pridgen even told him the basic terms of what that will was to be. Mr. O'Quinn was "uncomfortable" with a third party telling him what someone wanted in their Will – particularly, when the third party's wife (Jan Pridgen) was to be a beneficiary under the terms that were being related and she was not a blood relative. As Mr. O'Quinn, testified: "I went 'GULP' when I heard that." Nevertheless, the importance of Mr. O'Quinn's testimony on the "Undue influence" claim occurred when Mr. O'Quinn first went to see Dr. Smith, at his home, on September 25 to go over the terms of what Pridgen had told him. In that conference at Dr. Smith's home on Live Oak Parkway, Dr. Smith changed some of the items as they had been related to Mr. O'Quinn by Mr. Pridgen. Pridgen had told O'Quinn that Dr. Smith wanted to leave $100,000 to the "Fellowship Fund" at FBC. When Dr. Smith saw that, he changed it so it would be for Roy Piner's benefit. In addition, Pridgen had told O'Quinn that Dr. Smith wanted to leave $1,000 each to Jack, Erin and Lisa and Dr. Smith changed Lisa and Erin to $5,000 each. That certainly indicates a man who knew and understood what he was doing. Mr. O'Quinn apparently made those changes and prepared a final draft of the Will and returned to Dr. Smith's house on September 26. Mr. O'Quinn came an hour early and again went over all the terms of the Will with Dr. Smith with no one present except Mr. O'Quinn's paralegal. Only when O'Quinn was satisfied that Dr. Smith was singing a document that he intended to be his Last Will and Testament, did he allow it to be executed by Dr. Smith and witnessed by his friends and respected citizens, Frank Reynolds and Ed Rusher. *If we leave out all other considerations in this case and all suspicions that naturally arise from this Will, that testimony – standing alone – may be sufficient to allow a jury to find there was no undue influence exerted on Dr. Smith or require a judge to rule, as a matter of law, that there was no undue influence and dismiss our caveat.*

As you can tell, I am clearly troubled by our likely ability to successfully proceed in the face of the evidence that we have uncovered so far. While we were unable to do the depositions of Pat Jenkins, Carol Tucker or Jan Pridgen (time caught up with us) and they can be scheduled for a later time in September, I am not certain that we will be able to overcome the independent testimony of O'Quinn, Reynolds, Rusher and Richardson to establish undue influence. If we cannot produce some credible evidence to support this contention (that the Will was executed as the result of undue influence being exerted upon Dr. Smith by the beneficiaries), we stand a strong likelihood that this Caveat will be dismissed as having no legal merit. If it is dismissed in that manner, there is some possibility that the Estate could seek to recover its costs in defending this Caveat (including attorney fees incurred) from you individually. That could be, and more likely than not would be, an amount in excess of $100,000. While I do not believe that this is likely, it is and should be a serious consideration for each of you. None of us should doubt that O.K. Pridgen or Lonnie Williams would hesitate to bring such a claim if they were successful in "winning" this Caveat. Mr. Williams' near constant refrain of this being a "frivolous" Caveat would indicate that he is already considering that possibility.

Other issues developed:

Leaving aside for a minute the issue of your Caveat to the Will, there were a couple of other matters that were uncovered during our three days in Wilmington that may be noteworthy. They involve serious discrepancies between Mr. Pridgen's sworn answers to our discovery requests and his sworn answers to my questions during his deposition as compared to the information obtained from Mr. O'Quinn

145

and his files. In addition, we learned some information which would raise an issue as to whether or not Lisa and Erin should be the beneficiaries of $100,000 each as a "gift" from Dr. Smith to them – separate and apart from the bequest he made to them in the Will of $5,000 each. Let me elaborate on these points.

A. Mr. Pridgen's candor while under oath:

In my interrogatory #9 to Mr. Pridgen, I had asked him about the September 26, 2002 Will and specifically asked him if: (c) he provided any information to Mr. O'Quinn prior to September 26; (d) if so, what was that information; and (f) when did he first learn that he was to be the Executor. In his **sworn answer** to that Interrogatory, he said he told Mr. O'Quinn only that Dr. Smith wanted to make a new will and that he did not learn the contents (that he was named as the Executor) until after it was signed and a copy was delivered to him. When I asked him during his sworn deposition if he knew that his wife, Jan, was to be a beneficiary in that Will, he said he did not. In First Baptist Church's Interrogatory #15, they asked him what role, if any, he played "in procuring" the will of Dr. Smith. Under oath he said "None." In the Church's Request for Admissions #1 they asked Pridgen to admit that he "assisted" in procuring the will and he denied that – again, under oath.

For Mr. O'Quinn's deposition, I had issued a subpoena requiring him to produce his entire file with all the documents that he had in connection with the preparation and signing of Dr. Smith's Will on September 26, 2002. He complied with that request and we found notes in that file indicating that Pridgen had: 1) seen Mr. O'Quinn on the street in mid-September and told him that Dr. Smith wanted to make a new will (consistent with what Pridgen had sworn to be the truth). However, according to O'Quinn's notes of his "street conversation," Pridgen also told him that Smith planned to leave his estate to the church and "cut off out all of his nieces and nephews who paid little attention to him prior to Jimmy's death;" and 2) In addition, the day before Mr. O'Quinn was to go see Dr. Smith, Pridgen called him and (according to O'Quinn's handwritten notes) told him EVERY TERM AND ITEM THAT WAS TO BE IN THE WILL – INCLUDING THAT HIS WIFE WAS TO RECEIVE 10% AND HE WAS TO BE THE EXECUTOR! A copy of Mr. O'Quinn's handwritten notes of that telephone conversation with Mr. Pridgen on or about September 23 is included with this letter [omitted from this book].

We will await the printed transcript of Pridgen's deposition, but if he testified as I recall his testimony, then these "inconsistencies" will take on greater significance for obvious reasons concerning his continuing to serve as Executor of the Estate and even with his professional licensing Board. The Bar expects that its members will give truthful answers in sworn testimony in a court of law even if that truthful testimony may be adverse to a personal financial interest of the attorney.

B. Information of intended "gifts" to Lisa and Erin

We learned something else for the first time during Mr. O'Quinn's deposition. When he and his paralegal went to meet with Dr. Smith and go over the final draft of the Will on the 26th and, prior to the arrival of Dr. Reynolds and Mr. Rusher, Dr. Smith indicated yet another change he wanted to make in his Will. He had thought about Erin and Lisa and for reasons that he explained to Mr. O'Quinn, he had decided that he wanted each of them to have $100,000 rather than the $5,000 he had indicated a day earlier. Mr. O'Quinn immediately told Dr. Smith that would be an easy change to make in the Will, but he would have to go back to the office to do so. Apparently, Dr. Smith told him not to do that, but instead to tell O.K. – as his power of attorney – to go ahead and give Erin and Lisa $100,000 **then** *(immediately)* as a gift. Dr. Smith certainly had a right to do that if he wished to do so (after all, he had taken out more than $700,000 in cash in the preceding months from his account at FUNB and we still do not know what he did with all of that or whom he may have "gifted" with some portions of it). Mr. O'Quinn's paralegal has notes in the file in her handwriting confirming these instructions. After the Will was executed and Mr. O'Quinn had dropped the original of the Will off at the Pridgen office, he returned to his office where he immediately prepared a letter of instructions to Pridgen. It is dated September 26, 2002 and states, in relevant part:

"During my discussion with Dr. Smith, prior to signing the Will, he said he wanted Erin and Lisa Shelhart to receive $100,000 each. I asked him if he wanted me to revise his Will before he signed it. He said no, but for me to tell you to make arrangements to make a gift *now* of $100,000 each to Erin and Lisa in addition to the $5,000 bequest in the Will." (emphasis added)

147

He mailed the letter that day (and/or, he may have faxed it as he did not remember). When I asked Pridgen on Wednesday if he had received that letter or if he had ever done what he was instructed to do, he acknowledged receipt, but said he had not ever done what he was told "because Dr. Smith never mentioned it [to] me."

Based on this newly discovered evidence, I think that Erin and Lisa have a claim against the Estate for $100,000 each – independent of and regardless of the Caveat – and they possibly have a claim for interest due to them since September, 2002 (since they should have had this money and it could have been earning interest for them since that time). If so, it is my further opinion that any claim for interest would be directly against Mr. Pridgen since it was his decision to not pay the money and the Estate should not be penalized for his decision in that regard. For each of your further interest, I am enclosing with the Memo, a copy of Mr. O'Quinn's paralegal's handwritten notes of this conversation with Mr. Pridgen and Mr. O'Quinn's letter to Pridgen of September 26, 2002 instructing him to make the payments to Erin and Lisa [omitted from this book].

IMPRESSIONS CONCERNS AND RECOMMENDATIONS

After all of this, the issue remains of where do we go from here? Personally, I am convinced that, despite all that has been said and produced to date, that Lonnie Williams firmly and irrevocably believes that the Will is valid as is. He does not believe that Dr. Smith lacked mental capacity to execute it (and I do not know that we have any evidence to the contrary on that point or are apt to develop any) and, based upon the testimony of O'Quinn, Richardson, Dr. Reynolds and Rusher, he is convinced that he will win on the undue influence claim. Quite candidly, I am not certain what evidence we could develop to counter that position. This is true regardless of what Pat Jenkins, Carol Tucker or Jan Pridgen say in their depositions or what we might find if we located and discussed this case with the other care givers (Betty Parker or Wanda and Alicia – who were not really there much, if at all, prior to the execution of the Will.) Unless we have a strategy that is likely to produce evidence to support our claim for undue influence, we will be continuing to spend time and money without much hope of being able to make a recovery in the future. In addition, and as I indicated above, if we are ultimately unsuccessful in the caveat proceeding, you *may be individually liable* for the costs to the estate for having to defend the caveat.

As you will recall, this issue of whether we might be able to make any recovery or even be entitled to receive an award of attorney fees for the work of our firm in this matter, was a concern that I addressed when it became apparent that if we were only successful in setting aside the Will as to the bequests to Jenkins, Tucker, Phillips and Jan Pridgen, you had no legal interest to the estate and might, therefore, not be legally entitled to recover legal fees from the estate either. This is so because the law would say that those gifts "lapsed" because of wrongdoing and what they were to have received would go into the residuary estate. Since the "residuary estate" of Dr. Smith was divided so that 60% was to go to the Church and the other 40% was to go to the women, the Church would get it all. In order to "protect" your legitimate interest to proceed at that time, I had not limited our claims of "undue influence" to just the women in our Response to the Church's Request for Admissions. Instead, I had indicated that until discovery was completed, we would not know the effect on the "entire Will" of any undue influence that might have been exerted on Dr. Smith (a theory that, perhaps, Pridgen, et al had "included" the Church as a major beneficiary to make it "look better" when they got $2,000,000 and Pridgen was named the Executor and would expect to get a major fee). From the depositions of O'Quinn and Richardson, it appears clear that Dr. Smith was intending to make the Church his primary beneficiary for a long time[29] prior to the Will be [sic] executed (he told Jack Richardson about his desire to assist the Church in its "mission work" and its youth programs and he clearly had a long history of significant contributions).

The following matters need to be resolved at present:

1. *Fees:* Unfortunately, but realistically, this brings us back to the issue of time and effort being expended by this firm on what is essentially a contingent fee case which now seems to have little prospect for recovery being made upon which legal fees could be awarded to you or, on your behalf, to our firm. I am enclosing a copy

---

[29] When writing this Maxwell may not have been considering that Uncle Jimmy's previous will left nothing to the Church. At that time, Maxwell still did not know how deeply church leadership might have been involved in the planning of the will.

of our most recent "pre-bill" here in the office [omitted from this book]. As you can each see, I have already expended more than 200 hours on this case and Lori has spent more than 100 hours (you might note that her hourly rate charge for "legal work" is less than was Jan Pridgen's hourly rate for many "personal services"). To date, the fees earned (based upon time expended) exceeds $78,000. Obviously, I cannot continue to invest that type of time or effort into a contingent claim in the "hope" that the court might award attorney fees when that now appears to be highly unlikely. If we are to proceed, it would need to be on an hourly fee charge and I am not certain that would be a good expenditure of your resources – even if you were willing to pay those fees. There is also the prospect (which I believe is quite minimal) that the court could order you to reimburse the Estate for continuing to pursue the Caveat.

Having said that, you need to know that Mr. Hunter, on behalf of the Church, continues to want to pursue this matter and wants us to do so as well. I have spoken with him again this week. His, and the Church's reasons for wanting you to pursue your claims of undue influence would be, at least, three-fold: 1) if we were able to convince a jury that, based upon the seven (7) required factors, there was undue influence and the women were disqualified, then the church would get an additional $2,000,000; 2) if we assisted in pursuing an effort to have Mr. Pridgen removed as Executor, the church could contract with another attorney who might be willing to assist in closing the estate on an hourly basis (rather than the "commission basis" upon which Pridgen presently serves) and this would be an additional savings to the Church; and 3) since Mr. Pridgen is a long time member of the Church, if we continue the "attack" on him and/or the women, it saves the Church from having to attack its own. However, unless the Church were to agree that it will pay our fees, then this would be a "pro bono" effort on my firm's part for the Church. Since I am not a member of that Church, this is a "contribution" that I am not willing to undertake.

2. **Settlement:** I do need to let you know that Mr. Hunter also continues to believe that this is a case that should be settled and that any settlement as he contemplates it (and I assume that he has the Church leadership's "blessing" for this) would involve the intestate heirs (the eight of you) receiving some financial payment from the Estate. As he has often explained to me, he feels that the women have

some "risk" of being disqualified by a jury and that they *should* be willing to accept what they already have received as well as a portion of what they *would* receive under the terms of the Will (about $500,000 each). He has inferred to me that the women should be willing to give up $100,000 each so that the intestate heirs would then receive a total of $400,000 as would each of the women.[30] He has also suggested that his fees and our fees would be paid from the estate prior to any other distribution as well as whatever fees or commissions are "negotiated" with Mr. Pridgen and Mr. Williams. Obviously, under this scenario, the Church's only contribution would be what it agrees to allow to be paid as attorney fees or commission. However, as long as Mr. Pridgen and Mr. Williams remain in their present positions, I do not think that they are willing to entertain any idea or even consider that they have any "risks" in this case. Therefore, I do not believe that any settlement that results in any reduction in the amounts the propounder or their attorney would receive when they "win" this Caveat will presently be considered. Quite frankly, this whole concept is difficult to get a handle on since it is only a concept in the mind of Mr. Hunter. To even pursue such a course of action (which clearly contemplates continuing with the deposition schedule, further investigation of the other care givers and possibly adding Mr. Whaley to our deposition list, as well as seeking to have Mr. Pridgen removed) would require a substantial amount of additional time by my office which I am presently reluctant to advance unless we have some understanding as to how or whether our office can be and will be compensated for some of the time invested.

3. *Erin/Lisa's claims:* I do think that independent claims on behalf of Erin and Lisa for $100,000 each should be pursued. While I have not yet had time to research the validity of such a claim (promise of a "gift" that is thwarted by a third party), I would be willing to do so. If it develops that there is legal authority to pursue such a claim, and if Erin and Lisa requested that we undertake to pursue that claim on their behalf, we would be willing to do so on a contingent fee basis of 25%

---

[30] You can imagine the family's frustration at a suggestion that the eight intestate heirs should accept a settlement that required them to split $400,000 while "caregivers" whom they believed were exploiting their Uncle would get $400,000 each. Not to mention the Church, who seemed to be using the family as a hatchet man so that could wash their hands of the dirty work, would get about ten times that.

of any amount recovered. This would involve the filing of another lawsuit and the time and effort to bring it to fruition.[31] There will be no charge for the research to determine if a legal basis exists for the pursuit of this claim and that could help them decide if they want to proceed.

4. ***Pridgen's continuing role as executor:*** There is the issue of Mr. Pridgen continuing to serve as Executor over an estate in which he has a clear conflict (his wife is a beneficiary and neither of them are "blood relatives" of Dr. Smith) and whether there will be some professional issues with his licensing board based upon the transcript of his deposition and his previous sworn answers in discovery as compared to Mr. O'Quinn's notes. Unless we stay in this matter on some basis for some period of time, the issue of Mr. Pridgen remaining as Executor would be solely between him and the church. The "integrity issue" is one that I may have to confront – regardless of where this litigation is headed.

5. ***Future of Woodford Farm:*** Under the worse case scenario, Bill has the option to purchase the house and surrounding five acres at "its appraised" value. Quite frankly, I have not heard anyone indicate that FBC really wants the remaining acreage for a "retreat" facility so it is possible that they will be looking to sell the entire tract. As I had previously indicated, Mr. Hunter had told me that their appraisal had been completed. However, last week, he only had a copy of the independent appraisal of the house and five acres. I am enclosing a copy of that for each of you [omitted from this book], but you will see that this appraiser has put a value of $143,000 on that portion of the Farm. Clearly, if Bill wants to pay that amount, the Church would be willing to sell it to him (or any combination of Smith family members) for that. I would suspect that they would be willing to "negotiate," but I have had no conversations with the Church or Mr. Hunter. Quite frankly, and from information that Billy has sent, this seems to me to be relatively high as an appraisal ($12,000/acre).

Lori and I had lunch with Mr. Hunter after we completed the depositions last Wednesday. During that lunch, Mr. Hunter asked me

---

[31] No additional suit was ever filed

to "get a figure" that the family would be willing to pay for the Farm and/or a separate figure that you would be willing to pay for the house and five acres. He promised to take that to the Church and see what could be done. I assured him that I felt confident in saying that the family was not willing to pay $1.4 Million Dollars for a piece of property they believed should have stayed in the family as a bequest. Quite frankly, I believe that he still perceives some way of trying to have a settlement whereby the women and/or Mr. Pridgen would "assist" in any such payments being made by reducing what they might receive and consenting to let the eight intestate heirs receive that amount. I have nothing more to add to this, but wanted you to know of the discussion.

6. *Quick Claim Deed:* Finally, Mr. Hunter has prepared and gave to me last week, "Quick Claim Deeds" for each of you to sign. As you know, the Will gave the Farm and Brunswick County property to the Church. Had there been no Caveat, that would have been accomplished simply by filing the Will and some documents confirming the transfer in the respective Register of Deeds for Columbus and Brunswick County. Since there is a Caveat, filed that cannot be accomplished. Yet, someone needs to take responsibility for the maintenance, taxes, etc. on the properties. Even if the Church were to sell some or parts of these properties to you, it is logical that they assume these responsibilities for now. They will receive a similar deed from the Estate and are asking that each of the intestate heirs and their spouses also sign these deeds. There is no risk to you; you do not give up your rights to these properties if the Caveat were to be successful (they would have to be deeded back from the Church to the Estate) and it does ensure that someone will be looking after the properties. I am sending the original of these documents in the respective envelope for each of you (i.e. Billy and Jodie get their deed; Ebie and Sid get theirs, etc.).

Present Options:

To try to summarize what I perceive to be your options at this point in time, I would suggest:

1. The family could decide it has seen enough from the depositions, hearings, etc. that have taken place to date and is satisfied that it is unlikely that the Caveat will succeed. If so, you could further decide to no longer pursue the Caveat. As a result of such a decision, there would be no more expenses incurred by the family (financial or, possibly, emotional) and I do not believe that there would be any basis for the Estate to seek reimbursement for its expenses. There were clearly enough "suspicions" raised under the facts of this matter to cause a caveat to be filed and part of the reason that it was filed when it was is because the Executor was in such a rush to sell the personal property. If the family should choose this course of action, there would be no fees paid to this office unless the court should deem appropriate, which the executor would resist and I would think would be highly unlikely.

2. You could decide that you needed or wanted to continue with the Caveat. As you can tell from the analysis that I have done in this relatively long document, at this point I do not see a legal basis for ultimately succeeding in a Caveat proceeding. In addition, I am not confident that there is evidence available that has not yet come forward that will assist us in being able to prove Dr. Smith lacked mental capacity to execute the Will or that undue influence was exerted on him to get him to make the Will dated September 26, 2002. If I am correct in that analysis, then there is the high likelihood that the court will not allow you any attorney fees for our firm investing what is already nearly $80,000 in time and expense and which will surely be substantially more as more time is expended by us in pursuit of this Caveat on your behalf. Obviously, if I presently thought we had a reasonable chance of success, we would continue the course of action and anticipate that we would be successful in the Caveat or, at least, would raise such substantial issues, that the court would exercise its discretion and make an award of substantially all of our fees for the time invested. Unfortunately, I am not presently confident enough of that outcome to be willing to continue to spend the amount of time and effort that is going into this case solely on the "expectation" that the court might award some or all of your attorney fees.

At the same time, I had committed to take the depositions of the three remaining women and it was no one's fault that those were not

154

completed last week. I feel committed to you to complete those with no change in our fee agreement. I anticipate that we could do that in no more than two days (with one overnight stay). I would further anticipate that I would spend an additional 20 to 30 hours to prepare for, travel to and take those depositions. I will do that without changing our fee agreement so that we will all know what the women have to say.

3. After those depositions are completed, we will have to discuss how or whether to proceed further. If we do not uncover facts that could lead to us being able to present credible evidence to a court to support a valid continuation of the Caveat, our office could not continue to expend time at this rate without a change in our fee arrangement. I well understand that for the family, there are some issues presented in this matter that transcend whether the Caveat is ultimately successful or whether the intestate heirs make any recovery from the estate. Such issues as Mr. Pridgen's continuing to serve as Executor, the size and amount of fees that were charged by he and his wife to Dr. Smith while serving as POA, the "gifts" that the family believes were lavished on the care givers prior to Dr. Smith's death (and "accountability" for those gifts) are among issues that concern you. It may well be that the only way to attempt to uncover the true facts for any of those issues is to continue with the Caveat and utilize the discovery tools that are available. If I conclude that we are unlikely to be successful in recovering legal fees and costs from the Estate and you wanted me to continue working on this matter, we could convert our fee agreement so that, from that point forward, we would be paid monthly on the basis of charges for our hourly rate. It is possible that the Church would agree to assist in seeing that some portion of the then "back charges" were paid to retain our office in this case, but this is simply an issue that we would have to discuss and resolve.

4. If, after I have completed the research on the viability of claims on behalf of Lisa and Erin (which should be completed by the end of next week – September 15), it appears that there is a basis for them to pursue a claim for $100,000 each and possibly interest on those claims, and they want to do so, they will need an attorney. I think it is foreseeable that this would invoke a highly contested court proceeding. If they decided that they wanted our office to represent them in pursuit of those claims, we would be willing to do so on the basis of a

contingent fee contract of 25% of any amounts recovered for them with no fees being charged them if there is no recovery.

I know that this has been a lot of information for you to receive and analyze. After you have had time to "digest" it, I will look to hear from you so we can discuss how to proceed. Unfortunately, since Mr. Hunter wants to move forward on the deposition schedule, some of these decisions will need to be made sooner than later. I am sending Bob Johnson a copy of this Memo (without enclosures). I know that Bob has been a good friend to many of you for many years and has offered good legal services to some of you during that time. He referred you to me. It may well be appropriate to discuss these issues with him and I wanted him to know the background and status of our claims to date.

I do want all of you to know that I was professionally flattered to be afforded the opportunity to represent you and Lori and I continue to feel that it is a privilege to be able to seek out the truth on these many convoluted issues surrounding the last three years of Dr. Smith's life.

cc. Bob Johnson

......

The family felt that they were on the moral high ground, but Jim Maxwell's memo brought legal realities crashing down. The family had to face the very real possibility that they could "win" the trial, proving to a jury that the caregivers were unduly influencing Uncle Jimmy, and "lose" the estate to the church. Despite the family's certainty that crimes had been committed against their Uncle it seemed that without strong evidence of the church's involvement, the law wouldn't provide an avenue to pursue the wrongdoers. To the family, the First Baptist Church seemed all too willing to use the family as a hatchet man to take down the Pridgen's and the caregivers so that they could keep their hands clean and increase their bottom line. It looked like it was over for the family's Caveat. Jim Maxwell would keep his word and continue his best effort through the next round of depositions, but like the fictional character, it seemed that Maxwell "missed it by that much."

156

24. Depositions Part II
All roads lead to Rome
September 2005

Patricia C. Jenkins

Pat Jenkins testified that she started working for Uncle Jimmy's wife Iris in November of 2000.[345] She was employed, at that time, as a Certified Nursing Assistant (level II) through an agency.[346]

She seemed to have an agenda of her own about what she wanted to discuss in her deposition. Pat would talk at length about various subjects after being asked yes or no questions. When Pat was asked, "Were there other members of the family that you know, that would, from time to time, come to see Dr. Smith?"[347] She first talked about a time that Bill called to let her know he wanted to visit Uncle Jimmy at 9:30 am that day, and Pat said, "Okay." According to Pat, Uncle Jimmy decided, at that moment, to go to the Family Dollar Store. Pat said she asked Uncle Jimmy to stay at home and even called his power of attorney to ask for instructions. The attorney, Pat says, told her to go on to the store.[348] Bill, of course, would have arrived at the house that day with no one to show him in. According to Pat's testimony she and Uncle Jimmy returned to the house about 2:00 pm and Bill, his wife and his son arrived shortly thereafter. She testified that when Bill and Amy asked why they were stood up Pat said, "Well, are you trying to argue with a nurse that's here in the house?" (Note the use of the title "nurse" in her sworn testimony). Pat continued describing how Amy [a Registered Nurse] told Pat that she wasn't a nurse, then went on to describe how Bill was talking to his Uncle about his farm. Pat said to Bill, "Look now, we can't be talking about his property around his workers here. You need to talk with his power-of-attorney." Thereafter Pat describes how Amy became angry and "lit in on me again." then said, "I'm the nurse..." so Pat called 9-1-1 and asked them to send police. Pat said that when the police got there, Uncle Jimmy said, "Take her [Pat] downtown." Pat testified that Uncle Jimmy would "normally" tell the police to arrest her when they came to the house.[349] That's the sort of answer that could be expected from Pat if you asked her a question like, "Were there other members of the family that you know, that would, from time to time, come to see Dr. Smith?"[350]

Pat also addressed the January 2002 confrontation with Carrol Herring of Herring associates. Herring associates claimed a non-compete agreement existed and Pat would have to pay a commission to her for the work she did for Uncle Jimmy after Iris died.[351] About Herring, Pat Jenkins said, "She tells lies all the time. I know a lot of them, if you want to hear them."[352] Pat claimed that she was no longer needed as a nursing assistant after Iris died and Uncle Jimmy called her personally to ask her to come back to work in a different capacity. Pat even claimed that her answering machine recorded the call with Uncle Jimmy on tape.[353] When Bob Hunter asked about why she kept an answering machine recording of Uncle Jimmy since December of 2001 the conversation went on:

Hunter: How is it that you happened to keep this recording all that time?

Jenkins: Isn't it amazing?

Hunter: Yes, ma'am.

Jenkins: I keep everything. I document everything. That's what I'm trained for. And that's what--they trained me in my nursing profession when I first started, you keep up with all reports, and you keep up with everything, and I do.

Hunter: So you keep--

Jenkins: Uh-huh (yes).

Hunter: --your tape recordings from your home phone every time somebody calls you?

Jenkins: I sure do. I sure do.

Hunter: How many--

Jenkins: Somebody comes in—anybody calls or does something to me, I—never know when I might need it.

Hunter: How many tapes do you have?

158

Jenkins: How many tapes do I have?

Hunter: Yes, ma'am.

Jenkins: How many do you want to hear?

Hunter: Well, as many as Dr. Smith—

Williams: Just tell her—tell him, if you can, how many tapes you--

Jenkins: On Dr. Smith's situation?

Hunter: No, everybody's.

Jenkins: Everybody's?

Hunter: Well, let's start with everybody's and—

Jenkins: You haven't called my house. I don't have yours.

Hunter: Yes, ma'am. But let's just talk about all the tapes you have. How many tapes do you have?

Jenkins: I don't know.

Hunter: You have over a hundred?

Jenkins: I don't know.

Hunter: Well, where are they?

Jenkins: They're at home.

Hunter: Are they in boxes?

Jenkins: Yep.

Hunter: How many boxes have you got?

Jenkins: I don't know.

Hunter: Are they shoe boxes?

Jenkins: I don't know.

Hunter: You don't know how you keep your tapes?

Jenkins: That's my personal information.

Hunter: Yes, ma'am. I'm asking you about your personal information. Would you answer my question?

Jenkins: I have about four, five.

Hunter: Four or five tapes?

Jenkins: Uh-huh (yes).

Hunter: Are they little teeny tapes that fit in the recorder or are they big tapes?

Jenkins: Not all of them. Some of them are. Some of them are smaller and some of them are bigger.

Hunter: And how many--

Jenkins: Some of them, I save them, and some of them, I record over.

Hunter: How many tapes do you have relating to Dr. Smith's situation?

Jenkins: Smith, I have just the one.

Hunter: Just that one tape, that one phone call?

Jenkins: Uh-huh (yes).

Hunter: How is it you kept that one?

Jenkins: How is it I kept that one?

Hunter: Yes, ma'am.

Jenkins: I just kept it.

Hunter: Well, why did you keep it?

Jenkins: Because Dr. Smith called me back to work. I figure I might need it.

Hunter: And you have no other tapes at all--

Jenkins: No other tapes.

Hunter: --regarding Dr. Smith?

Jenkins: Regarding Dr. Smith. I have no more, that's the only one. That's the God's truth. That's the only one I have.

Hunter: Have you taken it to your attorney?

Jenkins: Have I taken it to my attorney?

Hunter: Yes, ma'am.

Jenkins: Yeah, sure have.

Hunter: And have you had it transcribed?

Jenkins: Transcribed?

Hunter: Yeah, have you had it typed up?

Jenkins: Typed up? I can hear it, I don't need it typed up.

Hunter: Did you have it typed up?

Jenkins: What do you mean, "typed up"?

Hunter: Have you had it transcribed and typed up—what the words are on the tape?

Jenkins: Well, you can hear what the words are on the tape. You don't need it typed up. It's very clear. Dr. Smith's talking. It's very clear.

Hunter: I understand--

Jenkins: Very clear, his voice--

Hunter: --if you listen to the tape, you might be able to hear what's on it. What I'm asking you is did you have it typed up and transcribed?

Jenkins: To put on the tape?

Hunter: No, ma'am. Did you give--

Jenkins: I don't understand.

Hunter: --the tape to somebody to type up what was on it, and do you have a written record of what is on the tape?

Jenkins: Like—like her? (Indicating) [I assume she is referring to the court reporter.]

Hunter: Yes, ma'am.

Jenkins: No. No, I didn't--

Hunter: Did you have it done by a secretary?

Jenkins: No, I haven't given—had it done by nobody. My phone at home did it. [354]

Later in the interview, Bob Hunter asked:

162

Hunter: Are you currently taking any medications?

Jenkins: Yes, I am.

Hunter: What medications are you taking?

Jenkins: I'm taking medication for menopause.

Hunter: Any other medications?

Jenkins: Estrogen medication.

Hunter: Are you taking any other medications, other than medications for menopause?

Jenkins: For menopause?

Hunter: Yes, ma'am. Any other medications?

Jenkins: Yes, sir.

Hunter: What other medications are you taking?

Jenkins: What medications I take? I take Strattera.

Hunter: Strattera?

Jenkins: Uh-huh (yes). For menopause.

Hunter: Other than the Strattera, are you taking any other medications?

Jenkins: Yes, sir.

Hunter: What are the other medications you are taking?

Jenkins: I take Depakote.

Hunter: And what is Depakote for?

Jenkins: Depakote is for my menopause.[32]

Williams: So both of those medications you just mentioned—

Jenkins: Yes, both of them.

Williams: Okay, now, is there anything else, other than for menopause, that you're taking, is what he wants to know.

Jenkins: For menopause?

Williams: Anything other than for menopause?

Jenkins: Yeah, I take Evista.

Hunter: And what is Evista?

Jenkins: It's for menopause.

Williams: Evista is for bones.

Jenkins: It's for my bones.

Williams: I happen to know what that one is.

Jenkins: Yeah, it helps with the bones and all.

---

[32] From Depakote.com, accessed 5/31/2019: DEPAKOTE comes in different dosage forms. DEPAKOTE® (divalproex sodium) delayed-release tablets, for oral use, and DEPAKOTE® ER (divalproex sodium) extended-release tablets, for oral use, are prescription medications used:
- to treat manic episodes associated with bipolar disorder
- alone or with other medicines to treat:
  o complex partial seizures in adults and children 10 years of age and older
  o simple and complex absence seizures, with or without other seizure types
- to prevent migraine headaches

Hunter: Other than these three drugs for menopause, are you taking any other medications?

Jenkins: No, sir.

Hunter: Those are all the medications that you are taking at this time?

Jenkins: Yes, sir.

Hunter: And were you taking these medications during the period of time that you worked for Dr. Smith after his wife died?

Jenkins: Yes, sir.

Hunter: Okay. Were any of these medications prescribed to you for any psychological conditions?

Jenkins: For psychological conditions?

Hunter: Yes, ma'am.

Jenkins: Due to menopause. See, menopause has something to do with your psychological.[355]

That conversation did not end there. Pat eventually testified that she was taking drugs prescribed by a Dr. Koff. Pat said, "I needed [Dr. Koff] to prescribe my medicines, because the doctor I had lost his license."[356] There was no shortage of evasive babble like this in Pat Jenkins's 169 page deposition transcript. I considered leaving her testimony out of the book because I don't believe any reasonable person could believe that Lonnie William's and Charles Meier's client was telling the truth. Jim Maxwell noted that, "At times, she exhibited almost multiple personalities and gave a clear appearance of one who would be entirely capable of and perhaps, likely to, exercise undue influence if she chose to do so."[357] It is difficult to sort out the truth from the lies sometimes, but in an effort to be fair I will note some of the claims Pat made in her testimony to support her case.

Pat Jenkins:

Said Little Jimmy said to a nurse about his mother Iris "If you don't give her something to shut her up, I'm going to have to kill her."[358]

Said she stayed and helped Iris when several other nurses quit because Iris was a difficult patient.[359]

Said she gave Iris CPR to prevent her from dying during a seizure.[360]

Said she did not accept gifts from Uncle Jimmy, other than gas money, while she was working for Iris.[361]

Said she worked for a Dr. Hunley and after his death she was sent a bonus check thanking her for the work she had done.[362]

Said Uncle Jimmy did not buy her any stock [363]

Said she was Uncle Jimmy's "companion", not his nurse.[364]

Said Uncle Jimmy called her "nurse" but she referred to herself as CNA II.[365]

Said she never talked to Uncle Jimmy about business.[366]

Said she never told Uncle Jimmy that anyone was going to put him in a nursing home.[367]

Said when Reverend Queen and Reverend Everette went with Billy to notify Uncle Jimmy that his son had died Billy "kept saying 'Uncle Jimmy, do you want me to be your power of attorney.'"[368]

Said Uncle Jimmy saw Otto Pridgen in Sunday school, but never at home until after Little Jimmy died.[369]

Said she would sit in the Sunday School class with Uncle Jimmy.[370]

Said she only accepted $12,000.00 in tips. She said the $36,000.00 that she admitted to in her interview with the detective included all her pay and tips. She said Uncle Jimmy made a false statement when he told the detective he had given her $90,000.00.[371]

Said she did not know what gifts Uncle Jimmy gave her daughter Theresa Crumpler, formerly Theresa Mozingo.[372]

Said she reported Linda's $2,000,000.00 check to Otto Pridgen because
She didn't know it was a joke
It was a lot of money to be written on a check
She felt the POA should be informed
She didn't want anyone to be looking for a missing check.[373]

Said she knew Billy was no longer had power of attorney when she claimed Uncle Jimmy said, "Get your GD ass out of my house, right now, you son-of-a-bitch" to Billy.[374]

Said she was in the house, but not in the room when and where the Will was signed.[375]

Said she did not provide "caregiving" to Uncle Jimmy until after June of 2003.[376]

Carol S. Tucker

Carol Tucker testified that she was trained as a CNA.[377] She says she doesn't recall any training on the ethics of accepting gifts.[378] She testified that Linda Phillips called her about working with Uncle Jimmy and Aunt Iris and she started working for them in March 2001.[379] She stayed on when Iris died and continued to work for Uncle Jimmy.[380]

Interestingly, she testified that after Otto Pridgen gained Uncle Jimmy's power of attorney some things changed in the house. She said that she was cut back to 2 days a week from four and Pat Jenkins had become "... the head boss, the head knocker, the head—head honcho."[381] It's interesting that she recognized Pat's new authority after Otto Pridgen took over his power of attorney from Billy.

Jim Maxwell also asked Carol Tucker about her interview with Detective Johnson while Uncle Jimmy was still alive. Maxwell asked her about her comment to the detective that Uncle Jimmy was probably going to leave half of his farm to Pat. When asked why she thought that she said, "I have no idea. Probably because I thought he—he thought a lot of Pat." She said that she never actually had any discussions with Uncle Jimmy about who he would leave his farm to so Jim Maxwell asked, "That was simply a guess on your part?" to which she responded, "I was probably mad at Pat that day." Maxwell asked her why she would have been mad at Pat and Tucker responded, "Pat and I didn't always get along... Just like two women in a kitchen."[382] I believe Carol Tucker was trying to hide something with her evasive responses. I believe that Pat had a somewhat hostile relationship with everyone in that inner circle, but it makes me wonder if the Pridgens and the other caregivers put up with it to keep the money flowing. Let's not forget that Pat testified that Carol Tucker was with her the night that Pat gave him those last three enemas.[383] If she helped Pat Jenkins with that deed, she might feel compelled to protect her partner.

Carol Tucker admitted that she accepted money from Uncle Jimmy above and beyond her pay. She called it gas money in her deposition, but seemed slightly evasive when asked how much he had given her. When asked how much he would give her at a given time she said, "Twenty, sometimes more." When asked what she meant by "more" she said, "I don't know, sometimes maybe forty."[384] This conflicts with the $40 to $200 she admitted to accepting in tips during her interview with Detective Johnson.

Tucker also testified that she accepted $3,000.00 in Family Dollar Stock and $1,000.00 in another stock. She said that she accepted $13,000.00 for a new car.[385] I think that Carol Tucker knew that she was doing something unethical when she accepted these large gifts because when asked if she used the $13,000.00 gift to pay off her car she said, "I put it in the bank, because I—the way things were going, I didn't know if they were going to ask for it back or what, so I just held on to it."[386] This is one of those answers that makes me have more questions. What was "the way things were going"? Apparently, things were not going perfectly smoothly in Carol Tuckers eyes and she was uncomfortable with some of the monetary transactions going on. It seems that despite her discomfort she did nothing to stop, or report, or change "the way things were going."

Carol testified that Uncle Jimmy "usually leaves kind of big tips when we go somewhere." and that she took Uncle Jimmy to the restaurant her daughter, Sharon Rodriguez, worked in. Carol testified that Uncle Jimmy gave Sharon a $4,000.00 tip.[387]

Jan Pridgen

Jan Pridgen testified that she never knew Uncle Jimmy prior to her husband's employment with him (which means she only knew him for about four to five months at the time Uncle Jimmy mentioned her in the will).[388] When asked why Uncle Jimmy was put on an allowance of a thousand dollars a day she testified, "I had to have a little meeting with him about this, because I just couldn't—we didn't want him to have a lot of cash on him. It was a safety issue."[389]

When asked about the $17,000.00 per month average billing that she and Otto charged Uncle Jimmy she testified, "For a couple of months, and that was when it was just papers and papers. And then, it steadily declined until October of 2003, it was seventy-four hundred for the month of October 2003. And then November it was back up to—it went between, I think it was fourteen and twenty-one thousand during that period of time, because he was no longer doing any of the shopping."[390] I wonder if they ran out of "papers" to sift through for him so they invented the grocery shopping scheme to continue billing the man outrageous amounts. At least they didn't bill him to attend his birthday party... oh, wait a minute... they did.

In a line of questioning Jim Maxwell asked her if she ever had any discussions with her husband, Otto Pridgen, about what Dr. Smith might be planning to do with his estate after his death. She replied, "I'm sure I did. I know we talked – I don't know whether it was before or after he made the will. I remember having discussions about leaving the opportunity for Dr. Bill – I don't – I don't think we discussed anything before he executed it though."[391] Further in that line of questioning she stated, "He [Uncle Jimmy] always said, 'I always retire my nurses.'"[392] I wonder if she felt that calling them nurses was a slip up, because she continued with a discussion of the term "nurse" during her testimony about the will as follows:

> He always said, "I always retire my nurses." That's a quote. So I didn't know, and in the south, I know that people – so many people have taken offense at the term "nurse," but I had a nurse when I was a child, and she was a black lady that took care of me. My brother had one, my little brother had one, and these were black ladies that wore white dresses, their uniforms, and they were nurses.
>
> And anybody – it's just an old southern thing, when somebody is taking care of somebody, whether it's children or old people, they're called "nurses."[393]

While there is no smoking gun in this commentary about "nurses," you start to get an idea of the kind of people Billy and his family were dealing with. I'll reiterate at this point that only white nurses were mentioned in Uncle Jimmy's will. All the black caregivers were excluded. If, as Jan Pridgen said, Uncle Jimmy always took care of his nurses, why didn't he do something for the black nurses?

Recall that Otto Pridgen testified that he knew nothing of the contents of the will until after it was executed as you read Jan Pridgen's response to a question about whether her husband spoke to Bob O'Quinn prior to his drafting the will:

169

I think I heard him speak to Bob O'Quinn, and I know he was telling him some things that Dr. Smith had said that he wanted in his will, and I didn't pay a lot of attention because I was doing something else. But I know that he had a conversation about that with Mr. O'Quinn.[394]

Reverend Michael Queen

Reverend Mike Queen testified that he had known Uncle Jimmy since August of 1986.[395] He recalls noticing a gradual decline in Uncle Jimmy's health.[396] Queen said that he seems to remember the first time he visited Uncle Jimmy's home was after his throat surgery which was approximately 12 to 15 years prior to this deposition (circa 1990-1993).[397] Reverend Queen testified about a record the church keeps of visits pastors make to "Shut-ins", or people who have trouble getting out of the home to go to church.[398] Reverend Queen's first recorded visit was in October of 1993. The pastors at First Baptist Church recorded two to three visits per year from 1994 to 2002 on that document. The only exception to that was in 2000 when they recorded no visits. In 2003 and 2004 Reverend Queen, reverend Everette and one other staff member recorded six and five visits in those two years respectively. Queen testified that his reasons for visits were "Just to maintain contact." Perhaps it is just coincidental that they doubled their frequency of visits to Uncle Jimmy's house in the years that they were trying to buy the New Hanover County Law Enforcement Center.[399] For now, I'll give Reverend Queen the benefit of the doubt. When asked if he ever discussed the "needs of the church" he responded "Well, I certainly talked to – I always thanked him for the money he put in the Pastor's Fund. I probably wrote him a note or two over the years thanking him in the early days when he would bring food for the Wednesday group there, but I never went to him about any need that the church had."[400]

Reverend Queen also testified that he thought Uncle Jimmy's wife Iris was a member of the First Baptist Church, but he doesn't remember seeing her in church.[401] Since so many of the propounders seem to be comfortable using words of the deceased in their favor, I will go ahead and note that I have heard people say that when Iris saw those pastors coming to visit her home she would say things like, "Here come those Baptists, asking for money again." She was Lutheran, and never joined the First Baptist Church.

Reverend Queen does not remember if he visited Uncle Jimmy after Iris died.[402] There was no record in the church's log that a pastor visited in December of 2001. He doesn't remember if he conducted Iris' funeral, or even if he attended the funeral.[403] Reverend Queen testified that he thinks he met Uncle Jimmy's son once "more or less just in passing."[404] Queen could not remember if he had anything to do with Little Jimmy's funeral service.[405]

He testified that prior to Little Jimmy's death he had only bumped into Billy coincidentally at the hospital, and had shopped in his store, but did not know him well.[406] He testified that the first conversation he had with Billy about Uncle Jimmy was after Little Jimmy. He describes, "The first I recall, and we may have bumped into each other in the hospital or something like that. I really don't recall, but the day of Doctor Smith's son's death, I had to call Billy." When asked, "You had to call him?" Queen responded "Well, I think either Jim or I, because he asked us to call. Doctor Smith asked us to call Billy."[407] His testimony makes me wonder if he didn't want to call Billy. I wonder if Reverend Queen felt disappointed that a family member might come between his church and this elderly man's estate. Again, I will give Reverend Queen the benefit of the doubt.

Reverend Queen continued to testify that the day Little Jimmy died he was notified by the Wrightsville Beach Police Department. The police officers asked him to meet them at Uncle Jimmy's house to break the news of his loss. Reverend Queen and Reverend Everette went to Uncle Jimmy's house together.[408] After they broke the news and the police answered a couple of questions for Uncle Jimmy they departed leaving the two reverends and the caregiver on duty that day who happened to be Pat Jenkins.[409] When asked if anything else took place during that visit Queen continued to testify, "...a moment after we had told Dr. Smith what happened that the caregiver, Pat, came in, crying rather loudly, and came to Doctor Smith and told him that she would not allow us to put him in a nursing home. And that's when I asked Jim ... I asked Jim Everette to take her out. ... She was crying, and the police officers and I were trying to explain things to Dr. Smith."[410]

This was good evidence for the family. This suggests that Pat Jenkins might have been trying to convince Uncle Jimmy he needed her protection to keep from being put into a nursing home. Now it

171

might seem refreshing that Reverend Queen would be so forthcoming with this little tidbit of information that seems damaging to the case of the propounders, but keep in mind that if Pat Jenkins was removed from the will, it would increase the gift to the church. Either way this was damaging to Lonnie Williams client, Pat Jenkins.

I have the perception that Lonnie Williams began turning up the heat on Reverend Queen at that point in the deposition. Queen testified that he told Billy that "someone had seen Doctor Smith in the bank taking out what they perceived to be a large sum of cash." Queen said that he could not remember who told him. [411] Lonnie Williams interrogated:

Williams: Now, Doctor Queen, you're telling me under oath that something as significant as getting that piece of information, and you don't remember who it was that said that to you?

Queen: I'm not certain.

Williams: Well, Doctor Queen, what is your best recollection of who it was that gave you that information?

Queen: I suspect it was a member of the church, because those are the people who usually call me in situations like that, but sometimes it's people outside.

Williams: Doctor Queen, now, don't bandy around with me, please. You know good and well what your best recollection is of who told you that information. That's pretty significant information.

You're under oath to tell the truth, the whole truth. What is the truth about who gave you that information?

Queen: I'm not certain. [412]

This banter about the cash withdrawal whistle blower went on for four pages of the deposition transcript before Williams moved on to another subject. [413] Queen would not reveal any leads as to who else in the church might have some information about Pat Jenkins' alleged misconduct. Next Williams asked him if he knew of any reason why

172

Uncle Jimmy was not competent to withdraw money from his account to which Queen responded, "No, sir." This prompted Williams to ask him why he felt it necessary to disclose this information to Billy.[414] Reverend Queen stated that he was just relaying "That someone had a concern that Doctor Smith might be – somebody might be taking advantage of him."[415]

Despite the fact that Queen testified that someone told him Uncle Jimmy might have been taken advantage of, Queen testified that he saw nothing wrong with the care he was getting from his caregivers.[416] He testified that Uncle Jimmy was angry at Billy when Billy suggested that he fire his current caregivers and hire new ones.[417] This would offer a reason to a jury for why Uncle Jimmy would disinherit his family. He testified that he told Reverend Jim Everette that he thought he had "messed up" by going with Billy to suggest he change his caregivers.[418] This makes me wonder if the Reverend cares more about maintaining his personal connection to this wealthy man than he cares about protecting him from people that might be taking advantage of him.

When asked if he or anyone else at the church talked to Uncle Jimmy about "what he would do, or what the church wanted him to do with his estate" Queen testified that he thought Reverend Everette had.[419] Later in the deposition remembered one conversation he received from Jack Richardson who was actually trying to reach Jim Everette about Uncle Jimmy's estate.[420]

He testified that he had known Uncle Jimmy since 1986, but his testimony leads me to believe he knows little about Uncle Jimmy's life outside the church.[421] The church records show Reverend Queen only visited Uncle Jimmy at home nine times in the ten years prior to the signing of the will.[422] He testified that he did not know Uncle Jimmy's extended family well. He said that he knew who Billy was, but that was about all he knew about him.[423] He didn't know who Larry Fowler was.[424] In many of his responses to questions about Uncle Jimmy's life Queen testifies that he does not know, or does not recall the information requested.

When asked if there is any doubt that the will did what Uncle Jimmy wanted it to do, he stated, "I don't have a doubt about that."[425] How does Reverend Queen, who knows so little about the man outside of his church life, and who claims to have never spoken to the man about his will, have no doubt about what the man was thinking when

173

he wrote his will? I can no longer give Reverend Queen the benefit of the doubt.

Reverend James Everette

Jim Everette testified that he met Uncle Jimmy in his 15 years as an associate pastor at the First Baptist Church, making rounds to Sunday school classrooms.[426] He testified that he built a personal relationship with Uncle Jimmy over the years, and made three or four trips to Uncle Jimmy's farm with him, but none of those trips were in the previous five years.[427] He testified that he had never been back to the river at the farm, so he may have been unaware that approximately 1/3 of the property was swampland.[428] Before the timber was clear cut you couldn't even see the paper mill that neighbors the property. It was very attractive woodland before the trees were cut. If you didn't know the land bordered a paper mill and was 1/3 swampland you might guess that it was extremely valuable during the real estate boom of 2004-2006.

Everette also made multiple trips to visit Uncle Jimmy in his house. Church records indicate that he made nine such visits in the ten years preceding the date Uncle Jimmy signed his last will and four of his visits were logged in the two years following that signature.[429] Much like Reverend Queen, Reverend Everette didn't seem to know much about Uncle Jimmy's life outside of church. He didn't know Jimmy's wife Iris as well as he knew Jimmy. He testified that he could not remember what her final illness was, or what nursing home she spent a portion of her final years in.[430] He testified that he didn't think Iris was a member of the First Baptist Church, and she "would never sit in the room with Doctor Smith and I, when we would visit."[431] (Ditching a conversation with the First Baptist Church preachers seems like something Aunt Iris would do). He also testified that he only saw Little Jimmy if he happened to be at Uncle Jimmy's farm or house while Everette was visiting. He testified that he remembered seeing Little Jimmy in church with Uncle Jimmy, one or two times.[432] Of Uncle Jimmy's extended family Everette testified that he didn't know Billy until just before Little Jimmy passed away and he had met Uncle Jimmy's sister-in-law, but he could not remember her name.[433]

At one point, he testified that, "My family doesn't have a lot of money and I don't fully understand bonds, and things being liquid that can be turned to cash."[434] As I read Everette's deposition, it seemed to

174

me that he was trying to paint a picture of himself as a simple Baptist preacher who had no knowledge or interest in financial matters. He testified that he knows "nothing about tax or charitable gifts, estates,"[435] and he testified that he "did not know anything about the size of Dr. Smith's estate…"[436]

Given that Reverend Everette claims to have known nothing about Uncle Jimmy's wealth at the time the will was written, consider the following parts of his sworn testimony in the very same deposition. He knew that Uncle Jimmy gave the church a bus (approximately a quarter-million-dollar gift).[437] He knew that Uncle Jimmy gave at least $100,000.00 to the church's Mission Fund.[438] While Everette says that he does not know "anything" about the man's wealth he must know, at least, that he was financially capable of making generous gifts. This denial of knowledge is also curious, considering Uncle Jimmy's banker, Jack Richardson's deposition testimony, where he referenced discussing with Everette, a 1031 exchange for one of Uncle Jimmy's properties in the amount of about a million dollars. The only property that Uncle Jimmy owned that could have possibly brought that kind of money was the family farm. Everette was a part of that planning effort before Otto Pridgen held Uncle Jimmy's Power of Attorney.[439]

When Everette was asked about conversations he had with Jack Richardson, and whether those conversations were being held for estate planning purposes Everette replied, "Yes, sir."[440] This leaves little doubt as to whether the preacher who knows "nothing about tax or charitable gifts, estates"[441] was working on Uncle Jimmy's estate planning, but this raises other questions. What was the nature of Reverend Everette's involvement in Uncle Jimmy's estate planning? Was he carrying out Uncle Jimmy's wishes? Was Uncle Jimmy telling him what he wanted in his will, or was Reverend Everette helping to shape Uncle Jimmy's decisions in some other way?

After claiming to know nothing of the contents of the will, Reverend Everette testified that he received a call from Bob O'Quinn, the lawyer who drafted the will, in which he was informed that Uncle Jimmy intended to leave money in a fund for Mr. Piner.[442] When asked if he had any "other information from any other source as to what the contents of Dr. Smith's will was, or was expected to be" Everette responded, "No, sir."

Recall Jack Richardson's testimony. Richardson testified that he remembers a conversation where Otto Pridgen (who claimed to know nothing of the contents of the will at that time) said that "the church would be taken care of" in the will.[443] Were Pridgen, Everette, and Richardson (the three legged stool) keeping these secrets from each other during Uncle Jimmy's estate planning?

After Everette testified that he had no "other information from any other source as to what the contents of Dr. Smith's will was, or was expected to be"[444] he was presented another piece of evidence, in Everette's own handwriting. Exhibit 17[33], as it was named for the court, contained personal notes from Everette's conversations with Jack Richardson. The text of Exhibit 17 is included in its entirety here:

Exhibit #17 page 1
DO NOT WANT DR TO:
LOOSE [sic] DIGNITY
Create Family Rift
Die w/o a will
*He does not have a will @ this point *
Dr. Smith's estate has the potential to have a large tax liability
>Stocks/Bonds/etc. are liquid and can be turned to cash
>We are reducing the size of the estate by selling timber
"Jan & OK are moving in interesting & creative ways to see Dr. Smith's wishes to come into fruition."
At O.K. insistence:
Series of 3 tests to prove D. competence
As soon as it is proven (w/in month)
A will will be written/drawn that day and signed.
Aug., 2002 Phone conversation w/ Jack Richardson

Exhibit #17 page 2
Charitable renewable Trust would probably be the farm.
>Jim E. & Small Team to handle this.

→Would like to see nephew get the home and a few acres @ it.
Church could sell house to the nephew

Piece #1   1. Write the will
                2. Purchase the property

---

[33] It was labeled exhibit 17 during depositions, and exhibit 428 during the trial.

3. CRT[34] w/in this year

Conversation Jack Richardson Aug. 2002

Sell the Farm
Gift it to the foundation
Can fund it from Stocks or farm
→ Jack Richardson ←
Go see Dr. Jimmy
<Will generate $500,000.00 a year>
For tax law purposes > Give the farm to a foundation

Have timber surveyed.
Cut the timber/sell it then give it
← →

Exhibit #17 page 3
Jack Richardson 9/25/02
<Dr. Smith is working on acquiring a piece of property in the same
block of the church
<To be gifted to FBC this year> (immediate gift)

Charitable Remainder Trust
(Dr. Smith would make an outright gift to FBC. FBC would sell the
property immediately and use those assets for purposes Dr. Smith
chooses./ We would then provide an income to Dr. Smith for as long
as he lives.
FBC put together a team to manage this

3rd <Jack would distribute from foundation>
Annual contribution to the church for general purposes.

4th Wants to give his caregivers assets, but this would come over time

. . . . .

---

[34] CRT: Charitable Remainder Trust. Reverend Everette referred to this as a
"foundation" in page 35 of his deposition.

Does this look like the notes of a man who knew nothing about Uncle Jimmy's estate at the time the will was written? Was Reverend Everette just taking notes, or was he leading the estate planning? Recall Jack Richardson's testimony (from chapter 19 of this book):

> Richardson was asked if he ever called Reverend Everette or Reverend Queen to tell them about the disposition of the will. Richardson answered "I'm fairly certain I did not call Mike Queen. I had—and it seems to me that I may have called Jim Everette to find out where things were, but I do not remember giving information about the will in detail or even—I don't know at what point I knew that the church was included."[445]

It seems Uncle Jimmy's banker thought Reverend Everette had a leadership role in the estate planning. The dates of Reverend Everette's notes indicate that he was involved in estate planning for Uncle Jimmy in at least the two months preceding the signature on the will. Richardson's testimony implies Everette's involvement began much sooner than that, perhaps before Otto Pridgen entered. Everette's notes also indicate that he was aware of some very specific details about Uncle Jimmy's financial situation. When asked about some of his own notes the preacher who "did not know anything about the size of Dr. Smith's estate"[446] testified as follows:

> ...Jack said that he thought the return of five percent would generate - - or that the five percent on the foundation, I guess the foundation would create five percent, or it could somehow get five percent a year. And that's when Jack - - that's why I wrote down the 500,000.[447]

Let's look at these numbers. $500,000.00 is five percent of ten million. Reading this makes me believe that Reverend Everette was working on a plan that would make the church the beneficiary of a ten-million-dollar estate. Given that Uncle Jimmy had somewhere in the ballpark of four million dollars in liquid assets at the time, and some people at that time seemed to believe that his land was worth about six million dollars, it makes me think that he was working on a plan that would gift most, if not all of Uncle Jimmy's assets to the non-profit corporation that pays his salary... the First Baptist Church.

To my knowledge, there is no law against a preacher helping one of his flock with estate planning, even if that preacher knows nothing about estate planning. **If** Reverend Everette had been working hand in hand with Uncle Jimmy, **and** was not trying to influence him unduly, then there would be no foul play. Like all else this case, it's not that simple.

It has been established that Reverend Everette had multiple conversations with Jack Richardson, and at least one luncheon with Richardson and Otto Pridgen, where Uncle Jimmy was not present.[448] When asked how many times he spoke to Uncle Jimmy about setting up a foundation with Uncle Jimmy's wealth to benefit the church, he said that he had only had one conversation with him on that subject.[449] The majority of Reverend Everette's involvement in Uncle Jimmy's estate planning seems to have been done in Uncle Jimmy's absence.

During the trial, accusations would be made that Uncle Jimmy's nephew Billy was trying to pressure him into making a will. Read note 3 under "DO NOT WANT DR TO:" in Reverend Everett's handwritten notes: "Die without a will." His notes explicitly state "At O.K. [Otto K. Pridgen] insistence: Series of 3 tests to prove D. competence." Who was trying to pressure Uncle Jimmy into writing a will?

The reverend who claims to know "nothing about tax or charitable gifts, estates" remembered the day he and Reverend Queen went to Uncle Jimmy's house to notify him that Little Jimmy died.[450] Everette testified that Uncle Jimmy said that day that he was thinking of making his nephew Billy his power of attorney. Everette testified that he told Uncle Jimmy that he "didn't think he had to make it [the decision of who would be his power of attorney] today or tomorrow."[451] Why would Jim Everette suggest to Uncle Jimmy that he postpone a decision like this if Uncle Jimmy was competent and had already made up his mind. Does this sound like Everette was trying to influence Uncle Jimmy's decision making? Keep in mind that Everette was already said to have been meeting with Jack Richardson about a 1031 exchange before this date. My instincts tell me that if Uncle Jimmy had chosen an agent from the church to be his power of attorney Everette would not have made the same recommendation for postponement. Everette also testified that he discouraged Billy from going to Uncle Jimmy's house at night to fire his nurses.[452] Billy does not remember any such advice from Reverend Everette.[453] How would

179

Everette have even known that Billy and his wife got a phone call from the detective and were rushing to Uncle Jimmy's side?

There was tension between the church and the caregiver/Pridgen team. The church hired separate council, and seemed to be trying to distance themselves from the caregivers, but what was their relationship like during Otto Pridgen's tenure as power of attorney? Recall John Newton, the timberman. Reverend Everette testified that after Newton cut Uncle Jimmy's timber, he started attending Sunday School classes at the First Baptist Church. Reverend Everette even asked John Newton to look at the timber on his grandmother's land.[454] I don't know if Reverend Everette was involved in Uncle Jimmy's timber sale, but it certainly seems that he was a part of some business partnerships that were blooming inside the First Baptist Church.

Newton wasn't the only one making connections inside the First Baptist Church. Everette testified that after Uncle Jimmy's death, Pat Jenkins started working for other members of the first Baptist Church, Hyton and Muriel Babson.[455] They say that all roads lead to Rome, but in this case, they seem to lead to the First Baptist Church.

Let's face it... preachers are influential people in our community. What good is a preacher who isn't influential? Where is the line drawn between influence, and undue influence? To answer it in this case, I look to one of the legs of the three legged stool. Recall that Jack Richardson testified about Uncle Jimmy's intentions for his farm as follows:

> The initial conversation around the farm was more inclined that—that this would probably be a family asset. And then the second—or later on it—it—it turned from a—becoming a family asset—still thinking family asset, but the conversation was that Dr. Smith's nephew--...--Nephew Billy's son, Dr. William Smith, would be financially able to maintain that farm. And so it was more of a condition that it—that it would be an opportunity for Dr. William Smith to have an opportunity to go after that asset or—if he chose to.[456]

180

25. Summary Judgment

Before that second round of depositions, Jim Maxwell wrote a letter to Billy Smith and his family warning them that they might not have a case. He notified them that he would not continue on a contingency basis. After the second round of depositions, he decided to go ahead with the case. Perhaps Maxwell felt that he had some new evidence to work with. Maybe he just felt like he was doing God's work.

Maxwell probably wasn't the only one who saw some weaknesses in the church's case. The Pridgen's and caregiver's attorney, Lonnie Williams, had some interesting interactions with Jim Everette during that deposition. Williams asked Everette if he ever heard that Uncle Jimmy was withdrawing large sums of money from the bank. Everette testified that Reverend Queen told him about that (I wonder if either of them warned the Babsons). When asked where Queen got the information, Everette testified that he didn't recall. Everette testified that sometimes they share information without sharing names.[457]

After that, Williams asked:

Williams: You're more rumormongers than anything else; is that what it is?

Hunter: Objection to the question.

Everette: No. No.

Williams: Just don't cite the source. Is that the rule y'all follow; be sure not to cite the source of where it comes from?

Hunter: Objection.

Williams: Would you mind answering the question for me one way or the other?

Everette: There are times when we cite sources, and sometimes we don't.

Williams: And when you're in a deposition under oath, is that one of the times you don't tell where critical information came from?

Hunter: Objection.

Williams: Is that one of the times?

Everette: I placed my hand on the Bible. I raised my hand, and I promised to tell the truth, the whole truth, and nothing but the truth, and that's what I'm doing.

Williams: Well, that's certainly what you promised to do. And so did Doctor Queen...[458]

When I read Reverend Everette's testimony, "I placed my hand on the bible...," it makes me think of all the religious leaders through history that have abused their position of trust.

With renewed enthusiasm Jim Maxwell continued his investigation into Uncle Jimmy's case. He lamented the limited time he had to work. Maxwell was simultaneously representing a former District Attorney who was accused of engaging in misconduct that led to the death penalty in a capital case.[459] He had to devote considerable time to that case as well as others which diminished his ability to expand his knowledge of Uncle Jimmy's case.

In addition to this frustration, new twists continually caused the case to evolve. Up to the 12th of October 2005 the First Baptist Church had aligned themselves with the Pridgens and the caregivers. On October 12th Bob Hunter filed a Motion for Partial Summary Judgment. The church was still maintaining their assertion that Uncle Jimmy had "sufficient mental capacity to make and execute a will", but the church was then asking the court to consider that the Pridgens and the caregivers had exerted undue influence to procure their shares.[460] The propounder's fracture was complete. The church's cards were on the table. The church was going after the farm as though the will was valid, and the Pridgen's and caregivers' shares as though they were procured by undue influence.

This did not escape Lonnie Williams' attention. The former member of the First Baptist Church referred to it as the "Worst Baptist Church" in an e-mail to Jim Maxwell in which he discussed scheduling of meetings.[461] In reply, Jim Maxwell suggested that Lonnie Williams should refer to the church by its correct name, and hinted that he had discovered information that could remove William's client as executor. Lonnie Williams replied:

> Mr. Maxwell,
> Thank you for your continuing advice. I will give it the consideration which it deserves…I have noted how well Mr. Pridgen is treated by the church of which he has been a member for 50 years. Fortunately, I was a member for only 25….[462]

To add to the friction between the propounders, Williams petitioned the court to pay the Pridgen's out of Uncle Jimmy's estate for discovering and settling assets of Jimmy's wife Iris that were "undiscovered" until 2005 (Iris died in 2001).[463] Hunter opposed the payment on behalf of the church because he could not understand how the Pridgens had not discovered these assets in three years as power of attorney.[464] Recall that the Pridgens were billing Uncle Jimmy approximately $17,000.00 per month to go through his papers (and to attend his birthday parties, get his groceries etc.).[35]

Lonnie's legal status changed when the First Baptist Church hired different council to handle their case. To fight the summary judgment that the church requested, he needed to talk to the First Baptist Church Board of Trustees. To speak with the trustees about the case, Lonnie Williams had to go through their lawyer, Bob Hunter, and formal legal channels. Lonnie had to have a subpoena issued to depose Carlton Fisher, the chairman of the trustees. Keep in mind that Lonnie Williams is a former member of the First Baptist Church and knows many of its members and its board of trustees as you read excerpts from the deposition.

---

[35] Iris' assets were "discovered" by Billy Smith. After Uncle Jimmy died and the family took custody of his house (bequeathed to them in Little Jimmy's estate). A statement for some stock Iris owned was delivered via the postal service to that address. Billy forwarded that piece of mail to the propounders through Jim Maxwell. I assume that the statements were mailed diligently by Iris' brokerage house monthly (or perhaps quarterly) for the entire time of Pridgen held the power of attorney.

Herbert Carlton Fisher

Carlton Fisher testified that he was Chairman of Board of Trustees for the church.[465] He testified that the following individuals were on the board of Trustees since the outset of the caveat: [466]

Willis Brown
Bertram Williams
Clay Collier[36],[467]
John Lennon
Claude Arnold

Fisher testified that he had no personal relationship with Jimmy outside of church.[468] Lonnie Williams explained to Fisher that he called Reverend Queen shortly after the caveat was filed to ask if the church had retained council. Williams went on to explain that Queen told him that the trustees instructed him not to talk to anyone about the case, then asked, "From whom did those instructions come?" to which Fisher replied "From the Trustees."[469] Fisher testified that the two attorneys on the board of Trustees "…had a great amount of input…" and decided that "it would just be best that the ministers don't discuss it."[470] It seems to me that information control was as important to the First Baptist Church as it was to Pat Jenkins.

Animosity between the propounders was never more apparent than during this deposition. Lonnie Williams wanted to know how the First Baptist Church came to retain Bob Hunter and the deposition proceeded as follows:

Williams: And how [w]as Mr. Hunter, Mr. Robert N. Hunter, Jr., seated next to you, how was the decision made to employ him?

Hunter: OBJECTION, and I'm going to instruct the witness not to answer. You're going to have to get a Court Order.

Williams: Well that's not a matter of privilege.

---

[36] Clay Collier, an attorney, and one of his law partners, Andrew Hanley, pleaded guilty, in 2017, to Willful Failure to File North Carolina Individual Income Tax Returns.

184

Hunter: It is a matter of privilege.

Williams: It is not a matter of privilege. You were not employed, and you were not the attorney for the church.

Hunter: Well, then you're going to have to get a Judge to have him answer that.

Williams: Mr. Hunter, you and Mr. Maxwell have preached ethics to me about how terrible my ethics are in this case, and then you're going to even though you admit that's not matter of privilege, you're going to instruct him not to…

Hunter: I didn't admit that it wasn't a matter of privilege. It is a matter of privilege.

Williams: It is not a matter of privilege.

Hunter: You get a judge to get him to answer that.

Williams: You weren't employed as attorney.

Hunter: Lonnie, get a judge to go ahead and tell him to say that.

Williams: Don't lean forward to me, Bob Hunter. By God, I've had enough of you already.

Hunter: Well, I don't care if you've had enough of me or not. Let's just…

Williams: Well, I'm telling you just sit back, make your objections, and keep your mouth shut otherwise. [To Fisher] Do you refuse to answer the question?

Hunter: Upon instruction he's refusing to answer the question.

Williams: I want him to answer for this record. [To Fisher] Do you refuse to answer the question?

185

Fisher: Repeat the question.

Williams: You don't remember what it was?

Fisher: Not after that I don't.

Williams: How was Mr. Hunter selected, Mr. Robert N. Hunter, Jr., of Greensboro, North Carolina, how was he selected as attorney for the church?

Hunter: And I've instructed him not to answer for the record.

Williams: [To Fisher] And I'm telling you that it's you who has to decide. Do you refuse to answer the question?

Fisher: I don't refuse. I know that we discussed a number of people, but I don't know exactly how we came to the exact conclusion.

Williams: And you don't have any best recollection about how Mr. Hunter was chosen?

Fisher: No.

Williams: You are under oath? Are you aware of that?

Fisher: Yes sir.

Williams: Was his name suggested by Willis Brown?

Hunter: OBJECTION.

Fisher: Someone brought up his name. I do not recall who. It was one of the Trustees.

Williams: Was his name suggested by Dr. Queen's son-in-law, who is an attorney in Greensboro?

Fisher: I do not recall.

186

Williams: Were the ministers present when the trustees had their meeting?

Fisher: No sir.

Williams: Did you know anything about the reputation of Mr. Hunter when his selection was made?

Fisher: His reputation?

Williams: Yes.

Fisher: What do you mean?

Williams: Did you know anything about Mr. Hunter before he was selected as the attorney for this church?

Fisher: No.

Williams: You weren't aware of - - You hadn't ever heard that he had for fifteen years been the Public Administrator of Guilford County?

Hunter: OBJECTION. I'm objecting to a continual objection to this line of questions. If it continues I'm going to ask that we adjourn and go to a Judge.

Williams: Any time you want to.[471]

Jim Maxwell sat quietly through the bickering between the propounders lawyers. Once it was his turn to cross examine Fisher, Maxwell asked questions concerning the appraisal of the farm property. He asked Williams why he chose a New Hanover County appraiser to look at the property instead of one from its location, Columbus County. Fisher said that the firm he chose is a reputable firm qualified to appraise land throughout North Carolina.[472] Maxwell also asked why four of the six comparables used were in Brunswick County and asked if fisher thought it would be fair to say that Brunswick county "...may be in fact one of the most rapidly developing most expensive pieces of real estate in the State of North Carolina at the present time". Fisher called the comparison apples to apples, but admitted the "Certain parts" of Brunswick County fit Maxwell's description. Maxwell also asked him if he thought that the 225,000 acres of land in the vicinity of the farm that International Paper had recently announced that it was planning to sell would have an impact on the fair market value of the farm Fisher replied, "It might."[473] Maxwell asked about the disparity between the recent $1,493,000.00 appraisal and the 2002 appraisal of $582,000.00 but Fisher said that he had no knowledge of the previous appraisal.[474] One of the last things Maxwell asked about was if the church had considered how to handle the fact that the 5 acres of land that Bill Smith was entitled to buy in the will was in the center of the 600 acre property and had no direct access to highways.[475] Maxwell was curious about why Uncle Jimmy would leave a provision for his grandnephew to buy this inaccessible piece of land. The best trial lawyer in North Carolina doesn't miss much, even when he is distracted by other cases. The church's board of trustees had not given that much thought to the problem of the landlocked lot.[476] I suspect that the true authors of the will didn't know the land well enough to consider this either.

.....

While no reputable lawyer could imagine that the facts in this case could pass the smell test there was still the problem for the caveators of proving their case within the boundaries of the law. In addition to Bob Hunter's motion for summary Judgment which would, if awarded, remove the Pridgen's and the caregivers from the will and move those gifts to the church, Lonnie Williams filed a motion for Summary Judgment claiming that "...the caveat fails to state a claim upon which relief can be granted, and there is no genuine issue of material fact and that Movants [propounders] are entitled to judgment as a matter of law on all issues and claims..." Essentially Williams claimed that there was no question as to the facts of the case and asked the judge to dismiss the caveat and allow the estate to be distributed as described in the will.[477] Williams backed up his argument with the evidence already submitted as well as sworn affidavits from the following individuals (Brief excerpts/summaries of the affidavits are found in parenthesis): [478]

Christy L. Jones, Ph.D. (Summarizing her prior diagnosis)

Dewey H. Bridger, III, M.D. (Stating that Uncle Jimmy scored perfect on the mini mental state exam)

William W. Hinton (Member of First Baptist Church, and recent employer of Pat Jenkins). (Stating that "Dr. Smith's nurses and Jan Pridgen provided him with excellent care and companionship")

Hyton W. Babson (Member of First Baptist Church). (Stating that Uncle Jimmy's choosing Pat Jenkins as caregiver and OK Pridgen as POA is evidence of good judgment and that Babson had employed Pat Jenkins to care for his own wife)

Gene L. McIntyre (Member of First Baptist Church)

Charles E. (Bud) Davis (Member of First Baptist Church) (Stating that Uncle Jimmy was close to his wife and son, but had never heard him talk about extended family)[479]

While Williams and Hunter were claiming that there were no material issues of fact to argue Jim Maxwell would argue differently. In an e-mail to Billy and some of his family members Maxwell described his plan to show the judge that Uncle Jimmy was "95 years of age and was in such a physical and mental condition that it was determined that he needed 24/7 care and someone to act as his POA ... to handle all his financial matters. He was surrounded 24/7 by the caregivers and the Pridgens and few folks outside that group had access to him. That he was confused about his estate (often inflating its value) and once gave a caregiver a $2,000,000 check. He also 'tipped' a daughter of one of his care givers $4,000 for lunch. He also allowed (with no apparent objection) a man who had never done any legal work for him to charge amounts ranging from a low of about $15,000/month to more than $25,000/month to serve as his POA (when Billy and young Jim before him had done this for free). He left Bill a piece of property that is totally landlocked and of questionable value. He wanted Erin and Lisa to each have $100,000, but never followed up to see if it was done. When told of Jimmy's death, Jenkins 'swooned' that she would not let 'them' put him in a nursing home although the only folks present at the time were two ministers, a police office[r] and a police chaplain..."[480]

If the propounders motions passed, the family's effort would be defeated. On the 5th of December 2005, the best trial lawyer in North Carolina was notified that he won his motion to deny summary

Judgment. Judge William A. Cobb found there was "a genuine issue to one or more material facts on the issue of whether or not James Henry Smith had sufficient mental capacity on September 26, 2002 to execute his Last Will and Testament... [and whether the Will] was obtained through undue and improper influence and/or duress upon James Henry Smith." This would allow the family to go forward with a claim of undue influence and lack of mental capacity.[481] This was a huge victory for the family, but it was far from over.

Before a jury could hear the case, North Carolina Law requires mediation. I suppose the family's desire to remove the Pridgens and the caregivers from the will completely was a hard point to negotiate from. Furthermore, the family wanted to pursue the propounders conduct in criminal court as well. However, the family was willing to negotiate independently with the Church. The family was primarily interested in the farm which the Church could have offered. The family hoped that the church would settle with the family by giving up the farm and then pursue the Pridgens and the caregivers in court for the rest of Uncle Jimmy's gift. It seems to me that the church wanted to maintain the perception that they were just caught in the middle of a bad situation. It seems that they were perfectly happy for the family to do the dirty work against the other propounders. Jim Maxwell described the church's position going into mediation in an e-mail to the family as follows: "As Mr. Hunter said (in recognition of the family's goals in regard to the removal of Pridgen and the disinheritance of all four women) the Church can 'negotiate' over a figure; it cannot negotiate principles."[482] The family had the impression that the First Baptist Church had no intention of going after the Pridgen's and the caregivers in civil or criminal matters if the family dropped their suit. I have the impression that the First Baptist Church Inc. would never let principles stand in the way of fundraising.

After the mediation, the family made the church a high/low offer. The family suggested an agreement that if the caveat was successful the family would take the farm and 20% of the estate. Then family would then GIVE the church the other 80% of the estate. This would mean that if the family won outright the church would still get about $4 million. If the propounders were successful, by this agreement, the church would give the family the farm and nothing else. If some of the sitters were removed individually (by undue influence) then the family would get the farm and 20% of the removed persons share (the other 80% would pass to the others in the residuary).[483] In an e-mail to the family Jim Maxwell described his reaction to the Church's response: "Like each of you, I was surprised and disappointed in the Church's response to our offer of a 'high/low' agreement which guaranteed the church everything it would get under an uncontested will, with the exception of the farm, if we lost, but we, potentially provide the Church with a higher 'net' recovery from the Estate if we won and had the will invalidated."[484] Maxwell went on to describe that the Church (in Bob Hunter's words) wanted nothing more and nothing less than the will provided them.[485] This was inconsistent with their previous attempt to throw the caregivers out. After this settlement rejection family members agreed that if they won the trial outright they would give nothing to the church except $100,000.00 for Roy Piner.

26. The Final Depositions
March, 2006

Before the trial, Maxwell needed to tie up some loose ends with two more propounder witnesses who had submitted evidence into the case. He did so with the depositions of Dr. Dewey H. Bridger III, M.D. and Christy L. Jones, Ph.D.

Dewey H. Bridger, III, M.D.

Dr. Bridger testified that he had been Uncle Jimmy's doctor since about May of 1998.[486] He testified that he administered Uncle Jimmy a Mini-Mental State Exam for competency [which includes tests like: "Hold up a card that says, 'Close your eyes.' So the subject can see it clearly. Ask him/her to read it and do what is says. Check the box at right only if he/she actually closes his/her eyes."]. Bridger said that Uncle Jimmy asked him to give him the exam because he had concerns about his memory and wanted to know if there was anything else that needed to be done.[487] It's interesting that he says Uncle Jimmy asked him for the exam, because in Uncle Jimmy's medical record there is a note dated 1 May, 2002 (the day of the mini mental exam and the day after the Pridgens took power of attorney) that says "His lawyer sent him to make sure he is doing o.k."[488] Another note dated 1 July, 2002 says, "Phone call from Jan Pridgen @ OK Pridgen law firm. She request appt. for competency eval. Called Dr. Christy Jones office and they will schedule. Advised Ms. Pridgen per Dr. Bridger that he does not feel Dr. Smith needs licensed medical care. – M. Dance, LPN".[489]

I have three concerns about this data. One concern is that I think there is evidence here that the Pridgens were pushing Uncle Jimmy to get the competency exams (that would hold up in court better than questions like, "Ask the subject to repeat 'No ifs, ands, or buts'" as in the Mini exam). A second is that Dr. Bridger made a recommendation against hiring licensed medical care. Third, that Dr. Bridger's testimony under oath during this deposition seems to be inconsistent with his notes taken at the time the care was given.

I don't know if Bridger has had any training in elder abuse, but if he was as familiar with elder abuse as Detective Cassidy (who spent a career fighting it), he would have known that most elder abuse is committed by unlicensed caregivers in the home.[490] Dr. Bridger's

192

analysis focused on Uncle Jimmy's health, however, and not some sort of criminal abuse, so he may not have peeled back the onion far enough to uncover any.

Bridger's testimony that Uncle Jimmy wanted the mental exam, and Bridger's medical notes that say Jan Pridgen called for a competency evaluation are not the only quirks in the medical evidence. Medical notes from the day after the Pridgens took power of attorney also state that Uncle Jimmy's son died and "he really has no one left to care for him."[491] I wonder who told Dr. Bridger's staff that Uncle Jimmy had no one to care for him. Another oddity is found in an August 17, 2002 entry from Dr. Bridger's office in which it states that Uncle Jimmy "Is present with his son and personal nurse."[492] This is weird, because as of that date Little Jimmy was already deceased. Dr. Bridger testified that he thought that entry was a mistake made by one of his assistants. He further testified about the man mistaken for Uncle Jimmy's son as follows: "I'm sure it was – I'm sure it was probably – it may have been Mr. Pridgen. I really don't know."[493]

Maxwell reviewed Uncle Jimmy's medical records with Dr. Bridger. There is a memo from Maxim Healthcare in Uncle Jimmy's records dated July 2002 that suggests that a Registered Nurse recommended to Jan Pridgen that all the caregivers in Uncle Jimmy's home be hired from a licensed organization. According to that memo Jan Pridgen agreed, "because of the legal side of it."[494] Did the Pridgen's try to fire Pat Jenkins and the other unlicensed caregivers, but fail for some reason? This reinforces my belief that the Pridgens would have to appease Pat Jenkins or lose employment with the man they were billing over $17,000.00 per month. That might explain why Jan Pridgen felt that all the caregivers should be from a licensed agency in July of 2002, but by September of 2002 Jan joined Pat as one of the "faithful caregivers" who were beneficiaries in the will.

About 8 months after Uncle Jimmy's last will was signed he was taken by one of his nurses to see Dr. Tracy H. Moore, apparently for "difficulty with voiding."[495] According to the medical record of that visit Uncle Jimmy said that he took a long time in the bathroom that morning, but he was emptying normally. That nurse, whose name is not included in the record, gives a different account and says that he has to strain to make urine. A bladder scan was done, but a physical exam was deferred that day because Uncle Jimmy was "slightly agitated and only grudgingly even consents to the bladder scan."[496] Dr.

Moore warned the "nurse" that the additional medications that he prescribed could impact Uncle Jimmy's blood pressure and asked to clear them with Dr. Bridger.[497]

Two months later Bridger wrote: "The pt is in today for an evaluation. He is just really kind of steadily going down hill. He is not sleeping well. He is weeping more and is complaining of some pain in his knee, The nevus appears to be much better. His BP looks like it is kind of low at this point. ... Probably not much we can do at this point and Dr. Smith really does not want much in the way of intervention. We will just see what we can do to keep him comfortable."[498] What happened to this man who was reportedly so healthy before he signed the will? What was changing in this man's life? About a year after the will was signed, Uncle Jimmy started taking Aricept for dementia.[499] His medical record reports that he would wake up in the middle of the night and clap his hands. During the day would request to have pillows on top of his head.[500] Three months after that report his medical record states that he is being given Ambien to help sleep in the evening, but stays in the bed all day and doesn't need that much sleep. He would get agitated and pull off his diaper.[501] Dr. Bridger must have really trusted Pat Jenkins and Uncle Jimmy's other caregivers because he suggested that he try to make diagnosis' over the phone to save the caregivers the effort of bringing him into the office.[502] Dr. Bridger never made a house call for Uncle Jimmy.[503] On 22 February 2005 Dr. Bridger signed Uncle Jimmy's death certificate.[504]

Dr. Bridger said that, in July of 2002, Uncle Jimmy did not need to have licensed caregivers because he "doing pretty well."[505] Below some excerpts from Uncle Jimmy's medical records that will indicate some of the issues that Uncle Jimmy was contending with during that time in his life. After reading through the excerpts you will have a better idea of what Dr. Bridger meant by "doing pretty well".

The excerpts from medical notes are in the following format:
[Date]: [Name of Dr. Associated with the Record]: [Medical information]

Prior to 1998: Drs. Unknown: Prostate cancer with surgical intervention, laryngectomy for laryngeal cancer two knee surgeries,[506]
May 5, 1998: Bridger: Vertigo, Pain in left lower abdomen, Fatigue[507]
April 27, 1999: Bridger: Skin infection.[508]

November 11, 1999: Bridger: Pedal edema, Enlarged Prostate[509]
August 9, 2000: Bridger: Fall with injury to knee and head (stitches). Healing satisfactorily.[510]
March 6, 2001: Wertheimer: Short of breath, Extremely dizzy.[511]
March 12, 2001: Smith: Atrial fibrillation.[512]
August 8, 2001: Bridger: Edema and dizziness.[513]
March 27, 2002: Hundley: Arthritis of knee and cervical spine.[514]
May 1, 2002: Bridger: "Lawyer sent him to make sure he is doing o.k. Mr. Smith's son died recently under suspicious circumstances and his wife died about 5 ___ ago, so he really has no one left to care for him." Occasional palpitations, mild dizziness. 30/30 on mental exam. Wrote "a letter to his attorney at his request, outlining findings."[515]
May 29, 2002: McManus: Evaluation for Hypertension: continue current monitoring.[516]
June 26, 2002: Hundley: Advanced degenerative arthritis in knee. Does not remember being asked to check with Dr. Bridger for more medications.[517]
July 1, 2002: Bridger: Received call from Jan Pridgen requesting appointment for competency evaluation. Advised Ms. Pridgen that Dr. Bridger does not feel Uncle Jimmy needs licensed medical care.[518]
July 1, 2002: Maxim Healthcare: "Nursing assessment completed on client. TC to Jan Pridgen, paralegal for client. She states that she rec'd a TC from Dr. Bridger's office stating he could not authorize CNAs in the client's home. Ms. Pridgen states she will contact this RN after speaking with the client. She states she is tired of dealing with this every day and wants an agency to take over. This RN recommended that all CNAs in the home be employees of this agency. She agreed because of the legal side of it."[519]
July 5, 2002: Bridger: Faxed records to Dr. Christy Jones.[520]
July 8, 2002: Bridger: Seems to be doing well, Joint pain.[521]
July 29, 2002: Jones: Initial intake for Neuropsychological evaluation.[522]
August 13, 2002: Jones: Neuropsychological evaluation.[523]
August 15, 2002: Jones: Neuropsychological evaluation.[524]
August 16 2002: (Note below Jan Pridgen's phone #): Pt. unable to hold urine is there anything they can do/take[525]
August 17, 2002: Urinary Frequency. "Is present with his son and his personal nurse."[526]
August 20, 2002: Mynatt: Frequency, urgency, urge leakage.[527]

September 4, 2002: Jones: Neuropsychological evaluation follow-up.[528]

September 7-9, 2002: New Hanover Regional Medical Center: Admitted for upper respiratory infection and complications at his laryngeal stoma site. Bradycardic with heart rate as low as 40bpm. Transient AV block. Blood pressure poorly controlled.[529]

September 10, 2002: Bridger: Bleeding from his tracheostomy. Mobitz type II heart Block. "At this time he is clinically stable, feeling good, and ready for discharge. He has around-the-clock home care at home."[530]

[September 26, 2002: New Will Signed. Not in the medical record]

September 30, 2002: Bridger: Cough, cold and bronchitis. "He is doing better today. Still coughing up yellow sputum. He seems to be much better."[531]

December 6, 2002: Almond: Stasis Edema, Possible Early CHF, Organic Brain Syndrome, Multiple medications.[532]

May 12, 2003: Moore: Difficulty voiding: "Pt. presents today accompanied by his caregiver... he communicates with me via his device, that he states that he is having no problem. He states he had a bowel movement before he made his urine and that changes his voiding pattern, and it did take a long time in the bathroom, at one point early in the morning today, but that he feels like he is emptying at about his baseline. The nurse however, gives a different history and states that he is current is awakening 4-5 X per night to urinate; and also that he is having to strain, he gets very red in the face when he is making urine. ... Physical exam is deferred today, as pt. is slightly agitated and only grudgingly even consents to the bladder scan. ... We will increase his Flomax to 0.4 mg p.o. b.i.d He is to remain on the Proscar. I asked his caregiver and other nurses who care for him, to monitor his blood pressure, use caution when he changes position and when he first awakens, as this could impact his blood pressure somewhat and to clear this medication with Dr. Bridger."[533]

June 2, 2003: Bridger: Peripheral edema.

June 8, 2003: Dafashy: Lower extremity edema.[534]

July 17, 2003: Bridger: "The pt is in today for an evaluation. He is just really kind of steadily going down hill. He is not sleeping well. He is weeping more and is complaining of some pain in his knee, The nevus appears to be much better. His BP looks like it is kind of low at this point. ... Probably not much we can do at this point and Dr. Smith really does not want much in the way of intervention. We will just see what we can do to keep him comfortable."[535]

July 31, 2003: Herring: Cough and congestion, poor family historian.[536]

August 2003: Hospitalization: Upper Respiratory infection, anemic, renal insufficiency.[537]

September 16, 2003: Bridger: Evaluation of S.O.B. and anemia. Seems to be improving.[538]

September 19, 2003: Bridger: "Pt is going through Dementia – all day spitting on Kleenex then rubbing his head – repeatedly. Start Aricept.[539]

October 31, 2003: Tinsley: Ruptured Appendix. Aricept helped agitation, underlying dementia not changed.[540]

November 11, 2003: Bridger: Pat – Re Dr. Smith/ Staying up all night – agitated/ confusion getting worse[541]

November 12, 2003: Bridger: Back to normal baseline. I&P

Congestive heart failure – stable.

Hypertension – continue Diovan/HCT 160/12.5.

Edema – use Lasix only as needed.

Reflux – continue Protonix.

Memory loss – continue Aricept 10mg per day.

Anxiety – continue Ativan 1mg once or twice a day as needed.

_____ - continue Proscar and Flomax and I will reassess him in 3 months. This appointment was greater than 25 minutes.[542]

November 18, 2003: Severe Anxiety. "Wakes up and starts to clap his hands for 20 in the middle of the evening & during the day requests to have pillows on top of his head."[543]

December 11, 2003: Bridger Yellow sputum from trach.[544]

February 6, 2004: Bridger: Insomnia, Agitated at night. Caregiver requests mood elevator.[545]

February 11, 2004: Bridger: Prescribes Lexapro antidepressant over the phone[546]

March 17, 2004: Bridger: Insomnia, pretty much stays in bed most all the time. They state he is given Ambien at 7 o'clock and another one at 12:30. He basically gets about an hour sleep from each one of them. He is up and awake pulling off his diaper, etc. He basically stays in bed all the time. I think his biggest problem is lack of activity. He just does not need this much sleep.

April 2, 2004: Bridger: "Excessive fatigue: Will cut Haldol back to 2.5mg qd and see how he does with this. I will see him back on an as needed basis. I've asked them to call before they bring him in to see if this isn't something we can handle over the phone before they make the effort to bring him into the office."[547]
April 23, 2004: Bridger: Insomnia.[548]
May 5, 2004: Bridger: Prescribes Aricept.[549]
February 22, 2005: Bridger: Dr. Bridger signs death certificate.[550]

Uncle Jimmy was diagnosed with Organic Brain Syndrome (OBS), about two months after he signed the suspicious will. If you look at some of the symptoms of OBS you will find among them, vertigo, memory loss, behavioral changes, and trouble performing daily activities.[551] These are all symptoms that Uncle Jimmy had long before his OBS diagnosis. Uncle Jimmy's brain disorder may have gone undiagnosed for over four years since his first diagnosed bout with vertigo. I believe he might have gotten a medical diagnosis sooner had his power of attorney not been so driven to show his competence. Some people seem to have the impression that Uncle Jimmy was an intellectual powerhouse in his later years, without mental decline or undue influence. His medical record paints a very different picture. While he was an intellectual powerhouse in his prime, he was not superhuman. In his old age, he was feeble... physically and mentally. Uncle Jimmy had good days, and bad days. Later in life, more bad than good.

Christy L. Jones Ph. D.

Dr. Christy Jones has a Ph.D. in neurosciences and neuroanatomy.[552] At the time of this deposition she was not licensed for clinical work.[553] She is, however, board certified in her field. Based on her deposition record I gather that she is quite proud of the work she has done in her field. When asked what kind of forensic work she has done she testified, "I've had several head injury cases for Home Depot. The one that settled about a year and two months ago was a twenty-million-dollar suit. A head injury case against a casino that was a five-million-dollar suit which settled just months before that. I've got another Home Depot case right now. A wheelbarrow wheel fell on a woman's head. There are other neurotoxicology cases. I had a [h]ead injury from, say, a car accident."[554]

198

When asked if any of the cases were tried in Wilmington she states, "No. These twenty-million-dollar cases – Wake County is the current Home Depot case. The large one, the twenty-million-dollar one, is the longest trial, civil trial, in the history of the Durham court system. That was in Durham, North Carolina. ... At least up to that time. I don't know if there's been one since. ... Actually, I won the case. They didn't get anything to speak of. They were suing for twenty million. I was on the defense side."[555]

I have the impression that Jones relishes the fact that her testimony can win a verdict. Jim Maxwell probably liked this comment that she volunteered because he would try to show a jury that Dr. Christy Jones was a hired gun, that is, hired to convince the jury that Uncle Jimmy was competent to write a will in 2002. I suspect Lonnie Williams worried about how arrogant Jones would sound to a Jury because at that point he interrupted Jim Maxwell's examination of Jones and said to Maxwell, "Does that make you feel better?"[556]

Jim Maxwell tried to get the deposition back on track and started "Well, I'd like to know, yeah. It would have been –"[557]

Interrupting, Dr. Jones continued on about her neuropsychological achievements in the legal system "I represented Home Depot and Grisham. ... Door falling on a child. ... I believe there was five hundred thousand that came either from Grisham or Home Depot, is what I was told later. And I think it was part of the damages. ... But Grisham settled out of court, against my recommendation."[558] It seems to me that Jones was so confident in her ability to control the outcome of a court case that she feels is appropriate to make recommendations about whether someone should settle or not rather than limit herself to offering a neuropsychological analysis.

Jim Maxwell got the deposition back on track with "Well, let's talk a little bit about Dr. Smith..."[559] Jones testified that her office was contacted to handle Uncle Jimmy's case. When asked how her office was contacted in Uncle Jimmy's case she testified, "Well, I am never personally contacted. My office manager is, and that would have been Maria Molina. And she would write on a sheet the referral source, as stated in my report, was an attorney. But the referral also came from the doctor's office. ... So it was a combination of Dr. Smith wanted an evaluation, then it was a doctor's office and an attorney. So it was some combination."[560] It's interesting to me that Jones' records show that her office was contacted by a lawyer, but she testifies differently. Given the fact that Dr. Jones was not directly contacted, I suspect that Maria Molina's notes are more accurate than Dr. Jones' testimony that Uncle Jimmy wanted the evaluation.

Later in her deposition Jones testified that she discussed with Uncle Jimmy, as she does with all her patients, his understanding of finances and that is how she learned that he wants to change his will.[561] Though she testified that Uncle Jimmy requested the competency evaluation, and she learned about the desire to change his will in a meeting with Uncle Jimmy himself, her neuropsychological report states, "There are issues regarding Dr. Smith's will and changes that he would like to make that prompted his attorney to request a competency evaluation."[562]

Jones testified that she got some of Uncle Jimmy's background information from Pat Jenkins because it was much quicker than getting it from Uncle Jimmy himself, due to the voice box he used to speak.[563] She testified that someone can have dementia and still be able to make decisions for themselves.[564] Jones testified that she asked Uncle Jimmy to count backwards from 100 by sevens and he made mistakes on two out of seven attempts.[565] She also said that he was oriented to year, but not month and day.[566] The "serial sevens" and the time orientation tests he scored imperfectly on are two of the tests he passed on the mini mental exam with Dr. Bridger. She testified that Uncle Jimmy was "very obviously oriented to person and place" but there was no test that asked him if he could name his nieces and nephews.[567] She testified that Uncle Jimmy told her that he wanted to disinherit his family and give money to his caregivers. She testified that she didn't remember him telling her he wanted to leave anything to the church in his will.[568]

She testified that she assessed that before Uncle Jimmy died his intelligence fell in the superior range. She admitted that she did not base that assessment on any testing done prior to hers, but that she assumed that he was very intelligent because he was a dentist and she "also knew that he accrued millions of dollars worth of income. And most people who can accrue that kind of wealth are fairly bright."[569] When asked why she assessed him as such even though her tests showed that he was in the 9th percentile for full scale IQ she said, "I gave the Raven's to get a better idea of IQ. The WAIS gave me some subtests that I wanted in terms of comprehension, for example. It's a good subtest to have when you are measuring capacity. Research has shown, research from the mid-nineties, that it's a good subtest for predicting capacity. And he scored at the 50[570] percentile for that."[570] I'll summarize this in my own layman's terms: Because Uncle Jimmy, as tested, showed a full scale IQ in the bottom 10 per cent of his age group, and scored average on another IQ test Dr. Christy L. Jones, Ph.D. assessed his intelligence as superior.

She testified that she made accommodations for him on tests to account for "his mobility and limitations with his hands, arthritis, as well as ability to talk." and that percentile scores he was given were for his age group, not the general population.[571] She also testified that she was not actually in the room with Uncle Jimmy while he was being tested.[572] How did she assess the effect that his physical limitations had on the testing if she wasn't in the room? I wonder if any of the other 90+ year-olds who have been issued these tests, to whom he is being compared, had mobility limitations or arthritis.

Jones testified that she assessed Uncle Jimmy's ability to handle his own finances.[573] She assessed that Uncle Jimmy "still had a concept of money that was reasonable."[574] She discussed his cash, stocks and his land with Uncle Jimmy. When asked if Uncle Jimmy knew what his assets were worth she stated, "I just remember that they were supposedly worth more than the check he'd written. ... What he said he wrote in jest, the two-million-dollar check that I mentioned in my report."[575] She did mention the check in her report, but her report didn't say that the check was written in jest in that report. The report said, "According to Dr. Smith, he reportedly gave a check for a large sum of money to a nurse for 'saving his life.' He was referring to the fact that he felt the nurse was keeping a family member from putting him in a nursing home."[576] There is no mention in the report that the check was a joke. In fact, Dr. Christy L. Jones used the fact that his assets exceeded the amount of the check he wrote as evidence that he understood his assets.[577] Why would a check written in jest be evidence that he understood the value of his estate? If it was just a joke, Uncle Jimmy could write a 2-billion-dollar check, and that wouldn't be an indication of competence or incompetence. There is no record that Dr. Jones spoke to Uncle Jimmy between the time that this report was transcribed and the date of his death. At what point did Christy Jones hear that the check was a joke? Who told her?

My research leaves me with the impression that these two professionals in healthcare might not be perfectly open and honest in their testimony. You would hope that these two would keep Uncle Jimmy's health a priority and put their personal feelings aside. You would hope that they wouldn't choose a side, but would let their science speak for itself. Unfortunately, the evidence is mixed as to whether they did or not. When asked about a report Dr. Charles Herring made in Uncle Jimmy's medical record that Uncle Jimmy was a "poor family historian" Dr. Dewey Bridger states, "I think it's probably – if you knew Dr. Herring, Dr. Herring seems to be a very impatient individual, and I'm sure he did not take the time to listen to what Dr. Smith had to say with his laryngectomy. I'm convinced that's what it was because Dr. Herring is a very dynamic individual and he – he doesn't have a lot of patience with things like that."[578] Rather than recognize that another doctor might have seen something that he missed, Bridger attempts to discredit his peer's analysis. Christy Jones sat with the propounder's law team after she took the stand, and stayed there (giving advice and handing notes to Lonnie Williams, according to one juror) while the family's expert witness testified.[579] Does that sound like an impartial witness or a hired gun?

I think that Dr. Dewey Bridger and Dr. Christy Jones trusted Uncle Jimmy's caregivers and the Pridgen law firm. Bridger must have trusted the caregivers enough to make prescriptions over the phone based on their input.[580] About her analysis of Uncle Jimmy's financial competency, Jones states, "He had an attorney who was – I have in his chart – managing his finances to write his checks."[581] If she based his financial competency partly on the fact that he needed a lawyer making financial decisions for him, she must have assumed that the lawyer was trustworthy. If the Pridgens and/or Pat Jenkins told these two doctors that Uncle Jimmy's family was out to get his money I think they would have believed them. If these two healthy, intelligent, well educated professionals could be led by the Pridgens and the caregivers, imagine how easily a ninety-plus-year-old man in declining health might be led by them.

27. The Guerette Investigations

Jim Maxwell was pouring full steam into preparation for trial. Maxwell needed witnesses who were disinterested in the outcome of the case who could offer information contrary to the propounders' more reliable witnesses. He hired Guerette Investigations to interview potential witnesses that could help the family's case. Guerette's team interviewed the following individuals:

Joan Teer (Friend of Uncle Jimmy's who tried to visit regularly)
Theresa Hondros (caretaker who worked for Uncle Jimmy)
Shirley Lovitt (Theresa Hondros' sister who has worked with Pat Jenkins)
Beverly Boykin (caretaker who worked for Uncle Jimmy
Clyde Gentry (Gardening buddy of Uncle Jimmy's)
Todd Allen Mozingo (ex-husband of Theresa Mozingo, daughter of Pat Jenkins)

Joan Teer

Joan Teer was a friend of Uncle Jimmy's. In Joan Teer's interview with Guerette's investigation team she said she felt caregivers made it difficult for her to visit Uncle Jimmy. The caregivers she remembered specifically were Pat Jenkins and Carol Tucker. Teer recalls common excuses that were given to her by these women were that her friend was sleeping, tired or just didn't want any visitors. Mrs. Teer also remembered a black caregiver whose name she could not recall. She said the black caregiver was extremely friendly and always let her visit Uncle Jimmy.

Mrs. Teer recalled some events about the caregivers that she found odd. She recalled a time when Uncle Jimmy was unresponsive and in poor health near death. At that time, she remembered the caregivers laughing and joking about "play money." She didn't think that the caregivers were doing this to entertain Uncle Jimmy because he was so unresponsive at the time.

Teer also recalled that Pat Jenkins and Otto Pridgen's wife Jan were talking to each other during Uncle Jimmy's funeral service. Guerette's investigation reports that the two "were yapping with each other literally during the entire service."

Teer also became fed up with the caregivers not allowing her to have private conversations with Uncle Jimmy. She asked Uncle Jimmy's sister-in-law about it and found out that the caregivers were not letting her visit at all.

Teer also told the investigative team that she knew many of the lawyers involved. She knew the family's lawyer, Jim Maxwell. She also knows of Otto Pridgen and Lonnie Williams. The report suggests that Teer has a low opinion of Pridgen and states that she was "very shocked that Lonnie Williams has taken this case and is representing someone like Otto Pridgen."[582]

Theresa Hondros

When Guerette's investigator explained his investigation into Pat Jenkins taking advantage of Dr. Smith's funds, Theresa Hondros said, "Pat, yeah, I can see Pat doing that." According to the report "Pat also has a mental problem and the company she used to work for, Herring and Associates could provide some information about Pat as well." [This makes me wonder... If this is true, why did Herring and Associates keep inserting Pat into people's homes? Remember, Herring and Associates is the company that wrote the letter to my cousin Jim telling him to pay a finder's fee of $2700.00 to mend the "rift"]?

The investigator reports that the first night that Hondros worked for Uncle Jimmy "Pat was packing up valuable silverware and other very valuable items to be put in bank trusts and vaults. She had all of the silverware laid out on a table and was polishing it and getting ready to be packed up. She said the expensive jewelry had already been packed up in vaults." Per the report, Pat was "crazy about men, money and jewelry. She had a way about her that she could get another man to give her anything or do anything for her. She also remembered Pat received extra bonuses from JHS [Uncle Jimmy] and other clients that they never gave her [Hondros] or other caregivers." The report states that Pat "always managed to work for elderly men or women where there was a lot of money or jewelry involved."[583]

Hondros' testimony fit in precisely with the family's perception of the situation. The Guerette investigator felt that she would make a good witness.

Shirley Lovitt

The Guerette investigator received a phone call from Carl Hondros shortly after interviewing his wife, Theresa Hondros. Mr. Hondros informed the investigator about his sister-in-law, Shirley Lovitt, who had also worked with Pat Jenkins. According to the investigator's report Lovitt gave a very similar narrative about how, in that previous employment, "Pat took full charge of the household and tried to run everything."[584]

Beverly Boykin

According to the report Beverly Boykin felt like the will was "a set-up on Pat Jenkins and the Pridgen's behalf." Before the investigator mentioned Carol Tucker's name, Boykin stated "I bet that old lady with the white car was left some money too wasn't she?" She also asked, "They only left money for the white caregivers, none of the black caregivers got any money, did they?" The investigator confirmed her suspicions.

Of course, I can't read Beverly Boykin's mind, but it is interesting to me that she said, "*They* only left money…" Uncle Jimmy was the only one man, so who are "*They*" that she believed wrote the will?

Boykin referred to Otto and Jan Pridgen as the "Overseers." Boykin asked the investigator if the Pridgen's received anything in the will, and again the investigator confirmed it. According to the report Boykin noted that Pat was very "in tune with all of the business going on with JHS [Uncle Jimmy] and the Pridgens." The report states that Pat and Carol would tell her "to be on her best behavior and not to be on the telephone when Otto or Janice came around because they were the bosses; they were in charge of the household." Note that Boykin was not told that Uncle Jimmy was in charge of the household.[585]

Clyde Gentry

According to the Guerette report, Clyde Gentry would visit Uncle Jimmy often and "would just have friendly talk." Gentry recalled that after one of his visits Jan Pridgen called him and wanted to know what he and Uncle Jimmy were talking about. Gentry reportedly told Jan Pridgen that it was none of her business. Gentry's visits became less frequent after that incident with Jan Pridgen because, according to the report, "he did not want to get mixed up in whatever problems were going on at his home."[586]

Todd Allen Mozingo

Todd Mozingo was a police officer in Charlotte, NC and was married to Pat Jenkins daughter during the period of time that she was driving to Wilmington to see Uncle Jimmy to "do his nails."

When Guerette's investigator first initiated his conversation with Todd Mozingo he was not allowed inside Mozingo's apartment. The investigator stood outside the apartment and attempted to explain the current situation with Uncle Jimmy's case. Before the investigator even mentioned his former wife, Pat's daughter Theresa, Todd Mozingo said, "Buddy, we've been divorced for a long time and I haven't had any contact with her." The investigators report states that Todd appeared to be "nervous and very jumpy" and asked the investigator if he knew he was a Charlotte Police Officer. The investigator thought this appeared to be an attempt to discourage the investigation. The investigator offered to tell Todd as many details about the case as he could to calm him. Eventually Todd started "spilling" his information to the investigator.

Todd Mozingo met Theresa in September of 2001 and married her 3 months later. They were married for 10 months.

The report states that the last time Todd spoke to Pat Jenkins was in October of 2002, when she called him "to cuss him out for divorcing Theresa. She was blaming him for upsetting Theresa and causing the divorce. He stated that she (Pat) is in fact Bi-Polar and does have medication she takes for the condition." The report states that Todd Mozingo claims to have never had any direct problems with Pat Jenkins other than the one time she called him after the divorce and that Pat "is not the type of person you can reason with or talk sense to. She has no sense of what reality is."

According to the report Todd feels his marriage to Theresa was a big mistake. Todd called Theresa "smoking hot" but stated that Theresa kept him in the dark about a lot of things. The report stated that Todd didn't even know that Theresa was taking anti-depressants until after they were married and that Todd "knew something wasn't right with Theresa and Pat, but he did not know for sure what was going on." Todd claims that before his marriage to Theresa he had an impeccable reputation at the police department. According to the report, during the divorce, she tried to go after Todd's retirement fund and "tried to get criminal charges and a restraining order against him."

Todd received a call from a private investigator while he was married to Theresa. That investigator asked how he was able to afford the home and Lexus SUV he had purchased. According to the Guerette investigation Todd told that investigator that he was not able to afford it all and had to sell the Lexus SUV after only a few months and later had to sell the home as well. According to the Guerette report, Todd claims to have had no knowledge of any money that Uncle Jimmy gave Theresa.

At the end of the investigator's report it states that Todd "hopes both Theresa and Pat rot in hell. If they were to walk out in front of a bus and get killed, he wouldn't care."[587]

28. The Trial

The mediation was wasted. The investigation was complete. First Baptist Church refused a final offer for settlement from the family. The family's final offer was to drop the caveat, if the church would allow them to buy the Farm from the church for one dollar, and if the propounders would pay the caveators' legal costs and fees out of the estate.[588] At that point there was nothing stopping the trial from going forward. Maxwell sent one last e-mail to the family reminding members that to have the mental capacity to make a will "one has to be a bit more competent than a 'cauliflower'."[589] Knowing what they were up against, the family braced themselves for the trial.

Civil Session of the Superior Court
Of New Hanover County, Wilmington, North Carolina
Before the Honorable John E. Nobles, Jr., Judge Presiding,
and a Jury

The trial started on April 12, 2006, Judge John E. Nobles, presiding. In the courtroom, on the left side, there were four lawyers from two legal teams. Lonnie Williams brought Charles Meier. Bob Hunter brought a surprise. Hunter brought Lisa Johnson-Tonkins, a female attorney who appeared to be African American. She had not been seen or heard from by Billy or Jim Maxwell before the depositions. The family wondered if the Church's lawyer, Bob Hunter, knew that this case reeked with racism and would try to wash the church's hands of some of this stink by putting a face in front of the Jury that wasn't as pale as the rest of the law teams.

With the propounders law teams sat the Baptist preachers, Otto Pridgen, his wife and legal secretary, the three caregivers, and on some days, a man in a wheelchair, Roy Piner. Family members believed Mr. Piner was wheeled in as a stage prop as an attempt to convince the jury that a greedy family was trying to take money away from a handicapped man.

Behind the propounders a group of about a dozen onlookers, presumably from the church congregation. Most of them were elderly, well dressed, and probably retired from employment. Occasionally, you could find another man sitting on the left side with the propounders who didn't seem to fit in with the rest of the crowd. The misfit was younger than the church congregants he sat with and was wearing a knit shirt instead of the button-down style most of the propounder's supporters wore. He sat with a pencil and notepad in hand. He was Ken Little, a journalist with the Wilmington Star News, and his articles on this trial would land on the front page of the paper.

On the right side was Billy Smith sitting beside Jim Maxwell and his legal secretary, Lori Rosemond. The three of them might have looked extraordinarily lonely, had there not been a larger than life man sitting behind them. One day, Jim and Billy introduced themselves to the man who said that he was Otto Pridgen's neighbor, and he was coming to the courtroom to watch Otto "go down." I think the only time during the trial that I remember seeing my dad smile and laugh was when he told me the story about that stranger sitting behind him in the courtroom. With all that was being said by the Pridgens, the caregivers, and the leadership of First Baptist Church, it comforted my dad to have someone in the room who was close enough to the propounders to know what they are made of and showing support.

I didn't get to see much of the trial personally, so my first exposure to it was through newspaper articles and e-mails from my family. When I finally got the transcripts of the trial I was disappointed to read what the jury got to hear, or more precisely, what they didn't get to hear. As you read, put yourself in the shoes of a juror, who doesn't know anyone involved, and is hearing it all for the first time.

Jim Maxwell led the examination of each witness, then the propounders would take turns in cross examination.

Testimony of
Dr. Frank R. Reynolds and Edward A. Rusher, Jr.

Rusher and Reynolds' testimony in court was much like their depositions. Their testimony was damaging to the family's case, but they were witnesses to the will, and Jim Maxwell had to get through their testimony. They played cards with Uncle Jimmy, and they testified that he was skillful, and showed no signs of impairment. They called the care he received "excellent." Reynolds didn't believe Uncle Jimmy was influenced by anyone.[590]

Under Maxwell's examination they testified that the caregivers were a constant presence around Uncle Jimmy. They also testified that they were not aware that Uncle Jimmy made withdrawals of approximately $700,000 ($9,000 per day) in the four months between the time that his wife and son died.[591]

Testimony of
Robert A. O'Quinn

I wanted the jury to get a clear picture of how O'Quinn assessed (or perhaps failed to accurately assess) Uncle Jimmy's mental health. Based on his deposition, it seems O'Quinn assessed a man who wanted to give a large gift to his "burger flipping" nieces as competent to manage his estate. I wanted the jury to see that Uncle Jimmy knew his nieces well before his mind started to decay, and knew that they are smart and well educated, despite the limited resources available to them during their childhood. I wanted the jury to hear that the mind of the man who celebrated the better part of a century of Thanksgiving, Christmas, and other holidays with his nieces and nephews had decayed so badly that he couldn't remember his niece Ebie, his nephew Fred's name, or that his nephew Jack Shelhart had died, but his grand-nephew Jack was alive. I wanted them to hear that O'Quinn reacted with "horror at the fact that a third party would be calling me and telling me what to put in somebody's will."[592] These issues were not made explicit to the jury.

Maxwell asked O'Quinn if he knew of any attorneys who made $20,000.00 per month serving as a power of attorney to which O'Quinn stated "...no."[593] O'Quinn told the jury that Otto Pridgen told him during a "chance meeting" on a sidewalk that Uncle Jimmy wanted to rewrite his will and noted where he would leave some assets, recalling "not to his kinfolk."[594]

O'Quinn's "certain amount of horror" stated in his deposition was softly quantified as "slightly horrified" in his court testimony.[595] He testified that Otto Pridgen dictated the contents of the will to him over the phone.[596] He testified that he did not know at the time of the drafting of the will or at the time of the trial whether Lisa and Erin were nieces or grand-nieces.[597] He testified about the three children of Uncle Jimmy's brother he wanted to leave gifts to. The unknown names forced him to leave blank spaces behind his outline labels "A, B, C".[598] He also testified that the "faithful employees" phrase came from Otto Pridgen.[599] He testified that he heard Otto Pridgen telling him that Mrs. Pridgen would receive 10% of the residuary of the estate he thought it an "inordinate event" but he did not discuss this with Otto at the time.[600] He testified that he didn't know the exact rule but if the will was executed as Otto was dictating it then Otto would receive approximately 5% of the estate as the executor of the will.[601] He testified that his recollection was that Pat Jenkins was with Uncle Jimmy the day he went to ask him personally about the contents of the will and Otto Pridgen came into the house while he was there.[602] He testified that he couldn't recall why there were two blank lines in his notes under Linda Shelhart's name.[603]

O'Quinn testified that he did not know if two of the blood relatives mentioned in the will, Billy Smith and Jack Smith, were two of the three nephews his notes ordered a provision for in the will.[604] To me the familial inconsistencies leap off the page, but to a juror who doesn't know my family any better than the Reverends, the Pridgens and O'Quinn I'm not sure how relevant they would seem.

He testified that on the day he dropped off a copy of the will at Otto Pridgen's office he never even walked into the office. His paralegal just walked across the street from O'Quinn's car and handed it to Jan Pridgen on the sidewalk outside their office. He was surprised to hear that Otto Pridgen billed Uncle Jimmy for a 30-minute conference with O'Quinn that day.[605]

He testified that as he reviewed the draft will with Uncle Jimmy he didn't question Jack Shelhart's missing name (or any other oddly absent family members).[606] He testified that he did discuss a change for Jack's sisters, Lisa and Erin. He testified that when he asked Uncle Jimmy if he wanted to give them each $5,000.00 Uncle Jimmy changed the gift to an immediate $100,000.00 instead of $5,000.00 after his death.[607] Based on his testimony I don't believe O'Quinn knew the family well enough to ask Uncle Jimmy why he wanted to include some nieces, nephews and cousins but exclude others during that interview. It's clear to me that Uncle Jimmy didn't have the mental capacity to recall these people he had spent so much of his life with… certainly not while under the influence of people who had 24/7 access to him. The question is: would the jury get it?

O'Quinn testified that while he was assisting the management of his son's estate Uncle Jimmy fired him and rehired him about 10 minutes later.[608] Does this indicate a man who has his life together, or a confused man?

He also testified that he billed Uncle Jimmy for the preparation of his horrifying will.[609] I'm slightly horrified that Robert O'Quinn, a member of the North Carolina Bar association, would draft a slightly horrifying will, then bill an elderly, confused man for it instead of reporting Otto Pridgen to the North Carolina Bar Association. I'm slightly horrified that Robert A. O'Quinn would accept a check for $1214.50 to draft this slightly horrifying will.[610] Guess who the chairman of the grievance committee for New Hanover and Pender counties was at the time of the trial... Robert O'Quinn. Guess who was also a member of the board of directors for the New Hanover County Bar... Robert O'Quinn.[611] Guess who never got disbarred for misconduct... Otto Pridgen. Is there some connection between these two guys that never made it to the surface during this trial? Was it just a "chance meeting" on a sidewalk that brought O'Quinn into this drama?

After Maxwell was done with his examination the two teams of caveators would have their chance to cross examine. They highlighted, through O'Quinn's testimony, that there were two witnesses to the signing of the will. The witnesses were upstanding members of the community. This was, perhaps, the most damaging information to the family's case, and very simple for the jury to see.

The Church's attorney, Robert Hunter didn't stop there, however. He repetitively called the will a "solemn document" during the trial.[612] Perhaps this was a subliminal message to the jury that those honorable members of the North Carolina Bar Association were doing their noble duty to perform the selfless task of producing this will for Uncle Jimmy's signature. Hunter also asked O'Quinn if any member of the church instructed him on how to distribute the assets to which he answered, "No, sir."[613] This testimony from a reputable lawyer makes me want to scream. O'QUINN GOT THE FIRST DICTATION OF THE CONTENTS OF THE WILL FROM A MEMBER OF THE CHURCH.[614] ONE THIRD OF THE THREE LEGGED STOOL!!! ANOTHER LEG OF THE STOOL, JACK RICHARDSON, WENT TO REVEREND EVERETTE FOR INFORMATION ABOUT THE WILL.[615] TWO OUT OF THREE MEMBERS OF THE THREE LEGGED STOOL WERE FROM THE CHURCH AND DIRECTLY INVOLVED WITH CONVERSATIONS ABOUT DRAFTING THE WILL!!! Under cross examination by Maxwell, O'Quinn would admit that he knew that Otto was a member of the church.[616] Nevertheless, this, "No, sir"[617] testimony delivered, by this legal professional to the jury, would help wash the stink off the hands of the church.

Testimony of
Otto K. Pridgen

In the midst of Otto Pridgen's testimony, while the jury was out for lunch, lawyers debated the relevance of some of his testimony. Judge Nobles said, "I think Mr. Maxwell absolutely has a right to call Mr. Pridgen an adverse witness. He is going off on tangents and I'm not sure if Mr. Maxwell is in control of that and it is an unusual situation."[618] At times Nobles had to direct Otto Pridgen to answer Maxwell's questions directly.[619] This is how that session began:

Maxwell asked Otto Pridgen if he had ever handled real estate matters in his professional work Otto Pridgen gave a long answer including "... in those days... Banks did not lend money for homes." Concluding with "... a young fellow, like myself, I got none of that practice."[620]

Maxwell followed up, "Okay. So you've never really practiced real estate law?

To which Otto answered, "Well in the past 10 or 15 years, I've – my wife is a crackerjack at handling that sort of thing, and she has a computer, and for the past 15 or 20 years, we've done quite a bit of that."

"But your wife is not an attorney, is she, Mr. Pridgen?" Maxwell continued.

"Well, I don't know." Otto answered, "You'll have to ask her that question."[621]

Otto painted a similar picture of himself for the jury that he did during the deposition. The jury would hear that he couldn't afford the same social clubs that Uncle Jimmy was a member in.[622] He said he did not know the Smiths beyond Uncle Jimmy, his brother Jack, and Jack's son, Billy, and daughter-in-law, Jodie.[623] He testified that Uncle Jimmy called him on his unlisted number (he was never asked if his number was listed).[624] He testified that he was beginning retirement planning but decided to take on Uncle Jimmy's case anyway.[625]

I think that what Maxwell was aiming for in his initial line of questioning is this: Why would Uncle Jimmy hire Otto Pridgen after a long successful life, in which he had never called on him professionally or socially, outside of church. Why would Uncle Jimmy, in his right mind, hire a lawyer with little experience in estate law? Otto explained, "It's like going to your physician and, when they come, you don't – when the doctor sees you, he doesn't say, why are you coming to me? There's better doctors down the street."[626]

To the contrary, competent doctors do refer patients to other doctors for expert advice. I think a competent lawyer would also. I don't believe Uncle Jimmy ever called Otto. Otto testified that he spoke to Billy's Lawyer's associate before he was appointed power of attorney. He testified that she told him "Billy had learned that large sums of money were being withdrawn by Dr. Smith from the bank, and that nephew Billy was concerned about that and wanted to know where the money was going and what was going on, and he had employed private detectives."[627]

At one point, Otto Pridgen began describing his version of why Uncle Jimmy decided to change his mind about giving the farm to family members. The church's, lawyer objected to the testimony.[628] It's interesting how the two propounders, sitting side-by-side in the courtroom, did their own little battle against each other to present and/or deny information to the jury. The Pridgens and the caregivers seem to want the story to be that Uncle Jimmy was angry at Billy for asking him to fire his nurses, and so he decided to write family members out of the will. The problem the church might see about this is that Reverend Mike Queen was at that same meeting with Billy, so why, then, would Uncle Jimmy give the farm to the Church? It seems to me that the church wanted the party line to be that Uncle Jimmy's son died and he never had any intention of giving the farm to extended family members, so he left it to the church.

Otto testified, "The first thing we undertook to do [as power of attorney], of course, was to start making an inventory of Dr. Smith's assets, of one kind or another, and we went to the bank. We interviewed Jack Richardson."[629] Would the jury wonder why that was the first thing he did for a man said to be competent, and aware of his assets?

Maxwell asked Otto "…do you know Dr. Dewey Bridger?"

"Not very well, I know him, yes." Otto answered.

"You knew that he was Dr. Smith's physician?" Maxwell asked.

"Yes."

"All right." Maxwell continued "In his office notes, which are exhibit 408 in this particular matter, on May 1, 2002, the day after you were appointed as his power of attorney, Dr. Bridger has in his notes, 'Patient comes in today for evaluation.' That would be Dr. Smith. "He's doing well. His lawyer sent him to make sure he's doing okay."

"Yeah."[630] With the point subtly made that the lawyer made the medical referral, Maxwell moved on.

Otto testified that He didn't know any of the caregivers prior to working for Uncle Jimmy.[631] He had heard that a private investigator had discovered Uncle Jimmy was being taken advantage of by those caregivers.[632] When Maxwell asked him "... what did you do to investigate the credentials, the background, the experience of these women who were going to be in charge, 24 hours a day, seven days a week..."

Otto replied, "... I did not see any reason, whatsoever, to do a criminal check or background check..."[633]

When asked about $9,000.00 per day leaving Uncle Jimmy's bank account Pridgen testified that he conducted his own investigation and discovered that the money was largely taken by Uncle Jimmy's son. When asked how he did the investigation he said he examined Uncle Jimmy's son's house.[634] When asked who gave him permission to enter the house he said, "I think I got it from Mr. O'Quinn's office..."[635] When asked if he had the permission of the owners of the house to enter (which at that time were 14 of young Jim's cousins) he said, "No, I had not, but I had received a call from Billy's son, Dr. Billy Smith. Dr. Smith ... called and asked me, he said, please investigate the death of my cousin."[636]

Why would Dr. Bill Smith call a lawyer to conduct this investigation? I called my brother, Dr. Bill Smith, and asked him if he ever asked Otto Pridgen to investigate Little Jimmy's death or anything else like that. He said, "No."[637]

When asked about the withdrawals that continued after Uncle Jimmy's death Otto stated, "I have no explanation for that Mr. Maxwell."[638] I think the jury would see through him, but their opinion of him would be formed in one impersonal day, not years of frustrating interactions with dire consequences for a family member.

Maxwell asked Otto if he terminated Linda Phillips employment after the $2 million-dollar check was written to her. He said, "No, I did not."[639]

Later Maxwell asked about a letter he received from Dr. Bill Smith stating "I am pleased to no end that you and your wife have begun to replace the current sitters with professionals from an agency... Given the behavior that you reported to me which led to the termination of Linda, I also feel that there is an obligation to report this to the appropriate authorities so that future patients are not similarly exploited."[640] Otto testified that he did not remember any such conversation with Dr. Bill Smith. Otto maintained that Linda left voluntarily.[641]

Later in the trial Maxwell asked Otto about some letters written within his legal and housekeeping staff. One was from Pat Jenkins addressed to Carol Tucker:

> "Carol, there is to be no discussion what-so-ever c [sic] Dr. Smith concerning schedule changes, salaries, a will, or any monies of any kind. When Dr. Smith brings up money subjects, please carry on another conversation concerning his health or activities for the day. We will not accept any phone calls coming into this home from Linda or Betty or visitations from either one. Further action will be taken where rules are not kept. Dr. Smith is to have no discussion c [sic] you concerning this letter.
> Thanks, [Signed Pat Jenkins, cc: O.K. Pridgen, II]"[642]

Maxwell asked Pridgen, "Now, who is in charge of the rules about whether Dr. Smith can speak to two caregivers who have been with him for a year?"

"I am." Otto answered.

"Okay." Maxwell continued, "Were you prepared, and did you authorize Pat Jenkins, to say that these two women who had been with him for almost a year or more could no longer even talk to him or come visit him?

"I did, and I'd like to explain my answer."

"Please do." Maxwell said.

Otto testified, "Dr. Smith, I'm sure had grieved a great deal after his son's passing and his wife, in December of 2001, but he pulled out of that; and after I started working for him, he was not grieving. He was very satisfied with his home and the people that were in his home. However, I knew, or simply thought, that if either Linda or Betty Parker came back, that it was going to turn into a crying party; that they would naturally express their sorrow over his losses, and I did not want him

216

to have to go through all of that. And, with that precaution in mind, I did not think they should come back and bring up that subject."[643] Would the jury see this as alienation of affection?

Having these matters laid out before the jury Maxwell started a metaphorical drum roll leading up to the climax of the examination of Otto K. Pridgen, attorney at law.

Jim Maxwell: Mr. Pridgen, over the course of the slightly over a year this lawsuit has been pending, there has been a lot of discovery, has there not?

Otto Pridgen: Yes, there has.

Maxwell: And the jury may not understand. Why don't you help them understand what discovery is?

OK Pridgen: You can do it better than I can.

Maxwell: All right. Well, let's do it with question and answer. Can discovery involve things such as one party submitting interrogatories, questions, to another party to be answered?

OK Pridgen: That's part of it, I guess.

Maxwell: Okay. And typically those are required to be verified as being truthful answers by the individual that answers the interrogatories, are they not?

OK Pridgen: Yes.

Maxwell: And some of those were submitted to you in this case, were they not.

OK Pridgen: I think so.

Maxwell: Okay. There is another document that's often used in discovery, which is called a request for admission, is there not?

OK Pridgen: Yes.

Maxwell: And, generally, there you – are required or requested to either admit or deny a statement that is made.

OK Pridgen: Yes.

Maxwell: Okay. And it is anticipated that, to the best of your knowledge, you will answer truthfully.

OK Pridgen: I did.

Maxwell: Okay. And another form of discovery that can sometimes be used are taking someone's deposition, where you actually ask them questions orally, the answers are taken down by a court recorder, much as we are doing today.

O Pridgen: Sure, sure, sure.

Maxwell: There were 14 of those done in this matter, including your deposition, which was done over two days. Is that correct?

O Pridgen: Yes, sir.

Maxwell: All right. And in a deposition, like here, you were sworn before you began the process of answering questions; is that not correct?

O Pridgen: Yes.

Maxwell: All right. Let me show you what has been previously marked as Caveators' Exhibit 448-G. I ask you to identify that.

O Pridgen: Okay.

Maxwell: Okay. What does it appear to be to you?

O Pridgen: It looks like a thick – these are photocopies of the response to the caveators' first set of interrogatories.

Maxwell: By whom?

218

O Pridgen: By me.

Maxwell: Okay. And that's a series of questions, several pages of questions, that were submitted to you, and you answered them. Okay. And if you would turn, please, to the very last page of that.

O Pridgen: That's where I signed.

Maxwell: It's more than just signed, is it not? Isn't it sworn before a notary to be truthful?

O Pridgen: Uh-huh.

Maxwell: Let me show you what has been marked previously as Caveators' Exhibit 448-B, and ask you if you can identify that.

O Pridgen: My responses to the Baptist church's second request.

Maxwell: That's the request for admissions that we talked about moments ago.

O Pridgen: Yeah, Uh-huh.

Maxwell: And those you're not required to sign. Those are signed on your behalf by your attorney, are they not?

O Pridgen: Yeah, Uh-huh.

Maxwell: All right. And now let me show you what has been marked previously as Caveators' Exhibit 448-K, and ask if you can identify that.

O Pridgen: This is my response to their first set of interrogatories, the Baptist Church's interrogatories.

Maxwell: To you?

O Pridgen: To me.

Maxwell: Okay. And on the last page, tell us what that is.

O Pridgen: Must be my signature – no, this is Lonnie, Lonnie Williams.

Maxwell: Look at the page before that, then. I'm looking to see if that's not verified.

O Pridgen: Lonnie Williams signed it.

Maxwell: Okay. Was your signature notarized there?

O Pridgen: I think Lonnie signed this, apparently, didn't he?

Lonnie Williams: I'll stipulate it was verified.

Maxwell: (To the court) It was verified. (To the witness) Mr. Williams has stipulated that it's an interrogatory, and they have to be verified by you, do they not Mr. Pridgen? You know, in the practice of law, interrogatories need to be verified by the person signing them.

O Pridgen: Well, these weren't signed by me.

Williams: If that's not in there, it was left out.

Maxwell: Thank you Mr. Williams. (To the witness) You heard Mr. O'Quinn's testimony that, on or about September 23rd, somewhere in that time frame, he's not sure, and after you had seen him on the street and asked if he could help draw a new will for Dr. Smith, that you called him and, over the phone, gave him a fairly detailed information about what was to be in Mister – Dr. Smith's Will.

O Pridgen: I heard him say that.

Maxwell: Okay. Let me direct your attention to the first document you have up there, which is the interrogatories from my client to you, and ask you to turn to Page 2. It's actually Page 7, I'm sorry. Look at Page 7. (To the court) I'm sorry I haven't introduced those. If it please the court, may I introduce Exhibits 448-G, K and B?

Judge Nobles: Yes, sir.

Maxwell: (To the court) I have copies of these for the – go ahead. I'm sorry.

Williams: May we approach?

Nobles: Yes, sir.

(AN OFF-THE-RECORD BENCH CONFERENCE WAS HELD)

Maxwell: I would tender those exhibits, and we have copies for the jury.

Nobles: That's allowed.

(A COPY OF THE ABOVE-REFERRED-TO EXHIBITS WAS GIVEN TO EACH JUROR.)

Maxwell: (To the witness) Let me ask you on the very first one, 448-G, if you would turn to what is the second page of what you now have before you, and what the jury has. Do you see that? And I direct your attention specifically to interrogatory number 9.

O Pridgen: Mm-Hmm.

Maxwell: And question C.

O Pridgen: Okay.

Maxwell: We asked you the question: "Did you provide any information to Mr. O'Quinn, either orally or in written form, prior to Dr. Smith signing the document on September 26th, 2002?"

O Pridgen: Mm-Hmm.

Maxwell: If you'll look down at the bottom of the page there you'll see 9-C where, under oath, you answered, "Yes". Is that correct?

O Pridgen: That's what it is.

Maxwell: All right. D, "If the answer to 9-C, immediately preceding, is "yes", please describe the information you provided to Mr. O'Quinn." And then please read what you swore under oath was the information you provided to him.

O Pridgen: "I told Mr. O'Quinn earlier that Dr. Smith wanted to make a will."

Maxwell: Now, as a practical matter and, in reality, before September 26th, you told Mr. O'Quinn a whole lot more than that Mister – Dr. Smith wanted to make a will, did you not?

O Pridgen: Is that a question?

Maxwell: I'm saying, is that true?

O Pridgen: I have no recollection of that.

Maxwell: Do you think Mr. O'Quinn is not telling the truth?

　　　Williams: Your Honor, I object to that.

　　　Nobles: Overruled.

Maxwell: You heard testimony, that he took notes from you as to what was to be in the will for Dr. Smith.

O Pridgen: I have no recollection of giving Bob [O'Quinn] the information he told me. I'm sorry, I just don't. I think that's what I said here, isn't it?

Maxwell: Well, what you said here is that, I told Mr. O'Quinn earlier that Dr. Smith wanted to make a will.

O Pridgen: That's right.

Maxwell: That would be the street conversation.

O Pridgen: I'm sure I told him, because I asked him if he would draw the will.

Maxwell: Okay. Well, let me change from what you gave as an answer under oath on the 29th day of July 2005, and ask you today, April 13th, 2006, did you provide the information to Bob O'Quinn that he sat up here and testified to?

O Pridgen: I have no recollection of this.

Maxwell: All right. Let's take the next question, and I'll come back to that. Let's drop down to F, 9-F on Page 2. "When did you first learn that you were to be named or had been named as executor of James Henry Smith's estate in the document signed on September 26, 2002?" If you'll look over at Page 3 and read for us what your answer is.

O Pridgen: Where are we now.

Maxwell: I'm sorry, it's 9-F, Page 3 of the document you have, top of the page, 9-F.

O Pridgen: 9-F?

Maxwell: Yes, sir, third page of what you have there in front of you.

O Pridgen: I've got it.

Maxwell: Do you see 9-F?

O Pridgen: Uh-Huh.

Maxwell: What's your answer?

O Pridgen: I have no recollection –

Maxwell: That's 9-E. I'm asking about 9-F. I don't mean to interrupt you. We'll try to move along. 9-F.

O Pridgen: "September 26th, after he executed the will."

Maxwell: Okay. If, in fact, you had the telephone conversation with Mr. O'Quinn that he has testified to at some length, that statement would not be correct, would it? You would have known when you called him that you were, in fact, being designated as the executor.

O Pridgen: I think my – I think my recollection is that, after he executed the will, at that point, I knew that he had designated me to be the executor.

Maxwell: But the question that was asked of you, Mr. Pridgen, was when did you first learn that you were to be named or had been named?

O Pridgen: I don't recall that.

Maxwell: So you're telling us, under oath, today that you did not know before a copy of the will was given to you on September 26th that you were going to be named the executor of James Henry Smith's will?

O Pridgen: I have no recollection of knowing that. When I saw the will, I saw that's what he had done.

Maxwell: You have no recollection that you ever had any discussion with Dr. Smith as to what was to be in his will, prior to September 26th, 2002?

O Pridgen: I did not – I did not discuss his will with him, before or after he drew the will.

Maxwell: Well, help us out Mr. Pridgen. As you sit there today, what do you think the purpose or basis for Bob O'Quinn's testimony was when he says that he talked to you and you gave him the terms of this will?

O Pridgen: I'm sure Bob's memory is a lot better than mine.

Maxwell: Okay. Let's move, if we can, to the next document in the pile, which is Page 5. These are the first pages of the second request for admissions given to you by the church.

O Pridgen: What is that number?

Maxwell: It's Page 5. Up at the top right, there's a little teeny five.

O Pridgen: 448-G, is that what –

Maxwell: Yeah, you can – that's fine. Look at 448-B. If you're looking at the full document –

O Pridgen: Okay. I've got it.

Maxwell: Have you got 448-B?

O Pridgen: Yes, sir.

Maxwell: Do you see request number 1?

O Pridgen: Yes, sir.

Maxwell: Admit – this is the church asking you questions.

O Pridgen: Yes.

Maxwell: Your church asking you this question. "Admit that you assisted in procuring the last will and testament of James Henry Smith." And what was your answer to that?

O Pridgen: Denied.

Maxwell: Okay. Why did you deny that?

O Pridgen: The word "procure" is usually used in a sexual sort of relationships.

Maxwell: Procure is sexual?

O Pridgen: The word "procure" has a bad interpretation, in my mind.

Maxwell: Okay. You are a licensed attorney.

O Pridgen: Yes.

Maxwell: You told us that. Are you familiar with Black's Law Dictionary?

O Pridgen: It's been a long time since I used it.

Maxwell: You used it in law school, didn't you?

O Pridgen: Yes.

Maxwell: Everybody uses Black's Law.

O Pridgen: Yes.

Maxwell: Let me read – you can see if you agree with this. The definition in Black's Law Dictionary for the word "procure" is to initiate a proceeding, to cause a thing to be done, to instigate, to contrive, bringing about, effect or cause.
Now what is sexual about that?

O Pridgen: Nothing, nothing. My – I've just been turned off by the word procure.

Maxwell: So because you were turned off by the word "procure" you denied that you initiated a proceeding, you caused a thing to be done, you instigated to bring about this will?

O Pridgen: This is very simple Mr. Maxwell. Dr. Smith told me he wanted to draw a will. I asked Mr. O'Quinn if he would draw the will for him, and that's what Mr. O'Quinn did.

Maxwell: Okay. Now, is it your testimony today that you did not have discussions with him to assist in procuring this will, or you do not remember having discussions with him.

O Pridgen: I did not discuss with Dr. Smith – he told me that he wanted to draw a will. What he put in that will is what came from Dr. Smith. That was his will, not my will.

Maxwell: Do you recall sitting in your wife's deposition, Mr. Pridgen.

O Pridgen: Mm-Hmm.

Maxwell: Do you recall her testifying that she overheard a telephone conversation between you and Bob O'Quinn where you were going over the terms of what was to be –

O Pridgen: I don't recall her saying that.

Maxwell: Okay. We'll let her talk about that.

O Pridgen: Yeah.

Maxwell: Okay. Well, let's continue. 448-K.

O Pridgen: Is that in the same stack?

Maxwell: Yes, sir.

O Pridgen: Yeah, okay. Here we are.

Maxwell: Okay. On interrogatory – this is an interrogatory now, not a request for admission, you've got that, 448 K?

O Pridgen: Yes, I've got it in my hand.

Maxwell: And if you will go to Interrogatory number 15. For the jury's group, that's Page 8.

O Pridgen: Okay. 15?

227

Maxwell: Yes, sir.

O Pridgen: Okay. Here we go.

Maxwell: The question there was, "What, if any, role did you have in procuring the will of James Henry Smith being propounded in this action?" This was a question directed to you, again, by your church, to be answered under oath, wasn't it?

O Pridgen: Yes. None.

Maxwell: None. That's your answer, you're sticking by it?

O Pridgen: Yes.

Maxwell: Okay. Do you recall being deposed on August 29, 2005, Mr. Pridgen, on or about that date? You may not remember the date. Do you remember being -- my deposing you?

O Pridgen: Yes, go ahead.

Maxwell: On Page 68 of that deposition, on Line 2, I asked you this question: "Did you know that your wife was going to be a beneficiary?" And we were talking about Dr. Smith's will. And your answer to that question was "No, I did not."

O Pridgen: Yes.

Maxwell: At any time since the caveators' interrogatories were asked of you, the church's interrogatories, the request for admission, or you gave the deposition and the answer I just gave to you, have you ever attempted to amend, change or modify any of the answers that you gave in connection with your knowledge of what was going to be in Dr. Smith's will, before it was executed?

O Pridgen: Not to my knowledge.

Maxwell: And that's because you do not remember ever having had any such discussions with Dr. Smith or with Mr. O'Quinn?

O Pridgen: I do not recall ever speaking to Dr. Smith about his will, other than he said he wanted to draw a will, and I said, fine, and I'll try to -- I may have told him, on that occasion, that I would ask Bob O'Quinn to see if he would assist him.

Maxwell: Okay. Then, in fact, you never talked to Dr. Smith, about the terms of his will?

O Pridgen: Yeah.

Maxwell: But if the jury should find that Bob O'Quinn is correct in his recollection, that you called him and gave him those terms of Dr. Smith's will, those would have been O.K. Pridgen's terms, and not Dr. Smith's, if you never talked to him about that.

Williams: Objection.

Charles Meier: Objection.

The Court: Well, sustained, I'm going to have to ask you to rephrase that question.

Maxwell: If you never discussed the will with Dr. Smith, prior to it being executed, you could not have passed on to Bob O'Quinn anything in regard to Dr. Smith's intentions, could you?

Williams: Objection.

The Court: Overruled. Go ahead.

O Pridgen: I can't answer that, really. I did not – my recollection is that I did not give Bob the – what he said I did.[644]

That was it: The climax to the big drum roll. I guess the real world isn't as spectacular as the movies. The question is, "Did the jury get it?" Who told the truth, Bob O'Quinn, Otto Pridgen, or neither of them? Their testimonies are incompatible.

Maxwell continued with questions about the timber cutting. Otto testified that he had the timber cut because "... Dr. Smith's cash position had been depleted..."[645] Maxwell then laid out some factual information about the cash in Uncle Jimmy's various bank and brokerage accounts and his dividends from investments at that time which amounted to about $3.7 million and asked, "So you decided, a business decision, to try and sell the timber at the farm to improve this $3.7 million?"

"Yes, sir." Otto answered.[646]

Maxwell asked more questions about the option not to get multiple bids for the timber and the opinion of Uncle Jimmy's farm neighbor Larry Fowler.[647] I was happy to see that Maxwell addressed the issue about the competence and motivation behind the timber sale, but I was disappointed that there were no questions about the phone call Otto made to Newton shortly before Uncle Jimmy's death, almost three years after the timber sale. This trial was about Uncle Jimmy's competence at the time the will was signed. It was not about the end of his life so there was a lot of information the jury would never get to see.

Maxwell questioned Otto about Uncle Jimmy never signing a check later than November 2003. Otto admitted to paying himself $225,000.00 in 2004 by signing checks made out to himself from Uncle Jimmy's account.[648] Otto also admitted to paying himself to attend a "shrimperoo" party at Bud Davis' house on Harbor Island which was, according to Otto's testimony, at least partially paid for with Uncle Jimmy's funds.[649] Otto also testified that Bud Davis was a member of the First Baptist Church and the "shrimperoo" was a Baptist function.[650]

Otto also admitted to charging Uncle Jimmy legal office rates to do tasks that could have been accomplished by less expensive laborers. His defense of that is that it would have been a "terrible mess" if someone else did tasks like grocery shopping for him.[651] He admitted to charging Uncle Jimmy for his attendance at the birthday party.[652] During Otto's depositions he asserted that the Smith family didn't visit often. Maxwell asked about his billing records where he charged Uncle Jimmy when Pat Jenkins called him to alert him that a family member was visiting which included at least 73 bills after Billy was fired as power of attorney.[653]

…..

After Maxwell finished Ms. Lisa Johnson-Tonkins cross-examined Otto on behalf of the First Baptist Church. Her cross-examination was much shorter than Maxwell's examination. Seven pages, to be precise, compared to 120 pages in Maxwell's initial examination. She highlighted Otto's admissions in his testimony that Uncle Jimmy was also getting advice from Jack Richardson, a banker, and David Whaley, an accountant. I think her main ambition was to distance her client, the First Baptist Church, from the Pridgen's and the caregivers. She didn't mention that Reverend Everette was said to be a member of the three legged stool. Among the things she asked, "During the period of May 1st, 2002, and October 1st of 2002, were you on the board of directors at the First Baptist Church?"

Otto answered "No."

She also asked, "Did you have any position of trust within the First Baptist Church?"

"No, other than I was one of their sinners." Otto answered.[654]

The Church didn't present much evidence that the will was executed lawfully, and without undue influence. I think they just wanted to wash their hands of the dirty facts.

…..

During Lonnie William's cross-examination of his client he endeavored to add some credibility to Uncle Jimmy's competence. Otto again testified that he didn't fire the caregivers because Uncle Jimmy liked them and Uncle Jimmy was competent to make that decision. Williams asked about the bank withdrawals "… there were no withdrawals like that after you became power of attorney, were there?"

"No, sir."[655] Otto answered (This testimony contradicts the known withdrawals from his account subsequent to Pridgen's appointment as power of attorney. Maxwell addressed this and more during his redirect).[656]

In another section of his law team's cross-examination, his other attorney, Charles Meier, read aloud some of Otto's requests for

231

admissions and responses to interrogatories. I assume that this was an attempt to get Otto's side of the story across to the jury. Interestingly, Meier read one of Otto's answers that states "Dr. Smith came to my office and requested me to serve him." Which contradicts his own testimony that it was a phone call that initiated their professional relationship.[657]

.....

During his redirect examination Maxwell asked if Otto thought it was his responsibility to make inquiry about $9,000.00 per day leaving the bank account. Otto testified "On several occasions, I discussed it with Jack Richardson. I did not ask Dr. Smith, at any time, what have you done with your money."[658] Did the jury catch that? If this testimony is true, it is more evidence that the three legged stool was operating before the signing of the will without consulting Uncle Jimmy. Otto testified again that "I have no recollection of Dr. Smith ever discussing his will with me."[659]

Maxwell later asked, "Were you aware, in the summer, or early fall, of 2002, that there were discussions under way between Jack Richardson, then at First Union, and at least with Dr. Jim Everette, either at First Baptist Church –

"No." Otto interrupted.

"—in connection – let me finish."

"Okay. Excuse me." Otto apologized.

Maxwell continued "—in connection with the possibility of creating a foundation for Dr. Smith."

Otto answered "No, I was not aware of those discussions."

"Okay. Did you at some point in time, become aware of those discussions?" Maxwell asked.

"I think it was when assistant pastor from the church, Jim Everette, was giving his deposition." Otto answered.[660]

Recall Jack Richardson's testimony that he and Reverend Everette's early meetings for Uncle Jimmy's planning occurred before Otto Pridgen gained power of attorney.[661] Maxwell asked Otto, "Did it ever cross your mind that if a foundation were created for Dr. Smith and substantially all of his liquid assets for which an executor might get a fee were transferred, that executor would not get a fee for that amount of money?"

232

Otto retorted, "Mr. Maxwell, that was the farthest thing from my mind."[662]

In an attempt to reconnect Otto to the church leadership Maxwell asked questions that would lead to Otto's testimony that in his childhood he was a "young deacon" and served as a Sunday school teacher, and that the First Baptist Church has been an important part of his life.[663]

The jury probably understood the basic situation at that point. The uphill battle from there for Jim Maxwell was to show the jury involvement from ALL the caregivers AND the church leadership. The propounders legal teams would not make this easy.

Maxwell finished up, "And finally, on a high note, I happened to, find, over the weekend, I noted that shortly after June 11, 2004, you had a half hour noted, and the quote was, 'Pat off jury duty.' Now I presume that's Pat Jenkins that you were trying to assist in getting relieved from jury duty."

Otto answered "I assume so. I mean, I don't have any recollection of that."[664]

Maxwell simultaneously showed the jury that Otto was billing Uncle Jimmy for frivolous things and showed people that were serving their civic jury duty that the propounders felt they shouldn't have to. I think Jim Maxwell probably is the best trial lawyer in North Carolina.

Testimony of
Linda Phillips

Linda Phillips testified that she had a CNA license at one point, but let it lapse.[665] In Linda Phillip's testimony she made a distinction between being a caregiver and a companion. She stated that she was a caregiver for Aunt Iris, and a companion for Uncle Jimmy.[666] When asked about how she came into the employment of the Smith family, she testified that she was referred by Margaret Banck, a friend of a family she worked for previously. Maxwell asked, "And based upon Ms. Banck's recommendation, what did you do?"

Linda testified, "She told me to call. She didn't say – she said call – she said, 'I would call Little Jimmy,' because she says, 'Dr. Smith' has a tracheotomy and you might not be able to understand him on the phone.' So she gave me Little Jimmy's phone number."[667] This is interesting testimony, given Pat Jenkins' and Otto Pridgen's claims that Uncle Jimmy called to ask them to work for him.

She testified that Uncle Jimmy never gave her a tip while she was a caregiver for Aunt Iris. She said she started getting tips when she worked as a companion for Uncle Jimmy. She maintained that she had never received any more than $500.[668] This contradicts what Uncle Jimmy told detective Johnson before he died, but the jury wouldn't have the opportunity to hear Uncle Jimmy speak.

Linda described the night that Billy and Jodie came to the house to let her know that about $800,000 was missing from Uncle Jimmy's accounts, and that they wanted her to go home. She said that when she went upstairs to say goodbye and tell him that she was going home, Uncle Jimmy said, "Goddamn it, Billy, you go home."[669] She testified, Billy and Jodie left the house. She testified that Billy was calm that night, and that she had never seen him excited.[670]

She went on to testify that she remembered Uncle Jimmy being mad about Billy, the preachers and a nursing home, but she didn't know details. It was about the same time, she claimed, that Uncle Jimmy said that Billy wanted to put him in a nursing home.[671] No one ever testified that Billy said that he wanted to put his uncle in a nursing home. If Uncle Jimmy believed Billy wanted to put him in a nursing home, who convinced him of that? That two-day period, when caregivers knew that Billy wanted them fired, might have been all the time they needed to turn Uncle Jimmy's aging mind against his family.

Maxwell asked her if she ever had to call the Pridgen's to make reports. She said, "No. And the thing – I would come in quite often after Mr. Pridgen became power of attorney, because he would be there with Dr. Smith, shooting the bull."[672] I imagine that "bull" cost Uncle Jimmy $150 per hour.

She testified that the $2 million check she received from Uncle Jimmy was just a joke.[673] She testified that she returned the check to Jan Pridgen when Jan asked for it.[674] She testified that she left employment there about three weeks later, because of a schedule change, not a conflict with the Pridgens.[675] This is not what Billy remembers. Billy recalled a long conversation with her where she noted that she understood why Billy came into the house that night to remove his caregivers, and that she would never work with Pat Jenkins again. Billy ended that conversation with the impression that she was fired by the Pridgens.[676] The jury wouldn't hear that.

234

When asked about her call to Billy and Jodie she said she did so to say she "...didn't have no vengeance toward them, and I hope they didn't toward me..." When asked if she said anything about Pat Jenkins during that call she said, "Well Jodie, I don't know Pat all that much. She comes and takes care of Dr. Smith. Dr. Smith doesn't have any complaints." She denied saying that she didn't want to work with Pat again.[677] It's amazing how different her memory is of that event than Billy and Jodie's.

Linda Phillips testified that her last day of employment there was July 6th, 2002. She said that she was unaware that Pat Jenkins circulated a letter to Carol Tucker saying that Linda was not to be allowed to have any contact with Uncle Jimmy from that point onward.[678] If she left on such good terms with the other caregivers, why the letter? Linda went on to testify that she never once called or visited Uncle Jimmy again, the rest of his life.[679]

.....

Bob Hunter cross examined first. Hunter made the point that she was not employed by Uncle Jimmy at the time the will was signed.[680] As questionable as her testimony might be, how could a jury be convinced that she participated in undue influence if she was not present at that time in his life?

She testified that she believed that he was of strong mind. When asked if he ever tried to convert her to the Baptist way, she said that she was already converted. She denied knowing that there was a large amount of cash in the house.[681] Hunter asked her if she ever asked Uncle Jimmy for money. She said, "No." Hunter ended there.[682]

.....

Lonnie Williams asked her about her previous employment. She testified that she provided the same kind of care and companionship to many others in the final months of their lives.[683] Williams asked her to confirm that the only times she saw Pat Jenkins was on Sunday mornings when Pat would relieve her shift, and she did.[684] She testified that she was paid by check signed by Uncle Jimmy or his son. She testified that "Carol was a fine caregiver."[685] She testified that Little Jimmy wanted someone to be with Uncle Jimmy because he was lonely.[686]

When Lonnie Williams asked her if she ever discussed with Uncle Jimmy, his intentions for the farm, she said that he intended to leave the farm to Dr. Bill Smith, Billy's son, because he could afford the taxes.[687] She then testified that later he decided to leave the farm to the church.[688] She testified that she mentioned this to Reverend Everette, saying, "Isn't it wonderful Dr. Smith is leaving the farm to the church?" She went on, "He just smiled at me."[689] Linda's testimony adds to my belief that Reverend Everette knew a lot more than he was letting on.

She testified that she never turned family members away, but sometimes Uncle Jimmy would.[690] She reiterated for Williams that she didn't leave the night that Billy asked her to because she didn't want to leave without Uncle Jimmy knowing.[691] She testified that she had seen Uncle Jimmy get mad at other family members also.[692] She reiterated, during Lonnie Williams' questioning, that she did not intend to cash the $2 million check.[693] Lonnie asked Linda if she told Carol about the time Billy came to the house at night, to which she replied, "Yes, I did."[694] Williams ended there.

…..

When Maxwell reexamined her, he asked what Carol's reaction to her story was. Linda said that Carol was surprised. Maxwell asked if she ever heard Uncle Jimmy complain about any of his family members, to which she replied, "Dr. Smith never mentioned his family members." She testified that she rarely saw family, but she worked the night hours. She reiterated much of her previous testimony in response to follow on questions.

Lonnie Williams re-cross-examined, asking if she gave notice when she left employment. She testified, "Of course."[695]
Linda Phillips was probably Lonnie Williams' best client. Family members perceived a change in her story after the revelation of the will, but the jury might not see that. How could the family prove that a woman who was not even present at the time the will was signed was engaged in undue influence? If the church and the other three "faithful caregivers" could be shown to have acted badly, Williams might win the entire estate for Linda Phillips.

236

Testimony of
Christy L. Jones

Maxwell wanted to show the jury that Dr. Christy Jones was a hired gun, not primarily concerned with Uncle Jimmy's mental health. Under his examination, she testified that she is a clinical neuropsychologist. She testified that she is a PhD, not an MD.[696] Maxwell asked about her professional website, advertising her services as an expert witness.[697] He asked about a case she had "where a door had fallen on a small boy, and the issue was whether or not he, in fact, had neurological impairment as a result of the door falling on him, hitting his head?"

"That is correct." Jones testified.

"And you testified that—" Maxwell attempted.

"Objection." Williams interrupted.

"Sustained." Judge Nobles ordered.

Maxwell continued, "Let's talk a little bit about – well, let me ask you this, not about the case specifically but, in that case, do you recall in your deposition testifying – and I think I quote correctly – actually I won the case."

"Objection." Hunter interrupted.

Williams injected, "Your Honor, I object to that and move to strike it."

"I'm going to sustain that." Nobles ordered. At Hunter's request the judge gave instructions to the jury including, "You will strike it from your minds and not consider any of it."[698]

Maxwell ceased his effort to show the jury that Dr. Christy Jones was a hired gun and continued with his examination of her testimony. Maxwell asked if her office had any contact with Uncle Jimmy's attorney, Otto Pridgen. Jones testified, "Dr. Smith told me when he got there that his purpose was to be there for his attorney, in terms of being able to make sure that he could make his will." She would assert that he was referred to her by Dr. Bridger, and deny that contacts were made by Pridgen before Uncle Jimmy's arrival.[699] Maxwell asked her to compare her current testimony to the original intake sheet from her office records that stated, "referred by… Attorney Pridgen." She explained that "… often, patients tell me they have very different reasons for being there than either their families or their doctors or lawyers say they're going to be there, or they think other

237

people referred them. So I write both in my blanks."[700] She would maintain that it was Uncle Jimmy's initiative that instigated the evaluation, and his reason to do so was to prove his competency to write a will.[701]

Maxwell started going through her notes line by line. "Your scribbled handwriting." Maxwell quoted. He guided her to the line in question.

"Okay." She answered. "Gave two million dollars about five weeks ago, check to nurse for saving his life." At Maxwell's request, she kept reading her notes. "Nurse keeping nephew from putting him in a nursing home."[702] Which is it, a reward for saving him from a nursing home, or a joke? Hopefully the jury would have the same question.

The notes address the death of his son, the revocation of Billy's power of attorney, and how his mother died in her eighties with a strong mind. Maxwell asked her if writing a $2 million-dollar check would be indicative of rational thinking. She testified that she assessed his land values. She knew he had a lot of money, because she knew he had hundreds of acres, and she had recently priced land for new office space. On a subsequent visit, she asked him to bring his check register to go over his understanding of money.[703] I can only assume that she didn't check to see if there was $2 million in that checking account. In 2002, Uncle Jimmy's checking account balance never exceeded $35,000.[704]

Maxwell asked her about her knowledge of real estate. She testified, "Well, if he really did have a farm that was somewhere between, I think he said 50 to 100 acres, somewhere in there, in Brunswick County. If an acre in Brunswick County would go for one to 200,000, in that neighborhood, it wouldn't take much for 50 to 100 acres of just one of his farms – let's take a conservative view, that's way over $2 million."[705] That might make his Brunswick County land worth as much as $20 million, and his Columbus County property worth $120 million. Dr. Jones' "conservative" estimate was way off. This basis for measuring his competence was chosen by a woman who wasn't competent in real estate assessments.

Maxwell asked her if she had heard anything about Uncle Jimmy's family except for the nephew mentioned. She testified that the closest family he had were nephews, nieces, and divorced spouses of nephews.[706] This testimony was odd, because none of Uncle Jimmy's nephews were divorced. Did Uncle Jimmy tell her that his

238

nephews had exes? That might be an indicator of incompetence that Dr. Jones missed because she didn't know his family. This is another odd fact, but it's unlikely that the jury would catch it, any more than Dr. Jones did.

Maxwell asked her if she remembered Uncle Jimmy ever mentioned leaving anything to the church to her. "No, I don't, and he may have told me, but his main focus would be – was to shift money from family to caretakers."[707] This is interesting to me, because I believe that even if Uncle Jimmy had the minimum mental capacity to make a will, he was very easily confused, and very easily influenced by those surrounding him. I think that if he was led to Dr. Jones office by Jim Everette, he would have been more likely to speak of gifts to the church. In fact, he was led to Dr. Jones office by Otto Pridgen and Pat Jenkins. I suspect that is why his mind was on gifts to his caregivers at that time. Again, the jury might not see this.

Maxwell asked questions to see if she was aware of a pattern of abuse where younger people take financial advantage of older people. Dr. Jones testified, "Actually, that's a good question, bus [sic] I see more elder abuse in my practice than any other kind of abuse, and 90 percent of the time, it's from the children."[708] Family members believe Dr. Jones was revealing her anti-family bias. While the jury wouldn't get to hear it, I'll add this excerpt, for my readers, from a true expert's book on elder abuse investigations, Thomas M. Cassidy:

> For the better part of twenty years, I investigated health fraud and patient abuse for the New York State Attorney General's Medicaid Fraud Control Unit. As an investigator, I saw firsthand the tragedies that can occur when elderly patients are abused, defrauded, or neglected. I also observed that elder fraud cases, once a rarity, are on the rise. One thing is true in every case of elder fraud and abuse: caregivers take advantage of their position of trust...[709]

Dr. Jones may have been right that children abuse elders in 90% of these cases, but Uncle Jimmy's child was not his caregiver in this case. Make no mistake about this: Dr Jones' area of expertise is neuropsychology, not elder abuse investigations.

Maxwell asked her about the $9,000 per day leaving his bank account. She testified, "... he had a sense of humor. And one of the things about his sense of humor was how much longer am I going to live? What am I going to do with it?"[710] I suppose an elderly man facing his mortality is entitled to a dark sense of humor, and to give gifts before the end of life. There are some questions I would have liked to hear, that weren't asked of Dr. Jones. I would have liked to ask her if a man who was an honest taxpayer his whole life started taking $9,000 a day out, and giving large gifts, untraceable by the IRS, would that be an indicator of undue influence? Would that be an indicator that he was no longer in control of his finances?

Maxwell asked her about the note in her records that states "accompanied by nurse, Patricia Coston Jenkins." Jones recognized Pat Jenkins in the courtroom, and testified that other references to Uncle Jimmy's "nurse" referred to Pat Jenkins.[711] Maxwell asked if any "red flags" went off when she discovered a caregiver might be a beneficiary of his will. "You bet."[712] She testified. She went on to explain that she relied on his test results to determine his competence.[713]

Maxwell reviewed the test results with her. She testified that he scored perfectly on the mini mental state exam that Bridger administered. She testified that when she asked him the date, he got the year right, but the month and day wrong. When she asked him to spell "world" backwards, she wrote "d-l-o-w" in her notes. She explained that she didn't count the missing "r" against him because she had trouble understanding his speech due to his voice box. She testified that he missed two of the first five answers on serial sevens test the (counting backwards subtracting seven each time starting from 100). She testified, "Which, at his age, was good."[714]

After a discussion about dementia, Maxwell asked Dr. Jones if Uncle Jimmy were diagnosed with dementia, would it impact her assessment of his ability to make a will. Jones testified, "It could. Dementia doesn't mean you can't make a will. Some people are lucky... As a dentist, one would predict that he probably had superior performance, and he also was a man who made a lot of money for himself. So he had a lot of reserve. And even areas where he is falling below where he used to fall, his low points are generally in the low average range. If people can't make a will when they fall into low average range... We're in trouble if you can't make a decision in the low average range."[715]

Maxwell asked her if she sat with Uncle Jimmy during the tests. She testified that her technicians administered the testes, and she was not actually present. When asked if she even saw Uncle Jimmy on his two follow up visits, she testified, "If I did, it would have been if I saw him in the hall, to say hi to him."[716] Her personal assessment of Uncle Jimmy doesn't seem to have been based on very much face to face time with him.

Maxwell led detailed discussion on the tests Dr. Jones' staff administered. During this discussion, Jones testified to the techniques she used to help him overcome his disabilities that she attributed to some of his testing problems. For example, she explained that she used tests that only required pointing to overcome his arthritis, and speech difficulties.[717] Maxwell asked her about her technician's note that read, "When he used this device, I understood his speech well." The note continued, "It was easy for me to understand his speech when facing him in the test environment."[718]

Dr. Jones was ready with the explanation, "What I'm telling you is he shortened what he would say… instead of being verbose, instead of going into detail, he would talk with shorter numbers or words."[719] I wonder, how much detail do you need to add when asked to spell "world" backwards?

Maxwell asked her, "As a result of the testing that you did, would there have been any difference in your opinion in Dr. James Henry Smith's processing the question[s], one, did you take your pills today; and, two, Dr. Smith, what pills did you take today?..."

"Not anything in my testing," she answered, "because I tested for aphasia but not anomia, per se."[720] I think what Maxwell was driving at was that if someone put a blank piece of paper in front of Uncle Jimmy, then asked him to write his will, he would have had great difficulty remembering his family member's names and understanding his assets. On the other hand, if someone sat with him and wrote for him, and said things like, "Would you like to make a gift to your church? How about your caregivers? How about your lawyer's wife?" He could answer yes or no to things like that.

Maxwell asked her what she told Uncle Jimmy about his results. She testified, "In his case, he didn't look like he had the pattern of deficits to look like an Alzheimer's dementia, which it turns out that probably was true, or he would have been very demented by the time he died. So we were on target there." To me she seems proud of her

241

diagnosis of an absence of Alzheimer's. She went on, "…if he looks like he had an Alzheimer's dementia, the next move would be to put him on a course of memory enhancement medicine, but that's not what it looked like…"[721]

"Were you aware that about a year after this, he was put on Aricept?" Maxwell asked.

"Aricept slows progression. He would still have to become progressively–" Dr. Jones stated, not answering the question.

"What is Aricept generally prescribed for?" Maxwell asked.

"It's prescribed for Alzheimer's" she testified. "It doesn't mean he had it…"[722] It seems to me that she was defending her diagnosis, and perhaps her reputation. She was not simply answering the questions.

Maxwell asked her if she had discussions with anyone from Pridgen's office from the time of the examinations to the time of the trial. She answered that she was called to be notified that Uncle Jimmy died, and she would be asked to testify.[723] I wonder what gave her the impression that Uncle Jimmy was not "very demented" before he died. His medical record reports that he would wake up in the middle of the night and clap his hands. During the day, he would request to have pillows on top of his head. He would ask his staff to take him home while he was in his bed at home (see chapters 12 and 24). Who told Dr. Jones that Uncle Jimmy was not demented before he died? It saddens me to think that, if his doctors saw the decline, he might have gotten medicine that could have improved his quality of life in his final years. I don't believe Dr. Christy Jones was simply evaluating his mental health. I believe she was only looking for evidence that he was competent to write a will.

As Jim Maxwell wrapped up, he asked her if Uncle Jimmy paid by check, or if Medicare covered it. She testified that Medicare will pay for her services, but Uncle Jimmy paid by a check that was signed by Otto Pridgen. Maxwell ended his examination there.[724]

…..

Ms. Lisa Johnson-Tonkins cross examined on behalf of the church. Under her cross examination, Dr. Jones testified that Uncle Jimmy was not referred to her by the church.[725] Jonson-Tonkins asked Jones to translate her "Low average" assessment of Uncle Jimmy into an A through F scale. I assume this is to put it into layman's terms for the jury. "B would be low average. C would be borderline." Jones testified. To most people, a C would be considered average. Again, I have the impression that Dr. Jones was curving Uncle Jimmy's results for the jury. Jones went on, "… if you are using the absolute score, not' saying there should be some adjustment for the fact that, one, we're having this man who is talking very slowly and we're timing it, or a man who is trying to move blocks as fast as someone could without severe arthritis."[726] It sounds like a curve to me.

Johnson-Tonkins asked how important it was to have a face to face interaction. "Very important…"[727] Jones testified. Johnson-Tonkins knew another expert witness would be called to dispute her testimony. That witness would not have the benefit of a face to face interaction. This is almost certainly an attempt to preemptively discredit that expert. I wonder if the jury would have perceived how little face to face time Dr. Jones had with Uncle Jimmy.

"You've indicated that, in speaking with Dr. Smith, that he spoke a lot about his church. Is that correct?" the church's lawyer asked.

Dr. Christy Jones testified, "It was quite obvious that the center of his life had been around his church for a long time; that he used his faith to drive a lot of his decisions."[728] Johnson-Tonkins ended there. I wonder if Uncle Jimmy's "quite obvious" feelings for his church were as obvious to Dr. Christy Jones as his real estate wealth and rumors that his family wanted to put him in a nursing home. What would the jury perceive?

…..

Lonnie Williams asked several questions about her training, education, and experience. Despite her lack of experience in real estate and elder abuse criminal investigations, Dr. Jones has an impressive neuropsychological resume.[729] This would be easy for a jury to see. Williams asked questions that enabled her to testify that she believed he was healthy enough that he didn't need treatment.[730] Williams asked questions that led her to reiterate the importance of a face to face interaction.[731] He asked her questions that enabled her to review the tests her staff administered, and reiterated that she believed he was competent to write a will.

Williams asked her if he was likely to be under undue influence. She testified, "That's a good question. There are a lot of mental health issues that cause people to be a little more submissive, if you will. And he certainly had a number of things going on in his life that could have made him depressed. His son was killed, his wife had died in a matter of months…" She went on to discuss another test, the Minnesota Multiphasic Personality Inventory II (MMPI-II). She testified that Uncle Jimmy's MMPI-II test results showed no signs of depression.[732] There was one more oddity in that testimony. She said that Little Jimmy was killed. Law enforcement never considered that a murder. I can't help wondering what she was told about him.

"Based on the tests that you made," Williams asked, "was there any indication that he was scared or under any other sort of attitude to indicate that he was under the influence of any other person?"

"No, not at all…"[733] Williams ended his cross-examination there.

…..

Maxwell had some immediate concerns in his redirect examination, "The MMPI, when you sent your studies, the raw data, to our consultant, the MMPI was not included. Is there any reason for that?"

"No, that was an oversight. I'm sorry… I'll get that to you. I don't know, is there a fax I can send to you tomorrow." She testified. That's not very timely, considering the hearing was underway.

"We can talk about that afterwards." Maxwell got the examination back on track. Given her statements about the importance of a face to face interaction, Maxwell asked her, if it would change the test results if an expert couldn't have a face to face interaction. She agreed that it would not.[734]

…..

Lonnie Williams asked one final question "Are there any board certified neuropsychologists in the Durham area, Dr. Jones?"

"Yeah, there are several." She testified, then she was allowed to step down.[735]

Testimony of
Dr. Kristine Herfkens

Jim Maxwell would call Dr. Kristine Herfkens as his expert witness to dispute Jones' assessment. She is also a clinical neuropsychological PhD. Jim Maxwell reviewed her resume, which is similarly impressive to Jones'. The court admitted her as an expert witness with no objection from the propounders.[736]

Herfkens discussed the distinction between normal and abnormal aging. She discussed Alzheimer's and other dementias. She testified that it would be better to have a face to face interaction with someone to make an assessment, but in her profession, she is sometimes asked to offer her opinion on data without personal interaction. She also testified that she reviewed some sworn depositions along with Uncle Jimmy's raw data, which would help her draw a better conclusion. She testified that she has handled a handful of cases for people who spoke with voice boxes due to a laryngectomy, or similar condition.[737]

Maxwell asked her if it seemed problematic to her that Uncle Jimmy's appointments were being arranged by an attorney and caregiver. Herfkens testified, "Well, it's not, in and of itself, a problem, but it does create – for me, it would create a need to be really aware of what's happening... there are different questions that have to be answered... When there is a caregiver who is accompanying a person – and first of all, somebody who is 95, often, is going to have some type of caregiver... so it's not that unusual. But when part of the question has to do with, you know, changing a will, or when other – when there's potentially a forensic question involved that will benefits somebody who is part of the evaluation, that's a concern... any time there's money involved or estate issues involved, I have to be concerned about that. That's part of my job. Then I also have to make sure that the information that I gather in that evaluation is free from influence by potentially interested parties as possible. And so that would be my concern, in terms of having a caregiver present who has the potential to benefit from the results of the evaluation."[738]

Maxwell asked her if she formed any opinions on Uncle Jimmy's functioning from the data she reviewed. "Yes, I did." She testified. "...it appears to me that Dr. Smith was suffering from mild dementia." She described how on some tests "... the problem wasn't just motor, because Dr. Jones' technician had made a note that she had to stop the test, that it was discontinued after he made a large number of errors and became confused about what the test was all about... "[739]

One of the other tests that was particularly problematic is a test called the Short Booklet Category Test, and this is a test where there's a series of pictures, and you have to find a pattern in the series of pictures through trial and error problem solving... and he made, really, a fairly enormous number of errors on it... There were other tests that were similarly impaired. So, for example, on a test of word finding, which I think Dr. Jones also mentioned specifically yesterday, and she spoke about anomia, and said, if I'm not mistaken, that Dr. Smith didn't have it... people are shown simple pictures, maybe things that are pretty much every day objects; a comb, or something like that, and are simply asked to give the word. And so when that's a problem is when it's at the tip of the tongue, where you know what you want to say, but you can't get the word out, that was also problematic for Dr. Smith... even making those concessions, his performance was pretty impaired."[740]

Maxwell asked her about the factors she considered as she looked into Uncle Jimmy's case. She said that Uncle Jimmy was "pretty bright" and "high achieving."[741] She noted that his status at the time of his exams showed significant decline. "... He had impairment in attention. He had impairment in expressive language. Even if I take that off the table because of the motor issues with his speech, we can disregard that, if you want, he had impairments in both verbal and visual memory, and he had some impairment in executive function, primarily nonverbal executive function. So he meets, from a cognitive perspective, the criteria for dementia. He's declined from his high level of functioning to a level that's really pretty darn impaired. In addition, based on the other information that I had from depositions and from Dr. Jones' report, this is somebody who was changing in his activities in daily living. He was signing checks, but not writing them. He wasn't responsible for all of the decisions of his day-to-day financial management. From what I heard yesterday, I think Dr. Jones said that she was aware that his attorney was managing his finances."

"Objection." Hunter interrupted.

"He had 24 hour help around the house." Herfkens continued.

"Hold on just a second." Judge Nobles paused.

"I'm sorry." Herfkens waited.

246

"I have an objection to that." Hunter stated.

"I'm sorry." Nobles stated.

Hunter went on, "My objection is that this goes beyond the test results, and this is going into all sorts of things that she did not base her opinion on, these other factors, and I object to her testifying about them now."

"Overruled." The judge ordered.

Dr. Herfkens continued, "...Dr. Smith wasn't managing his finances and also he had 24-hour care in the home. Now, that doesn't necessarily mean he couldn't do anything, but I personally don't – am unaware of most people having 24-hour care if there hasn't been something that's changed about their activities in daily living. So there's evidence that something was changing about the way this fellow was able to manage his day-to-day business. And that, in combination with the test results, clearly points to dementia."[742]

Maxwell asked about his IQ. "... this guy was not terribly impaired on his IQ testing, but we are also talking about somebody whose premorbid IQ probably was well above 120, and his full scale IQ at the time of this testing was 80. That's a huge difference... this kind of difference in IQ doesn't occur naturally."[743]

Maxwell addressed more tests, and their consequences. She testified that, on one test "he was performing worse than 94 percent of his age peers. Now, this only goes to age 89, so it's not exactly his age peers, but compared to 89 year olds." Herfkens testified that, "By itself, it certainly doesn't suggest that he can't make a will. People with dementia sometimes have the ability to make wills and manage finances. It depends on a bunch of factors layered together."[744]

Maxwell asked her if it could impact on elements of the law, such as a person's knowledge of his family, or his estate, or an understanding of what he's getting ready to do with the will. Lonnie Williams would object to this, and the judge would sustain his objection. The jury wouldn't get to hear her opinion on that.[745]

Maxwell asked her if the test results indicated to her that Uncle Jimmy was having problems. Williams objected again, but was overruled.

"Yes." She testified. "... in terms of doing verbal abstract reasoning, he was functioning worse than 91 percent of his age peers. So there are a number of indicators in this battery that his problem solving and his reasoning skills were pretty well diminished."

Maxwell was ready for his punchline. "In your opinion, Dr. Herfkens, would an individual with the test results that you saw for Dr. Smith in 2002 be more susceptible to influence of outside sources than, perhaps someone who functioned at a higher level?"

"Objection." Williams interjected.

"Objection." Hunter followed.

"Overruled." Judge nobles ordered.

Dr. Herfkens testified, "That's one of the risk factors, one of the things that we know to be, from research, with people who have dementia, because they're losing abilities in a variety of areas and are more susceptible to being manipulated and abused. That's one of the reasons we have elder abuse laws. We have child abuse laws and we have elder abuse laws, specifically because those are the groups that are most vulnerable to being manipulated by other people."[746]

.....

Lonnie Williams led the cross examination. Williams led with a series of questions that highlighted that Dr. Herfkens was hired by the caveators to the will. He was apparently trying to cast her as a hired gun. "... Dr. Herfkens, you knew that he [Maxwell] was looking for an expert witness to testify that Dr. Smith lacked some mental capacity, or was suffering from some disorder, didn't you?"

"What I knew was that he had asked me to review some records and offer my opinion." Dr. Herfkens testified.

"You knew that what he was looking for in contesting the will was an expert witness who would disagree with what Dr. Jones said." Williams pressed.

"Objection." Maxwell injected.

"Overruled." Judge Nobles ordered.

"That's of no concern to me." Herfkens went on.

Lonnie Williams continued, "Well, whether it was of any concern of yours or not, you did know that, didn't you Dr. Herfkens?"

"I was aware, as I am any time I work with an attorney, that every attorney has their own agenda, but their agenda is not my agenda."[747] Herfkens stood her ground.

Williams continued to ask her questions about her knowledge that her client, Maxwell, was contesting a will. He asked her about her hourly rate. He asked her about board certification in her field. He compared her curricula vitae to Dr. Jones'. Williams noted that Jones is board certified, but Herfkens is not. Herfkens testified that it wasn't a requirement in her field, as it is in medicine. Williams noted that she is not a diplomate of the American Board of Professional Neuropsychology. He talked about boards that Jones was a member of, that Herfkens was not. This attempt to discredit her testimony went on for twelve pages of her transcript before he asked his first question about a fact in the case.[748]

"You do agree that it's easier to evaluate a patient if you have a chance to have a face to face meeting and interact with them, I believe you said, did you not?" Williams asked.

"Oh, absolutely it is."[749] She testified.

Williams asked if she had access to Uncle Jimmy's medical record prior to her evaluation. She testified that it wouldn't have added much to her analysis since she knew Dr. Bridger didn't detect any cognitive problems.[750]

Williams asked if she was in a position to offer an opinion as to whether he was competent on the day he signed his will. "No" she testified. He asked her if she was able to express an opinion as to whether Uncle Jimmy was under the influence of anyone at the time the will was signed. Again, she testified, "No."[751] Williams asked her to define the "mild dementia" that she identified in Uncle Jimmy. She testified that was "... identifiable impairment in one or more areas of cognitive functioning, and some change in their activities of daily living..."[752] Williams made the point that he was a 95-year-old being compared to an 89-year-olds in some tests, and younger in others. She testified again, that Uncle Jimmy was not scoring in the average range for his age.[753]

Williams went back to discussing her billed hours, then ended his questioning.

.....

Bob Hunter began, "... Mr. Williams has covered most of the ground I would cover..." Under his cross-examination, Herfkens testified that her testimony was not a medical diagnosis, she did not know what caused Uncle Jimmy's dementia. Hunter asked if she would have given him different tests than Jones did. She testified that she would have given him some of the tests Jones did, and probably would have selected a few others as well. She went on to testify that "appropriate conclusions" can be drawn from the tests administered.[754]

Hunter discussed the differences between her and Jones' conclusions. Herfkens made the point that some of their conclusions were "very different."[755] Again, Herfkens testified that the testing indicates dementia, but she could not determine a cause of the dementia from her study.[756]

Hunter re-discussed the fact that she didn't have the opportunity for a face-to-face interview with Uncle Jimmy. Again, she testified that this would have been desirable. Hunter asked her to quantify the importance of a face-to-face interaction, but Herfkens said that she couldn't quantify that.[757]

.....

Maxwell began his redirect examination with a metaphor, "… as a teacher in a school you're asked to do a second set of grading… The first teacher says he got eight right. You look at it later and say that he got nine right, or seven right, do you need a face-to-face to be able to know whether or not the test results are properly and correctly interpreted?"

"No." Dr. Herfkins testified.

"Objection." Williams interrupted.

"Overruled." Judge Nobles ordered.

Herfkens went on to testify that second opinions with no face-to-face interaction are standard practice in her field. Maxwell asked about the decline in Uncle Jimmy's score from a perfect 30 of 30 in the mini mental state exam to the scores he received on Dr. Jones' tests. "… It's pretty unusual." Herfkens testified.

Maxwell's final question was, "… based upon your findings of mental impairment that you've described, the dementia, and you expressed no opinion on mental capacity, no opinion on undue influence, the answers to whether or not those conditions, either or both, existed, would depend, would they not, on external factors that you were not presented in connection with the testing that you were asked to do?"

"Yes." Herfkens testified.

"Objection." Williams injected.

"Objection." Hunter followed.

250

"Overruled." Judge nobles ordered.

"That's all. Thank you very much." Maxwell ended.[758]

The two neuropsychologists' testimony would have been a lot for the jury to digest. It is hard to imagine how their testimonies would have influenced a jury.

Testimony of
Michael Queen

Mike Queen testified that he was the head pastor of the First Baptist Church and had been for 20 years.[759] He graduated from Wake Forest University in 1968, and went home to West Virginia from there to go into business with his father before he went to Southeastern Seminary, near Raleigh. He served at a church in Greensboro, NC before leading the First Baptist Church in Wilmington.[760]

Queen testified about the charity work the church does in the community. He testified about the "Smith" classroom named after Uncle Jimmy's father. He testified about the charitable acts that Uncle Jimmy did for the church, such as bringing vegetables for church meals.[761]

Maxwell asked if he knew anything of Uncle Jimmy's continuing financial commitment to the church. Queen mentioned a $100,000 gift that Uncle Jimmy donated with a restriction that only the interest should be used. Queen went on to say that Reverend Everette went to Uncle Jimmy to ask if they could use some of the principal. At that meeting Uncle Jimmy pledged almost $100,000 more.[762] Queen testified in his deposition that he "never went to him about any need that the church had," but it seems someone from the church did (see chapter 22). Queen went on to testify that Uncle Jimmy wanted to buy the church a bus. Queen said that, "… we contacted a dealer and we found – I believe the bus had 400,000 miles on it, and you could get it for 180,000, or something like that…" Uncle Jimmy offered a new bus, he testified, "And so we did some further research and found a manufacturer in Mexico that made buses, and we were able to buy one for approximately 241,000, and Dr. Smith gave the money to purchase that bus."[763] Reverend Queen seems to know some pretty specific details about that transaction for someone who claimed to know little about him financially. Queen went on to describe Uncle Jimmy's other contributions to church funds, such as the pastor's fund, which Queen would use to pay for luncheons, and the like.[764]

Queen testified that he knew the farm had been in the family for many years. He testified that he didn't know much about Uncle Jimmy's family, except for his wife, Iris, who he said was a member of the church. He testified that Iris did not regularly attend services. He testified that he had a sense that Uncle Jimmy's family was important to him.[765]

Maxwell asked him if he remembered it being reported to him that large sums of money were being taken out of the bank account. Queen testified, "... someone said to me that they had seen Dr. Smith at the bank a couple of times and that he appeared to have a large amount of money sticking out of his shirt pocket, and they thought that was a bit unusual."

Maxwell asked if the informant expected him to do anything about that. "Yes, I think so" he testified. When asked what he did about it, Queen testified, "Well, when Mr. Smith was made the power of attorney, I made him aware of that." When asked if he ever told Uncle Jimmy's son this information before he died, Queen testified, "No, sir... I just didn't have the occasion to do that in – and it didn't seem like it was any of my business."[766] I wonder why Reverend Mike Queen felt that Uncle Jimmy's finances became his business right after his only son died. This point was made very subtly in the courtroom. I wonder if the jury would have even noticed.

Queen testified about the time that he and Jim Everette visited Uncle Jimmy with the two police officers to notify him that Little Jimmy had passed on. Pat Jenkins was on duty that day, he recalled. He said that Uncle Jimmy began to cry when he got the news. The officers answered a few questions for Uncle Jimmy, then excused themselves, leaving Uncle Jimmy with the two preachers. Queen went on, "Somewhere during that time, while the officers were still there, Ms. Jenkins came in and spoke to Dr. Smith and said for him not to worry, that she wouldn't let them put him in a nursing home, and that seemed a little awkward at the moment. And I think she and Jim [Everette] then stepped back out of the room." He testified that they prayed and spent some time together, then "... I don't know whether he said it or whether I suggested calling his nephew, Billy, but he agreed that that was the person to call, and I think I excused myself and Mr. Everette came in and I went to the phone and called Billy..."[767].

252

Queen would testify that after that day Billy "...came to see me a couple of times; a few phone calls raising questions about the sale of timber at the farm, raising questions about how much money had been withdrawn from the bank, but fairly quickly in that process, after Mr. Pridgen had been named the power of attorney, he began to share that information with Mr. Everette more than me. Jim Everette was very close to Dr. Smith, and I assume that that was why most of the information went to Jim."[768] This information that the jurors would receive is different than some family member's view that after they went, with Reverend Queen, to tell Uncle Jimmy that they thought he needed new caregivers that Queen was "on the outs" (see chapter 8). The jury wouldn't see that.

Queen testified that he thought Billy was acting "in the best interest of his uncle" the day he tried to remove the caregivers.[769] He testified that Uncle Jimmy became red in the face and refused to switch caregivers.

Maxwell asked Queen if he ever recalled Uncle Jimmy discussing his long-term plans for the farm with him. Queen testified, "The only time Dr. Smith ever said anything to me about the farm, he made a comment to me one day that he didn't know what he was going to do with the farm. He said he'd like to keep it in the family but that Dr. Bill, his great nephew, is the only one that would be able to afford to pay the taxes on it, and that was the only comment that he made."[770] Before the will was written, family members had the impression that Reverend Mike Queen believed that Uncle Jimmy's intent was for the farm to stay in the family (see chapters 13, 15, & 20). To the jury, Queen would say he "...didn't know what he was going to do with the farm."[771]

.....

Charles Meier would cross examine on behalf of the caregivers. Meier asked Queen about Uncle Jimmy's charitable giving, and the Piner Fund (for Roy Piner). Queen discussed the disabilities he was born with, and the charity work done on his behalf.[772] The family believed that the church's attorneys were trying to paint a picture of a greedy family that wanted to take money away from this disabled man. The jury wouldn't get to hear about all the family negotiation attempts prior to the trial that would have protected Roy Piner.

Queen testified that he knew Ms. Jenkins, and Meier asked Queen if he believed that the care Uncle Jimmy was receiving from his caregivers was "very good," to which Queen testified, "Yes, sir."[773]

Meier asked Queen (in reference to the day he went, with Billy and his sons, to Uncle Jimmy's house, to discuss removing caregivers) about the time he said he felt the family had Uncle Jimmy's best interest in mind. Meier went on to ask, "... at least two of these gentlemen you had never met before, is that right?"

"That's right." Queen testified.

"You didn't know – never knew Billy very well at all." Meier continued.[774] It seems he was trying to illustrate Queen's assessment of a family acting in Uncle Jimmy's best interest as an uninformed decision. Meier went through much of Queen's previous testimony again, spending significant time on testimony that Uncle Jimmy got mad when family members tried to remove the caregivers.[775]

Meier asked Queen if Otto Pridgen was a member of the church. "Yes, sir" Queen testified. He then asked if Otto Pridgen and Uncle Jimmy were friends. "They were in the same Sunday school class" he testified. He asked Queen if he ever relayed any information about Uncle Jimmy's unusual bank withdrawals to Otto Pridgen, as he had to Billy. "No, sir" he testified.[776]

Meier asked if Queen remembered Uncle Jimmy's ruptured appendix, and if he noticed a decline in his health after that. Queen concurred.[777] This last question might suggest that his loss of competence occurred after the will was signed. He asked Queen if church members were offering communion to Uncle Jimmy in his home, and if he knew the church members who signed affidavits submitted as evidence on behalf of the propounders. Queen testified affirmatively. Meier ended there.[778]

.....

Hunter then cross examined Queen on behalf of his church. He asked Queen about the records of church visitation for Uncle Jimmy. Queen verified that he and other church leaders visited Uncle Jimmy at home and in the hospital, and made these records.[779] Hunter asked several questions that allowed Queen to discuss his friendly relationship with Uncle Jimmy.[780]

254

Hunter asked him how he learned that the church was a beneficiary in the will. Queen testified, "I think the way I first learned that was from Jim Everette..." Queen denied having any discussions about this with Uncle Jimmy. Hunter asked if he felt Uncle Jimmy was competent the day the will was signed. Queen testified, "Yes, sir." Queen went on to give some examples, including, "He was always able to express himself. He had to speak with the little voice box thing, and sometimes he would have to repeat himself, but I was able to communicate with him."[781]

.....

When Bob Hunter finished, Maxwell re-cross-examined Queen. Maxwell asked about the hard feelings that might have been felt by Uncle Jimmy after he joined the party to discuss removing the caregivers. Queen testified, "I don't know whether they were patched up, I just never felt any distance between us." Maxwell asked if a reduction in Uncle Jimmy's contributions to the church after that event might be an indicator that Uncle Jimmy was more upset than the Reverend thought. "I don't know what that indicates." Queen testified.[782]

.....

Maxwell didn't show the jury a smoking gun with Reverend Queen. Queen would seem to be a good witness for the propounders, particularly the church. There were some oddities in his testimony that the family would see, but a juror might not. Nevertheless, he would put a friendly face on the church for the jury to see. Reverend Jim Everette, on the other hand, was one leg of the three-legged stool. If the jury could see him, it might be a different story.

Testimony of
Dr. William T. Smith IV

Dr. Bill Smith testified that his Uncle Jimmy had decision making capability around the time that the will was signed.[783] On the surface, it may seem like this is damaging to the family's case, but recall that the family's primary claim was not incapacity, but undue

255

influence. I believe the jury would recognize that Dr. Bill Smith and his family members were honest.

Bill Smith also testified that, "We wanted him [Uncle Jimmy] to have a sound mind just like with any family member." [784] Understanding this statement is critical to understanding the family's failure to recognize Uncle Jimmy's dementia early on. Subconsciously, we wanted to see Uncle Jimmy as a strong and healthy person more than anyone else. Despite Dr. Bill Smith's medical experience, he was not an impartial observer when it came to Uncle Jimmy, and he didn't have a lot of the information that was revealed during the discovery phase of this trial.

About the attempted removal of caregivers, he testified, "I think our intention was to terminate all the caregivers and replace them with temp agency workers and figure out who were the culprits and go from there." [785] While his testimony might make a claim of incapacity more difficult for the family, I believe the jury would find him honest, and in stark contrast to some of the propounder's witnesses.

Testimony of Janice Pridgen

Jan Pridgen testified that she was her husband's paralegal. [786] She noted that before she started working for Otto in 1974 she worked for a firm that included Mr. O'Quinn (another interesting connection in this case). [787] When asked if she had any special courses or certifications as a legal assistant she testified, "In North Carolina, after you've done it for so many years, you're considered to be a paralegal." She and Otto worked alone, with no other employees or partners. [788]

Jan testified that the first time she met Uncle Jimmy was when he came to their law office to hire Otto as power of attorney. She admitted that it was less than 5 months later that he included her in his will. [789]

When asked why she was billing Uncle Jimmy $75.00 per hour to do his errands she testified, "Well, we discussed it, as we have talked about, trying to get someone to run errands at a much less rate than $75 an hour; but, if I did that, then I'd have to train them, I'd have to check the receipt against the money that was spent against what came into the house. There was a lot of specialized shopping. Dr. Smith took a lot of vitamins. And as an example, he, one time, wanted some tea tree oil.

Well, I've never - - I didn't know what tea tree oil was; and, with Dr. Smith's speech problem, Pat told me he wanted pea tree oil. Well I didn't know what that was any more than tea tree oil. So I would ask Pat, what did he need, and she said pea tree oil. I said, what is that? So it took me a little while to figure out what they were getting. He told me to go to Cross Seed out on Market Street to get it. So I went out there, and they didn't have it. They told me to go someplace else. So I went and got it. And he wanted it for nail fungus, that's why he wanted it, but - - and since I - - after that, saw I could get it in a lot of different places. I didn't have to go all the way out to Cross Seed."[790]

Can you see why Jan Pridgen's time was worth $75.00 per hour? I can't. When asked why she didn't send one of the other caregivers who were employed at a lower rate to run those errands she went on "...My daughter was - - she's 35, I think. She has two children. She's a stay-at-home mom, and she would just beg me, Mama, can't I help you do something? You're so busy. You don't have any time for anything. Can't I go for you? And I couldn't even let my own daughter, who I would think would be able to do as good a job as I did. Dr. Smith told me to do it."[791]

When asked about her husband Otto's testimony that he never discussed the making of a will with Uncle Jimmy she testified, "My husband's memory is not good..." When asked about her deposition testimony where she said she heard Otto discussing the terms of the will over the phone with Bob O'Quinn she recanted saying, "Well, somebody told me a long time ago what the word assume means. And, after thinking about this very hard, I didn't hear anything. Dr. Smith came in to talk to Mr. Pridgen about a will. He told the caregivers, I want to talk to Otto about a will... So he came in, he went in Mr. Pridgen's office. They sat in there and talked. I was out in my office, and I can't hear what they're doing, what they're saying. And at that time, as my husband had for years, he would always have me get so-and-so on the phone for me... So I got Bob O'Quinn on the phone. I told him Bob O'Quinn was on the phone. Dr. Smith was with Mr. Pridgen. I shut the door and left. So it was an assumption."[792] What would the jury believe?

Jan was asked to read a memo to the jury, regarding a conversation she had with Maxim Healthcare on or about July 1, 2002. Jan read:

"Nursing assessment completed on client. TC" – I guess it's telephone call – "to Jan Pridgen, paralegal for client. She states that she received a TC from Dr. Bridger's office stating that he could not authorize CNAs in the client's home. Ms. Pridgen states she will contact this RN after speaking with the client. She states she is tired of dealing - - tired dealing with this, every day and wants an agency to take over. This RN recommended that all CNAs in the home be employees of this agency. She agreed because of the legal side of it.

Jan denied memory of that conversation.[793] She was asked if she remembered multiple phone calls arranging a meeting with Dr. Christy Jones on Uncle Jimmy's behalf (which corresponded with her billing records). She denied memory of that.[794] Later they discussed the billing records showing a record of "J.M.P. [Jan M. Pridgen] reading Dr. Jones's report and O.K.P. [Otto K. Pridgen] reading Dr. Jones's report."[795] When asked why it was important for the two of them to read the report on September 4, 2002 she testified, "It was important to me to know about Dr. Smith. He had these tests, and I had - - I asked him to have a test; and when he was doing them, I did know he was being tested, and he said it's a crock of ... but he said the word. He said it's a crock of ... He didn't like being tested at all."[796] This is yet another contradiction: Did Uncle Jimmy want to have the tests done, or didn't he?

Maxwell asked her if the testing being done was in contemplation of a new will to which Jan replied, "I don't remember anything about a will."[797] Jan seems to want to make it clear that her knowledge of the competency test was independent of the timing of the drafting of the will. She simultaneously contradicts Dr. Jones' testimony that it was Uncle Jimmy that wanted the evaluation.

When asked about the note that Pat Jenkins wrote to Carol Tucker, instructing her not to have any discussions with Uncle Jimmy "about schedule changes, salary, his will or monies of any kind." Jan testified that she knew about the letter, and went on,

We were trying to establish a pecking order, so to speak, and wanted Pat to be the head nurse. This is what Dr. Smith called her. This was the position that she was in at the house, and I – we wanted her to communicate with the other caregivers. And

258

Mr. Pridgen was concerned, after these ladies lad [sic] left the job, that they might want to come visit with Dr. Smith and, as he said, he was concerned about everybody getting sad about Iris being gone. And another thing that he was concerned about, that I recall, was that, because Dr. Smith had liked these ladies that were there, Linda and Betty, that it would make him sad that they weren't there any more, if he saw them again. So that was the purpose in my conversation to Pat, and she prepared that handwritten note...[798]

Would the jury see compassion or control in her actions? Maxwell saw the discrepancy, and asked Jan Pridgen, "Why, in your opinion, would it have been bad for Dr. Smith to see Betty Parker or Linda Phillips if, in fact, he had a great affection for them, as you describe, and your concern was that he would be sad if he saw them?" She restated that it was because she didn't want him to be sad, then Maxwell moved on.[799]

Maxwell questioned her on the notes in her billing records that indicate that Pat was passing information from Uncle Jimmy about what he wanted in his will to the Pridgens. This, of course, is inconsistent with previous statements that she didn't know anything about his will, and doesn't want the caregivers discussing it.[800]

Maxwell asked her about the letter from O'Quinn, stating that Uncle Jimmy wanted to give an immediate gift of $100,000.00 to Lisa and Erin. She testified that, rather than addressing it with Uncle Jimmy, Otto would just wait to see if Uncle Jimmy brought it up again later, and that "we weren't going to encourage him to deplete his estate, prior to his demise."[801]

After the trial, Lisa discovered that Uncle Jimmy wanted to give her this gift. She felt distressed about this, but not for the reason you might think. She knew nothing about the gift during Uncle Jimmy's life but was concerned that Uncle Jimmy might have believed his wishes were carried out by Bob O'Quinn and Otto Pridgen. If so, he might wonder why Lisa and Erin never thanked him. Lisa was devastated (and I think Erin feels the same), not because she didn't get the money, but by the thought that her Uncle might have been hurt.[802] The jury would not get to see Lisa's view of the facts.

Maxwell asked Jan about the $619,216.00 that she and her husband billed Uncle Jimmy in the 34-month period from April 27,

2002 (acquiring the power of attorney) to February 22, 2005 (the date of Uncle Jimmy's death). She was asked if they had ever done any work for any other clients that they billed at that rate, to which she testified, "No, sir."[803]

When Maxwell asked her if Uncle Jimmy deteriorated mentally and physically, Jan testified, "I don't think he deteriorated. Mentally, he never deteriorated."[804] Her assessment is inconsistent with his medical record, but that is what the jury heard from Jan Pridgen.

Maxwell's questions about her billing for groceries, hardware and other shopping trips goes on through 15 pages of the court transcript. He asked about her many trips to Lowe's hardware, Sam's club, Wal-Mart, Eckerd's drugstore, CVS drugstore, Harris Teeter grocery store, Baskin Robbins ice cream, et cetera, every day for over 1000 days she served as Uncle Jimmy's power of attorney's assistant. She billed $75.00 per hour up to 12 hours per day in those 1000 days, weekends and holidays included. Many of those hours were for shopping trips. Seven hours were attributed to "clean out linen closet."[805]

She also billed him about 40 hours over 4 different days for reupholstering chairs. Maxwell asked, "Tell us about your reupholstering experience and your business of reupholstering chairs for Dr. Smith."

She testified, "Dr. Smith had two chairs in his foyer that were tattered, and I asked him if he would like to have them recovered, and he said, 'Yes'. So I went and picked out some fabric and took it to him, for his approval, and he said he liked it, and so I started reupholstering his chair... after I spent a little time on it, I realized it was going to be too time consuming and that I needed to have them done by someone else. So I did not go on with that."[806] If Jan billed him 40 hours for upholstering, at $75.00 per hour, that makes $3,000.00 for her time, not counting fabric, and she didn't finish the chairs. She claimed to have done more than just upholstery on those days to earn her fee.

The list goes on and on. She billed him $300.00 for taking him to lunch. She billed him $300.00 and Otto simultaneously billed him $600.00 to go to a Sunday School party with him (and it was Otto's own Sunday School group).[807]

Maxwell asked her about billing to handle phone calls from "Rosa, Wanda, Carol, whoever was there." Jan Pridgens billing notes for these calls have a little triangle that says "8:30" and another that says "7:40 off." Then it has 11.2 for the time. Maxwell asked Jan, "...I assume that that represents from 8:30 a.m. to 7:40 p.m., representing 11.2 hours, is that correct?"

"Correct." She replied.

Maxwell continued, "You were on the clock at $75 an hour from 8:30 to 7:40 on that day and every day that we have one of these sheets in which there's a triangle at the top and a triangle at the bottom. Is that fair?"

"Yes, sir." She replied.

"Did you not eat any time during that date?" Maxwell asked.

"Nope." Jan testified.[808]

Maxwell asked her about a note in her records referencing a time when the police were called when Dr. Bill Smith (Billy's son) and his family were visiting. Jan testified that she "... asked the officer if he would please ask Dr. Bill and Amy to just leave for right now... and talk to Pat and see if we could make an arrangement where they didn't cross paths again."

Maxwell asked about a note in her records that says, "Dr. Smith said he wanted everybody to stay... That would have included Bill and Amy and their daughter."

Jan testified, "Yes, sir. Dr. Smith, as everybody has testified, had a good sense of humor, and – but he didn't want anybody – he didn't want Pat to leave and he didn't want Dr. Bill to leave. And when he made the comment about, arrest the lady in the white [Pat Jenkins in her nurse's outfit], that was one of his famous little jokes that he made quite often. He would – when the police officers would come, when the alarm would go off at the house and they'd come and he'd always tell them to arrest the lady in white, just because it was a funny thing he said."[809] The frequent police visits aren't as funny to the family.

She testified that later in Uncle Jimmy's life she billed him for many calls from Pat and others referencing Alzheimer's, dementia, clapping his hands at night, claiming that he has $30 billion, and keeping a pillow over his head.[810] This is the same woman, who, on the same day, in front of the same jury, testified that, "Mentally, he never deteriorated."[811]

She testified that she billed him for 82.7 hours of tax preparation even though he had a full time CPA.[812] That's over $6,000 to the Pridgen law firm before Uncle Jimmy got the bill from the CPA. You would think at those prices the Pridgens would have noticed that Iris' accounts weren't all settled in the three years that they managed his estate. The accountant billed another $7,000.[813]

Maxwell asked about another note in the Pridgen billing record, "Call from Pat. Carol threatened her in Alicia's presence." Jan Pridgen explained that as a "spit spat... just one of these little anger venting things."[814]

.....

When Maxwell finished, Bob Hunter began his cross examination. He asked her if she had a relationship with Uncle Jimmy before Otto Pridgen gained his power of attorney, to which she testified, "No, sir." He asked if a relationship of care and affection developed in the 5 months from the beginning of her employment to the date the will was signed to which she testified, "Yes, sir."[815] On the subject of large cash withdrawals, Hunter asked her if she ever asked Uncle Jimmy what he did with the money. She testified that it wasn't her place to ask. He then asked if those large amounts of money were going as gifts to his son and caregivers "... wouldn't it have been a taxable event which you, as the bookkeeper, would have had to report and list as a distribution for that year, that taxable year?"

Jan Pridgen testified, "Mr. Whaley was aware of everything that happened, and that is his expertise, not mine."[816]

Hunter asked her if she saw family visitors other than Billy, his wife, or Bill and his wife, and if Uncle Jimmy showed care and affection for them. She denied seeing any other visitors from the family [I and many other family members visited when we were in Wilmington]. On Uncle Jimmy's affection, she testified, "After the blowup with Billy, Dr. Smith tended not to talk with Billy."[817] This testimony was interesting to me, because of her earlier testimony that she didn't know Uncle Jimmy before she was employed there. This implies that she would not have known Uncle Jimmy during the "blowup," so how could she know what Uncle Jimmy's relationship with Billy was like before then. Her sworn testimony fits into the propounders' claim that the family was disinherited because of some family misconduct, but what knowledge is her testimony based on? The family could easily see through this, but would the jury?

Hunter asked Jan Pridgen about her husband's memory problems. She testified that she tries "to be very patient and just enlighten him as best I can."[818] Hunter asked if her memory, "superior" to her husbands, would help her recall a conversation, in her law office, about a will for Uncle Jimmy. "I don't remember" she testified.[819]

She testified, to Mr. Hunter, that she had never heard Uncle Jimmy suggest that he wanted to make out a will. When asked if the visit to Dr. Bridger was to establish competency for a will she testified, "I can't answer that... No, I don't know." Hunter then asked why a letter was desired, to prohibit discussions about a will among the staff, if no such discussions were being had. "Well apparently, Dr. Smith had come in, because he had it on his mind." She testified.[820]

Hunter asked her about the timing of the discussions about the will in the house, and the 2-million-dollar check that was made out to Linda Phillips. He established that some discussion about the will was had while Linda was still employed.[821] This was a subtle point to be made to the jury. It was a major boost for the family. This could imply that Linda was employed when undue influence occurred. The family believed that there was solid evidence to show that Reverend Everette, the Pridgens, Pat Jenkins, and Carol Tucker were guilty of undue influence. Linda was the Achilles heel. Jim Maxwell may be the best trial lawyer in North Carolina, but Bob Hunter didn't miss much either. If the church's lawyer could show that Linda was connected to the dirty side, he might increase the church's share, if he could convince the jury that the church's hands were clean. It seems Lonnie Williams' clients were getting attacked by both sides.

Hunter asked her if she had any awareness of discussions about the will involving Jack Richardson, to which she testified, "There was a discussion about a foundation for the church."[822] I wonder if she detected that Hunter was driving a wedge between the caregivers and the church when she answered that question. She seemed to return fire at the church's law team. While on the stand, she denied knowing about Otto's involvement in the planning of the will, but she seemed to remember the other two legs of the three legged stool.

.....

When the church's legal team finished, Lonnie Williams cross examined his client. She testified that she never took anything from his shopping trips for her own use, her long hours diminished her quality of life, that his personal records were a mess, that she worked with his banker, Jack Richardson, that she gave instructions to the yardman, that she did specialty shopping, that she did the payroll, the tax preparation, that she prepared for storms, and that she paid bills.[823]

She testified that she had the alarm systems for both his residence, and his farmhouse put into her name. She testified that, "… the alarm was going off at the house it seemed like every time they left, but there was a malfunction in it, as far as we could see."[824] This testimony reminds me of the time her son, Kip Pridgen, got stuck in the mud at the farm house, and had to call a farm neighbor to pull him out. The next day, the gate was closed, but the lock was missing. The alarm was cleanly cut off the wall. There was no sign of theft or vandalism (see chapter 9).

Lonnie Williams presented pictures of Uncle Jimmy with the Pridgens and Pat Jenkins at his side, like his Sunday School parties, and a Christmas dinner at his house. He asked her why Maxim would suggest having their own employees hired instead of Pat and Carol. She testified, "Well, they'd get more money."[825]

Lonnie Williams helped her make a point to the jury that Uncle Jimmy's most severe indications of dementia came after the will was signed. [826] Williams went on, asking Jan Pridgen to identify a propounder's exhibit. She testified, "This is a declaration of a desire for a natural death, signed by James H. Smith on August 10, 2003" (11 months after the will was signed). There were two witnesses to that document, both members of the First Baptist Church (George D. Nicklen and William W. Hinton). The document was notarized by Jan Pridgen. [827]

Williams showed Jan an exhibit that listed checks signed by Uncle Jimmy's own hand, presumable another indicator of competence. There were some checks in that list that were signed by Otto Pridgen.[828] Finally, Williams presented financial statements showing that Uncle Jimmy's liquid accounts had grown in the time that Otto Pridgen held the power of attorney from $3.8 million to 5 million.[829] I believe Williams would have liked the jury to believe that this indicated expert management of Uncle Jimmy's affairs. That is where Williams ended.

…..

In redirect examination, Maxwell picked up where Williams left off. Maxwell asked if the Pridgens bought or sold stocks Uncle Jimmy's behalf, or advised him on the purchase or sale of stocks. She testified that they did not, but that she monitored the accounts daily. Maxwell mentioned, "These were simply investments Dr. Smith had before you ever came on the scene." She concurred.[830]

Next Maxwell asked her to take another look at approximately 100 pages of checks signed by Uncle Jimmy and Otto Pridgen. Maxwell asked her, "Can you find a single check in there for reimbursement from Dr. Smith to you or your husband, which was ever signed by Dr. Smith, a single one?

"No, sir." She testified, "My husband signed all of those."[831] When Uncle Jimmy paid an outsider, he signed the check himself. When he paid the Pridgens, or when the Pridgens paid themselves out of his account, Otto Pridgen signed the check. Did Uncle Jimmy even know how much the Pridgens were paying themselves. Did the jury catch that?

Maxwell asked if the declaration of a desire for a natural death was signed less than four weeks prior to a notation that he had Alzheimer's. "Yes, sir." She testified. She added, "As I said, that was my terminology on that, the Alzheimer's word."

Maxwell finished by asking her, "And did I understand you to tell Mr. Hunter that, at no time since you read the will the day it was delivered to you... neither you nor your husband have ever sat down and figured that if, in December, '04, there was $5 million in just these accounts, and there was apparently another account, at least, high performance account that may have had another million dollars in it, that the two of you have never sat downed [sic] and figured out what your 10 percent of that amount would be..."

"No, sir" she testified.[832] I ask the reader: If you were reading a will that left something to you, would you be at least a little bit curious about what your gift would be?

.....

In Bob Hunters recross examination he focused on the cash values of the bank accounts and the timber sale. He asked, "... when the Woodford Farm was timbered... where did the money go?"

Jan Pridgen testified, "We opened up a high performance money market account, because it yielded more interest than the cap account."

"Okay." Hunter continued, "And how much money was initially deposited in the high performance money market account?"

"I don't remember. It was the first two checks, I believe, from the timber, and I don't have that." She testified.

"Totally, over time, within an approximation of $30,000 one way or another, how much was the net total you received from all the proceeds of timber sales?" Hunter asked.

Lonnie Williams attempted to answer for his client, "I believe, total, according to Mr. Maxwell's figures –"

"Hold on a second. Hold on a second." Judge Nobles stopped him.

"I can't answer that." Jan Pridgen stated.

Nobles got the court back in order, "Go ahead and ask your question."

"Do you recall?" Hunter asked.

"I can't give you that figure right off the top of my head." She testified.

Hunter added, "If your counsel says it was $1,100,000, was that approximately correct?"

"That was for Woodford and Brunswick." She testified.

Hunter went on, "All right. And none of that money, as I understand it, not a dime of that money, was deposited in the Wachovia cap account."

"Correct." She testified.

"And it was put in a high performance money market account."

"Correct." She testified.

When Hunter finally got to his punchline, Pridgen had agreed that all that was left of the $1.1 million dollars worth of timber, sold off of two properties, was $113,827.29.[833] Again, Hunter seemed to be hunting his co-propounders.

. . . . .

Lonnie Williams finished up by asking her if the sale was reasonable because Uncle Jimmy had little cash on hand.[834] Maxwell finished up by making the point that she testified that she chose to employ Pat Jenkins and Carol Tucker, instead of people under the cognizance of Maxim Healthcare to save money. He made the point that Wanda and Alicia (from Maxim) were being paid about $35,000 per year. Jan Pridgen agreed to those figures, and to the estimates that Carol Tucker was being paid over $60,000 per year, and Pat Jenkins was being paid over $47,000 per year, neither of these amounts included gifts.[835]

Testimony of
Patricia C. Jenkins

Jim Maxwell started his questioning of Pat Jenkins by asking her to confirm her name and residence. He then asked her if she was currently employed outside the home, for pay. She confirmed that she was currently employed by Hyton Babson.[836] This is the Same Hyton Babson that is a member of the First Baptist Church, and signed an affidavit for the court stating that hiring Pat Jenkins showed good judgment on Uncle Jimmy's part (see Chapter 24). Maxwell noted that Pat had been wearing a white nurses uniform to court for the previous 2 weeks, and asked her if she would be leaving court and proceeding to one of her care giving jobs, to which she replied, "I may, if I like, correct."[837] It seemed odd to the family that Pat Jenkins would wear a nurse's uniform to court.

He asked her if she was married, and if she ever worked for her husband's previous wife before she died. Pat testified, "I worked for his wife for four months through Eldercare, and then I was single, and I was dating someone. And a year later, Jim asked – he ran into me and asked me if I'd like to go out and eat. And I said, 'Well, give me a call, and I'll see.' So he called me. He asked me for my phone number, he did not have it, and I give it to him and he called me, invited me out to eat and, two weeks later asked me to marry him. I told him it would take me three months, I would have to think about it. I didn't know him that well because, see, I was working 10 hours with his wife when I went in. I didn't know Jim. I wanted to get to know him before I decided whether to marry him or not." To the family this sounded like a story to show the jury that her relationship with her husband did not start while she was employed to care for his wife.

She admitted to accepting small tips, and to asking her daughter to cut Uncle Jimmy's toenails once a month. She said she asked her daughter to stop coming when the family asked her to stop.[838] He asked if Uncle Jimmy ever called her a "head nurse." Pat testified that she would call herself a "Nursing Assistant II."[839]

She denied denying visitation.[840] She explained Uncle Jimmy's claim that he had $30 billion dollars as a joke.[841] She attributed the times he was clapping his hands at night and putting a pillow over his head to "one of the medications" and claimed that she was "the only one qualified to assist him with medications."[842] Maxwell asked her about the Aricept he was taking, to which she replied, "Aricept is supposed to be for Alzheimer's, senile dementia, but he [Dr. Bridger] gave it to him [Uncle Jimmy] for another reason."[843]

Maxwell began to set the stage for his big finale. He asked her about her licensing. Pat testified, "A CNA II [Certified Nursing Assistant level 2] can accommodate – they take care of traches, clean out traches and take care of tracheotomies. They do osteotomies, clean osteotomies. We do the blood glucose check, we take out pick lines, and I have the list, long list, if you'll let me get my records... If you'll follow me one day, you'll see how good I am." Maxwell asked her to expand on what training was required to receive a certificate as a CNA II. She testified, "I had to keep up a CNA I license, and I have to keep up my CNA II license, which both are inactive right now with the state of North Carolina."

"Okay, what does that mean?" responded Maxwell.

"Also – excuse me. I also do enemas. I'm allowed to give enemas to patients. A CNA I cannot to that, that's why we have CNA II." [844] She went off on a tangent.

Maxwell accepted the tangent, and asked if a CNA needs a doctor's order to clean out traches, and to administer enemas. On cleaning a trache, Pat testified, "Of course, there's a doctor's order, of course." About enemas, "I don't have to have an order for an enema. I can do that, as a CNA II assistant."[845] This statement she made to a jury is troubling. A CNA II is not allowed to give an enema without an order from someone with that authority if he or she is working with a hospital or nursing facility. Working outside of this type of supervision, a CNA II would have to make arrangements with the individual cared for, or the family on his/her behalf (or someone with a power of attorney).[846] What is troubling is that Pat Jenkins repeatedly cited her license and her authority to give enemas as a nursing assistant, out of one side of her mouth, and saying that she was employed as a sitter, not a nurse, out of the other. Would the jurors understand the significance of the actions of this unsupervised CNA?

Maxwell moved on, and Pat testified that she has 25 years of experience working with hospitals and individuals. When asked if any other patients or clients gave her a significant bequest, as in the will in question, she testified, "I don't know what that is. I have no idea what Dr. Smith has left me, and I have no significant amount to know what he's left me at this time. Ten percent. I don't know what 10 percent of all that is."[847]

Maxwell asked her how she came to work for Iris Smith. In testimony that takes up two pages of the court transcript (briefly summarized here) Pat said that she got a call from an agency to help Iris while she was hospitalized, that Iris was throwing her bedpan at people, that Pat solved her bedpan problem by offering a bedside potty, and that she followed her from the hospital to a nursing facility. She went on about serving her breakfast, helping with her showers, and telling her son she would have eggs when she wanted them, "... don't you worry, Mr. Smith, we'll make sure your mama has her eggs, then she started getting her eggs."

Judge Nobles interrupted, "Ms. Jenkins, let me stop you for a second. Try to listen to his questions real carefully and answer them. You've confused me.

"I apologize. So, anyway – I apologize." Pat Jenkins said.
"Just listen. He'll ask you another question." Nobles tried to get the witness back on track.

"So she got her eggs." Pat finished.[848]

Maxwell continued asking about her employment relationship through Eldercare, during Iris' life, and subsequent departure from that agency. He asked if it was her understanding that after Carol Tucker, Linda Phillips, and others hired outside of eldercare and other agencies, if she was the only licensed provider at that time, to which Pat testified, "Correct."

Maxwell asked her about her transition from working for Iris, under the oversight of eldercare, to working for Uncle Jimmy, independent of any agency. Pat testified that she left employment there for two days, then Uncle Jimmy called her back. She said that she told Uncle Jimmy that Little Jimmy would be taking care of him from then on, and that she said, "Have a nice day now," then hung up the phone.[849]

Maxwell asked, "Did I understand, from a prior deposition, that you actually tape-recorded that conversation?"

"No, sir, you're wrong. I did not say that." Pat testified.

"Okay. Tell me what you said." Maxwell continued.

"I said to you, my tape – my phone rang, I did not get to it fast enough, and my phone picked – the recorder automatically came on

269

before I could pick it up, and it automatically recorded it." Pat went on, "See, what happens is, when you have a phone and an answering machine that's connected together – my husband sold them. I don't know nothing about them, but he sold them, and it automatically just picked up. The answering machine came on, and I picked up the phone, and he went to talking. I didn't know the dag blasted thing was recording, and I just went ahead and talked and, when I got off the phone, I hung it up. So later I thought, you know, Little Jimmy said that he didn't need me, and I asked my husband, I said, 'Hon, Dr. Smith called me. Does that phone in there record? Maybe I should have recorded that to make sure, in case there was a mix-up there with them.' He said, 'Yeah, the phone automatically picked it up and it's recorded.' I said, 'Save that for me. I may need it to see whether Dr. Smith wants me to take care of him.'"[850]

Maxwell continued, "The reason you kept the tape was for what reason?"

"To let you know that Dr. Smith really wanted me to take care of him" she testified.

"To let me know?"[851] Maxwell asked.

The jury wouldn't get to hear the more outrageous deposition conversation.

Maxwell asked her about trips to the bank to withdraw money. Pat testified that she drove him to the bank some of those days. She claims no knowledge of what he did with the money. "I never ask him about his money. I don't even get in my husband's money. I didn't ask him nothing about his money, huh-uh. That's one thing women don't do, is ask men about their money."[852]

When asked about Little Jimmy's death, she testified that it devastated and hurt her. She said she knew it was going to hurt Uncle Jimmy, "No matter what Jimmy was, he was his son and he loved him. He may not like his ways, but he loved him."

"What do you mean, no matter what Jimmy was? What was Jimmy?" Maxwell asked.

"Well, he had a boyfriend." She testified. "What do you call them?"[853] I believe this was her attempt to damage the family's reputation through Uncle Jimmy's son's homosexuality.

Maxwell refocused the questions on the moment when police officers came into Uncle Jimmy's house with the preachers from the First Baptist Church to notify him that his son died. Pat testified, "And

270

they came in, and I told – I went in there, and I said, 'Dr. Smith, it's going to be alright. You're going to be alright.' Billy put his father in a nursing home[37], and he was scared he was going to go to a nursing home, and I knew he was, and I could tell."[854] The family knew this claim was false, but the jury was hearing all this for the first time. Later in this interview Pat would admit that no one talked about Uncle Jimmy going to a nursing home before they told him about his son's death.[855]

"I don't understand why we got into a discussion about Billy and his father in a nursing home when you're telling us about people telling Dr. Smith his son died…" Maxwell continued.

"Because Billy begged Dr. Smith for his power of attorney."[856] Pat testified. Again, the family knew this wasn't true, and this testimony contradicts other evidence that suggests Uncle Jimmy asked Dr. Queen to call his nephew for him to ask him to take the power of attorney.

Later in the interview Maxwell asked, "Do you recall in your deposition when I asked you this question, you indicated that you did not recall even saying anything about a nursing home to Dr. Smith?"

"Well, I may not have recalled it at the time but, right now, I remember." Pat testified, "… I'm not going to – if the preacher said it, maybe I said it. I don't know. I don't recall it, though."

Maxwell asked, "Now at some point, did you understand that Dr. Smith asked somebody, Dr. Queen or somebody, to call his nephew Billy?"

"I didn't hear that… I believe it if you say it. I didn't hear it. I don't know." She testified. [857]

Later in the interview Maxwell asked her about the time an investigator (Detective Ken Johnson) came to the house and talked to the caregivers about Little Jimmy's death, to which Pat responded, "Correct. I wasn't there." That was another falsehood that would be easily disproven (see Chapter 8), but this must have been extraordinarily frustrating for Jim Maxwell.

Maxwell asked if she was still taking her medications, Strattera and Depakote.

---

[37] Billy's father Jack, made his own arrangements to move to the Brightmore assisted living facility in Wilmington when his wife Whit developed dementia. After Whit's death, Jack was hospitalized, and was discharged to a rehabilitation facility. He passed on in that facility. This testimony Pat Jenkins gave the jury about Billy putting his father in a nursing home is simply not true.

"Right, exactly. I sure am." She testified.

"Okay. Depkote is a medication that's often prescribed for folks with bipolar or mood disorders, is it not?" Maxwell asked.

Pat responded, "It doesn't matter – that is correct, but it has something to do with menopause…"

"And no one has ever suggested that you might have a bipolar condition or a mental disorder, and that was the reason for this medication being prescribed." Maxwell asked.

"No, not that I'm aware of." She testified.

"Okay. And Strattera is often prescribed for ADHD." Maxwell added.

"It doesn't matter. I still have to take it because of my menopause…"[858]

Maxwell asked her about the $2 million-dollar check, and she testified that she didn't think Linda Phillips would cash it. When asked why she reported it to Otto and Jan Pridgen, she said she just didn't want to have a check unaccounted for.[859] She was asked about how much time she spent on the phone with Jan Pridgen. According to some of those estimates she spent thirty minutes per call, six to eight times a day some days.[860] Pat noted an example of a phone call regarding Wanda Day calling in sick.[861]

Maxwell asked, "Okay. You picked out Wanda Day because she happens to be sitting here and you know she's going to testify in this matter?"

Pat challenged him, "Well I don't care. I'm not in least worried about Wanda testifying. Do I look scared?" [862] That was foreshadowing as to what would come in Wanda's testimony.

When Maxwell asked her if she ever took Uncle Jimmy to his country club, she started to babble again, "I took him quite a few times. He loved going to the country club. He went with [his son] Jimmy to the country club while Iris was alive, and I would take him and Iris, both, over there. Iris loved going to the country club. Little Jimmy met us at Sam's, when he was going with his boyfriend. They met over there, and he would get things for his self. His daddy would buy them, and I'd be with Little Iris, have Little Iris, and Dr. Smith would push his own cart. He would push the cart while I helped Little Iris, and Little Jimmy would be giggling down one aisle, and he'd run down the next with his boyfriend. That's all I know…"

Judge Nobles would interrupt again, "Held [sic] just a second. Ms. Jenkins, try to answer his question and don't go off on a tangent."[863]

Maxwell asked her why Uncle Jimmy was given three enemas a few days before he died. Pat testified:

> I have a patient in that situation now. But when a person gets into that age, normally women, especially, and men, they're a little bit further behind. It's not as bad on a man, but with – but it does come on them. At 90 – he's in his nineties. That's why Dr. Smith took stool softeners and drank all that Mylanta, because the muscles in the intestines do not push down the bowels like they would at a younger age. It slows down, okay? So about three days before Dr. Smith finally died, three days before, we went to put him in bed, Carol and I. It took two of us to put him into bed. He had slowed down quite a bit at this time. He had been slowing down for six months to a year. He had been slowly, slowly going down. And I had been – we had been feeding him Ensure and purees before the Ensure with a little cup. I tried to feed him to keep his system up, you know, and be healthy until then.
>
> And we went and put him to bed, and he went aaaaah, like that. I said, "Carol, let's get him in bed." I didn't want him to hit the floor. So we got him into the bed. When we did, I checked him out, because usually people – the BMs will come out. So I looked, and there was feces out the rectum, so I took and got a baby enema, and I put up there and I got a specimen out of the rectum; and when I did get the specimen out, there was some blood, and he was bleeding from the rectum. So I called Maxim. Maxim sent the RN over, Linda Strawcutter, the RN, and she told me, she says, "Pat, don't move him." She checked him out and she said his vital signs had dropped down to about 45. I think the top number was about 45 over 40, something like that. And she checked his pulse, and she says this happens with older people. It's called free bleeding. She says, "Do not turn him over, just let him lay there. We know he's been going, so just let him rest comfortable."
>
> So that's what we did until he passed away, and the family was called and they came by to see him a couple of days

before he died, and then I was called when he passed away – well, when he – well, Carol called me that morning he was about to pass away, about 4:00, and I got up, put on my clothes, went over there and stood by his side and all, and then they took me on out of the room, because I was – I hated to see the man pass away. I'd been with him and his wife for quite a while. So I went on in the dining room and, when the undertaker came, and all, and they got him ready to go out the door, they said, "Ms. Jenkins, you'll have to sign him out of the house." I said, "Well you can get his power of attorney." I said, "The power of attorney could go ahead and do it," because it hurt me. And he says, "No, you're the only one that can sign him out of the house. You're the head caregiver here, licensed caregiver. You're a licensed caregiver, so you're the only one can let him go out." So I had to sign him out.[864]

This is where Maxwell would end his examination. It was an awfully long answer to the question about why he had three enemas right before he died. In her own words, she gave him the enemas "about three days before Dr. Smith *finally* died." I don't believe that the undertaker told Pat that she was "the only one" who could sign him out of the house. At that point, that was the least troublesome question about the case.

…..

When Hunter, the church's lawyer, cross examined, he led off with questions about her medications. He asked if her psychiatrist prescribed them, to which she replied, "Yes, sir." When Hunter tried to continue, she interrupted, "And my medical doctor, my medical doctor, and he." She testified that her medication came from both her psychiatrist and her medical doctor.[865]

Hunter moved on and asked her what Uncle Jimmy's relationship was like with the church, to which she testified, "…he liked his church…" She denied knowledge about why Betty Parker, a black caregiver, might have been left out of the will.[866] He asked her about a time that Dr. Bill Smith tried to visit. She testified that Bill called beforehand, but Uncle Jimmy told her to take him to Family Dollar. She continued to testify that she told Bill that he could not talk to Uncle Jimmy about business, he had to talk to his power of attorney.

274

She went on to testify that Bill's wife, Jodie [mistaking her name for Bill's mothers name], told her, "I'm the nurse. You ain't the nurse."[867] Pat continued to testify that she called 911. She testified that the police officer told her that if Bill said anything to her that she should not respond.[868]

Next Hunter asked about numerous 911 calls. She testified, "There were a lot of calls. Because of that, Little Jimmy said that – he took me in there and showed me. He said they called people out to try to fix it..."[869] She blamed the 911 calls on the house's alarm system. That is inconsistent with the police reports that indicate there were no calls prior to Little Jimmy's death. There were 8 calls made from November 29, 2002 to February 10, 2005. The nature of the incidents were listed as "Breaking and entering", "Property Damage", "Larceny", and "Domestic Disturbance" (See chapter 14). Pat's testimony was false, but the jury might not see through this.

Hunter asked her who helped Uncle Jimmy with grocery shopping before the Pridgens arrived. She testified she did, and at the time she was paid $13 per hour. He asked who was in the house when the will was signed. She testified that she was, but didn't speak with Uncle Jimmy, or anyone of the other caregivers, or anyone from the church about it.[870] She testified that there was no romantic involvement, and no relationship of care and affection between her and Uncle Jimmy. She called it a "professional, caring relationship."[871]

Hunter asked her if she had her license that day. Pat testified, "I sure do. They're with the state of North Carolina."[872] Hunter ended his cross examination there.

.....

Lonnie Williams asked her to reiterate how she cared for Uncle Jimmy's wife, Iris. He asked her if Uncle Jimmy liked the nursing home that Iris was in, and she testified that he did not. He asked her to reiterate that she was called by Little Jimmy to come back to work for Uncle Jimmy. He asked her to identify pictures of Uncle Jimmy having Christmas dinner with Little Jimmy.[873] Much of Pat's testimony is related to what she claimed dead men said.

.....

275

In Maxwell's redirect examination, he asked Pat why no family members were at Uncle Jimmy's Christmas party, when they had been together during previous Christmas celebrations. Pat testified that, "...they could, any time they wanted to."[874] This is starkly different than the family's belief that they were being isolated from Uncle Jimmy. Maxwell asked if it was a surprise that, after Iris' death, Uncle Jimmy chose to let her go, but retain Carol Tucker, Linda Phillips, and Betty Parker. She testified that it was not surprising, because Uncle Jimmy would save money.[875]

Maxwell asked Pat about her inviting her husband to go to Uncle Jimmy's house after Little Jimmy died. "Do you recall in your deposition you told us that you called your husband because you wanted a witness?"

Well – well, I just wanted somebody there, in case they told me I need to go home..." she testified.

"Why would you have been let go when Little Jimmy died, when it was Dr. Smith that you were caring for?" Maxwell asked.

"I never know."[876] Pat responded.

Maxwell asked her about previous testimony about Uncle Jimmy pointing to her and saying, "...arrest her, the woman in the white."

Pat testified, "I wasn't in the house, Mr. Maxwell."[877] Again, this must have been extremely frustrating to Maxwell, to hear testimony so different from the depositions.

Finally, Maxwell asked her if she ever heard any family member say that they planned to put Uncle Jimmy in a nursing home. "No, I did not ever hear them say that." Pat Jenkins testified. Maxwell ended his examination there.[878] What would the jury believe?

Testimony of
Carol Tucker

Carol Tucker testified that she had completed 11 weeks of training for her CNA certification.[879] She testified that she and Linda Phillips had worked together in the past, and that Linda is the one who called her to work for Iris and Jimmy.[880] She testified that she accepted tips and reimbursement for gas from Uncle Jimmy. These payments, she testified, were about $20-40 per week. She testified that on four different occasions he went to the bank with her and bought her $1000

276

in Family Dollar stock each time. She testified that "He wanted everybody to have Family Dollar stock." She testified that she no longer owned the stocks.[881]

Jim Maxwell asked her about a time that Uncle Jimmy helped her with her car. She testified that she was involved in an accident, and her car was totaled. She testified that the car she lost was a gift from her previous employer's family.[882] Maxwell had just made a new discovery: Uncle Jimmy was not the first employer she had accepted large gifts from. She testified that she made a $5,000 down payment on a new car and Uncle Jimmy gave her a check for $20,000 to pay it off. She testified, "We went to the bank, and Jack Richardson, he talked to him, and he gave me the check, and Jack told whoever the teller was to cash it for me, and I put it in the envelope and give it back to Dr. Smith. And when we got home, he said, 'Now, get me that bill," and I gave him the bill, and it was 13,000, maybe 483 something..." When asked if she actually paid off the car with that money, she testified, "I put it aside, because everything was such in an uproar I thought I was going to have to give it back."[883]

"Okay. [Little] Jimmy was still alive when that occurred, if it was March." Maxwell pointed out.

"Yes, and he knew about it." she testified.[884]

Maxwell asked her about taking Uncle Jimmy to the restaurant where her daughter worked. She testified that she drove him to Jacksonville, NC. She testified that he tipped her daughter $4,000 that day at her restaurant. Again, she testified that this was before Little Jimmy's death.[885]

Maxwell asked her about going to the farm with Uncle Jimmy. She testified that he would usually stand by the car or sit in the car and watch them pick vegetables. Maxwell asked her about the time she told the detective she thought Pat was going to get the farm from Uncle Jimmy. When asked why she told the detective that, she testified, "I don't know. It just come in my mind."[886]

Maxwell asked her how he felt when Billy and his family came to visit. Carol focused her answer, "Well, after he was mad at Billy, he didn't want him to come back..." She testified that Uncle Jimmy still talked to Billy's wife, Jodie. She testified about Billy's children, "Oh, he [Uncle Jimmy] loved those children."[887] About Sid and Ebie[38], she

---

[38] Ebie is misspelled Evie in the transcript.

277

testified that Uncle Jimmy reacted "so-so" to their visits. When asked about his grand-nieces Lisa and Erin, she testified, "He loved to see them because they were pretty." She testified that she never heard him say anything negative about any family member other than Billy.[888]

Maxwell asked about the large bank withdrawals. She testified that she would drive him to the bank on her work days, and she would hand a check that he wrote to the teller, then hand the envelope that would come back to him. She testified that when they would get back to his house he would put that money on the plate in a shelf in his kitchen.[889] It's amazing to me that the people working in that house knew that $9,000 a day was going onto that plate, but no one can agree on where it went from there.

She testified that Uncle Jimmy got mad at Billy when he gained his power of attorney. When asked if their relationship ever warmed up, she testified, "It seemed like one time he was kind of talkative to him."[890] When asked about a note in Jan Pridgen's records about Billy offering to spend Christmas Day with Uncle Jimmy so the caregivers could have the day off, Tucker testified that she didn't remember, and didn't take the day off.[891]

Carol Tucker testified that after Uncle Jimmy's appendectomy her hours changed from her four day a week shift, to living in the home 7 days a week, 24 hours per day. She testified that she kept a log of events when she was there, but when Pat, Wanda, and Alicia were also there, they maintained the log. On the day the will was signed, her note in the log mentions "Preacher Everette came by about an hour." She testified that she knew Reverend Jim Everette, and pointed to him in the courtroom.[892]

.....

Ms. Lisa Johnson-Tonkins cross examined on behalf of the church. Carol testified that there was a caring relationship between herself and Uncle Jimmy. She testified that she never discussed the will with Uncle Jimmy before it's execution. She reiterated that Uncle Jimmy loved "the Smith children." She testified that he also loved his church.[893] She testified that she went to church with him a few times when Pat couldn't. She testified that he was upset when his son's beach house passed to his nieces and nephews through his son's will.[894]

.....

278

Lonnie Williams cross examined next. Williams asked about three pages worth of questions about her service to Aunt Iris and her previous employer.[895] He asked her if Uncle Jimmy could walk up until the time of his appendectomy. She said he could. She testified that he quit driving about the time that his son died. She implied that she was glad he quit driving because he drove too fast. She testified about his tips to the waitresses at Hooters. Johnson-Tonkins asked if he liked to help the waitresses who were college students. Tucker testified, "He liked them because they were pretty, too."[896]

She testified that she didn't know she was a beneficiary in his will until after he died.[897] She testified that she didn't deny visitation, and only once informed Billy and Jodie that he was lying down and wasn't ready for visitors.[898] She testified that she would sometimes sit with Uncle Jimmy and his visitors, and sometimes she would use the time that visitors were with him to take care of other things around the house.[899]

She testified that Uncle Jimmy was not intimidated by her, or Pat, or any other caregivers.[900] She asked her a question about a conversation that she might have overheard between Uncle Jimmy and his son, and the Judge stopped the examination and excused the jury for a discussion.

.....

While the Jury was out, Lonnie Williams explained to the judge, "She would testify – if she had not been stopped, she would have testified, within two weeks of the death of Iris Smith, that she heard Little Jimmy talking to his father and telling him, you promised me my mother's money; that you should not make your checks for more than $9,000, because they raise a red flag; and that she had seen him, on a number of occasions – she had seen Dr. Smith give money to Little Jimmy. I think that's important information and, in view of the amount of information that's come in for the caveators about the $9,000 checks, that evidence is entirely proper and competent.

Maxwell offered, "No objection to the last part of that with what she saw. I do have objection to the first part. I mean, that's double hearsay from two deceased people." The judge agreed with Jim Maxwell.[901]

.....

279

In the absence of the jury, Lonnie Williams began a voir dire examination of Carol Tucker. She testified that Uncle Jimmy's son said, "Daddy, you promised me mother's money." She testified that he said, "Whenever you make them [checks] more than 9,000 the red flag goes up."[902] With that on the record for another day, the jury returned.

．．．．．

Williams continued, "Carol, did you ever have occasion to observe Dr. Smith give cash money to Little Jimmy?"

"Yes." She testified.

"On how many occasions, Carol, did you see him do that?"

"Over the time that – I don't know, two, three, four times…"[903] So $9,000 per day went to the plate almost every day, and on three or four days she saw some go to Little Jimmy. Even if that is true there is still a lot of money unaccounted for. I can't help thinking what a great scapegoat a man who died of a drug induced heart attack makes. Let's not forget that the withdrawals continued for weeks after his death, until Billy initiated efforts to stop that.

In Williams' final questions, Carol testified that she took him to functions at her Mormon church, and she identified herself in pictures with Uncle Jimmy at social events. Carol testified that she believed Uncle Jimmy thought more of Pat than the rest of his caregivers.[904]

．．．．．

In Maxwell's redirect examination, he asked about the car Carol Tucker's previous employer gave her. He noted that this occurred after she worked with them for 9 years and helped her with her finances. He asked her about a will that would leave her 10% of a large estate after only working there 18 months. She testified, "I don't know the figures." He asked her about instructions to call the Pridgens and notify them of visitors. She testified, "It wasn't my call… No. It was the other girls. Not me." She testified that she did call to inform them if Uncle Jimmy was leaving the house.

His last question referred to a note in their log that indicate Uncle Jimmy woke up at 7 pm getting ready for the start of the day, without realizing that the day was over. Carol testified that was true, and Maxwell ended there.[905]

Lisa Johnson-Tonkins asked two final questions. Carol testified that is isn't uncommon for elderly people to get their day and night mixed up because of their sleeping habits. She also asked her to testify that her note that "Preacher Everette came" was timed at 4:00.[906] This would indicate that Reverend Everette's visit was the day the will was signed, but after the fact.

With the caregiver's testimony on the record, Jim Maxwell moved on.

Testimony of
Larry Fowler

Larry Fowler testified that he farms 75-80 acres of land in the vicinity of Uncle Jimmy's Woodford farm in Columbus County, NC. He testified that his family's land neighbors the Woodford property. He has been in that area since 1965.[907]

When asked how long he has known the Smith Family, he testified, "Well, my family has knowed him for – great day, back 50, 60 years probably. I met him when I was just – I mean, I can go back as far as I can remember..." Larry described him as "part of the family."[908]

"I hunted the property all my life..." Larry testified. "... he [Uncle Jimmy] didn't have nobody to ... keep people from trespassing... I kind of took it over." Larry built and maintained gates on access roads to the property. He mowed about a mile of dirt roadways for Uncle Jimmy.[909]

Maxwell asked if he knew any of Uncle Jimmy's family. He listed some of his brothers, nephews and grand-nephews.[910] Larry knows this family better than any of the church leadership or caregivers.

Maxwell asked him about farming the land. He described the plot he rented from Uncle Jimmy every year, and how he would simultaneously plant Uncle Jimmy's garden for him. Larry testified that he had walked that land his whole life and knew it well. Maxwell asked him about the timber on the property before it was harvested. "It was mixed pine and hardwood. It had some real pretty pine." He testified.[911] Maxwell asked what he knew about clear cutting the land.

He testified, "Yeah. I didn't know about it until this guy named John Newton, who was the timber buyer for Squires Timber, and he came by and wanted me to show him some roads, and he wanted permission to use our road to haul timber out. He was a young whippersnapper. He was pretty excited about getting that timber. As a matter of fact, he told me, said, 'I haven't slept in three days.'"[912]

An objection was raised to that and sustained.

"He's going to be a witness..." Maxwell started, but dropped it there.

"... without telling us what Mr. Newton told you about it, what did you learn about the timber?" Maxwell continued.

Larry said that when he heard that the timber was going to be cut he went to Uncle Jimmy's house to try to stop it. As he began to describe his discussion with Uncle Jimmy, Lonnie Williams objected. When overruled, Williams asked and received "a continuing line of objections."

Larry testified that Uncle Jimmy told him that he got almost a million dollars for the timber. He asked Uncle Jimmy if he got an appraisal from anyone else. He testified that Uncle Jimmy said he got two appraisals. Larry testified that Uncle Jimmy said that he drove a tractor around the land to show the timber company representatives what they could and couldn't cut.

"Have you seen Dr. Smith on a tractor any time within the last two or three years before he made that statement?" Maxwell asked.

"No. I knew better. I knew when he made that statement, I knew right then, I said, there's no way he'd be on a tractor, driving around that farm in the kind of shape he was in. And, as a matter of fact, he hadn't been on a tractor since [Young] Jimmy died, because I've been right there, and the tractors ain't been moved. He wasn't on no tractor showing people where the timber was."[913]

Maxwell asked if Larry had experience selling timber. Larry testified, "We've sold timber, my family and adjoining properties... And that's what really got me upset, was the fact that the timber was so good that he had, it was the very best."

Williams objected again. Nobles overruled again.

Larry continued, "I went to him to see if anything could be done, because I knew what he was getting was not enough money."

Larry testified that Uncle Jimmy was very happy about the sale and he "didn't have the heart to tell him..."

282

Williams objected, and was overruled again. Larry testified that he told other people he knew in the First Baptist Church about what was happening, "And Otto sent word back for me to mind my own business. I never said nothing more about it. I figured nothing more could be done."[914]

Maxwell asked if he continued to hunt and farm the land. Larry mentioned that he heard that pine was going to be replanted on the land where it was clear cut, and the plowed fields. This would prevent Larry Fowler from farming the acreage he had in the past. He went to ask Uncle Jimmy if he wanted to keep renting him the land. He testified that Uncle Jimmy said, "Yeah." Larry testified that he paid him then and there.

Maxwell showed him exhibit 433, and sked if he could identify it. "That's the check I gave Dr. Smith." Larry testified. "... it won't but just a few days after that, Pridgen contacted me and told me that I wasn't to have no more business dealings with Dr. Smith..." He went on, "...He said Dr. Smith wasn't capable of conducting business... that everything was to be done through him [Otto Pridgen], from now on."[915]

Larry testified that Uncle Jimmy gave him a tractor. (There was a note in Otto Pridgen's billing records: "Call from Pat. Dr. Smith said that he wanted to leave the tractor to Larry Fowler")[916]. When Uncle Jimmy died, he testified, "... Ms. Pridgen, she made several phone calls to the house, telling me they wanted the tractor back, and one time she called me and told me that if I didn't carry that tractor back down there, she was going to call the sheriff. Well, I'd had enough of it, her continually calling me – and I believe that's Mr. Williams there. I received a letter from him, too, saying it's unfortunate I don't have something in writing about that tractor, and that I needed to turn it over." Larry contacted a lawyer to handle that issue for him. Maxwell ended there.[917]

.....

Bob Hunter cross examined on behalf of the church. Some propounders claim that Uncle Jimmy became angry at the family when they started talking about what they were going to do with the farm after his death. Larry Fowler testified that he never heard anything like that. "They hope it stayed in the family for years to come, and he said,

'I hope we're neighbors for years to come.'"[918] Maybe Hunter saw a dead end. He stopped questioning there.

.....

Williams began on the defensive, "Mr. Fowler, you claim that you got a letter from me. I'll ask you to rethink your thoughts, and I'll ask you if Mr. Williamson did not write to O.K. Pridgen when he – when you got him into the case and I responded to Mr. Williamson's letter. I never wrote you before you got Mr. Williamson in the case, isn't that true?"

"I believe I got a letter from you." Fowler answered.

Williams asked if he had a letter. Larry didn't have it with him in court. Williams asked if he had given the letter to Maxwell in the year leading up to the case. Larry testified, "No. As a matter of fact, they're the ones that brought it up, that they knew it was in the will for me to have the tractor. I never told them. They already knew..."[919] The family's knowledge of Uncle Jimmy's desire to give the tractor to Larry came from the Pridgen billing records.

After his self-defense, Williams asked, "Now, the sale of timber, Mr. Fowler, wasn't this timber well past the maturity when it should have been harvested?"

Larry testified, "Well, you don't know much about timber, neither, I can tell." Larry went on that the timber went to Clinton, Keener lumber. "... they buy nothing but the very, very best."[920]

Lonnie Williams asked if Larry believed Uncle Jimmy was mentally competent to give him the tractor at that time. "Well, he told me I could have it, and I took it." He testified. Larry did not believe that he was incompetent at that time.[921] It's interesting to me that the propounders tried to reclaim the tractor as though it wasn't Uncle Jimmy's wish to give it to Larry Fowler, then use the gift as evidence of his competence in court.

Lonnie Williams discussed the hunting on the land with Larry Fowler, then asked if he felt Uncle Jimmy was competent to accept the check he gave him to farm the property. Larry testified that he was probably not incompetent at that time.[922] Williams ended there. This would defend the will against lack of competence, but the family's primary claim was undue influence, not incapacity.

284

Testimony of
Margaret Banck

Margaret Banck testified that she lived in Wilmington her whole 88-year life, except when she was away for school, and had known the Smith family ever since she met Uncle Jimmy's sister Octavia in 1938.[923] Maxwell asked her about her knowledge of the family. "Well, a great family, every one of them..." she testified, "... going back to when Iris was at Racine Drive, I went out to see her that day, and Dr. Queen came in and she introduced me, and she said, "Margaret's a Lutheran' and, being Swedish, she had been Lutheran. She said, 'Once a Lutheran, always a Lutheran.'..." She went on about her close relationship with Uncle Jimmy's family, including their son.[924] Margaret Banck testified that she knew Linda Phillips. And that she believed she was a capable caregiver.[925]

She testified about some trouble she had visiting Uncle Jimmy, "After Little Jimmy died, I went over there and paid my respects, and then I went back the next day and took a cake, and then I went back in the kitchen... and I sat back there with him and was talking to him when, all of a sudden, this young woman came running in the room and jumped in his lap and, of course, that was a little shocking to me. But right afterwards, this other person came in, and she said, 'glad to see you again.' I did not recognize her, and she said, 'This is my daughter, but it's Jimmy's adopted daughter.' When I got to the door, I asked Linda, I said, 'Who are those people?' She said, 'Pat Jenkins and her daughter.'"[926]

Margaret said that she asked Linda Phillips, "Why did you leave the Smiths?" She testified that Linda said, "I didn't like what was going on."[927]

.....

Lisa Johnson-Tonkins only asked Margaret Banck if Linda had a reputation for truth and veracity. Margaret testified, "Yes, I thought so."[928]

.....

285

Lonnie Williams began, and noted that he and Ms. Banck has known each other for a long time. Margaret concurred.[929] She testified that Uncle Jimmy was not offended by the young woman jumping in his lap. She said that she was the one that was offended.[930] Lonnie Williams asked, "In fact, when you and I chatted about this back on the 25th of July of last year, you said you were horrified that she would sit in his lap and hug his neck, horrified."

"Well, I was." She testified, "I mean it's just not the conduct that I'm used to seeing people … behave."

"I quite understand that you were not used to that." Williams injected. Ms. Banck never married. I wonder if this was a personal jab at her from Lonnie Williams, who knew her personally.

"Did you tell them you asked me to be on your side, too?" The witness asked of her interviewer.

"No, ma'am, I didn't ask you to be on anybody's side." Lonnie Williams was on the defensive again. "You quickly told me, as soon as we got on the phone, that you were on the Smith's side. Isn't that right?"

Margaret answered, "You said the Smith family didn't get along, and I said that they did."

"They didn't argue with each other, the Smith family didn't ever argue with each other?" Williams asked.

"I wasn't there if they did." She testified.[931]

Later Williams asked, "And Ms. Banck, I don't mean to be ugly or rude to you, but isn't a lot of your time spent playing bridge with other women and gossiping about everything in the world that comes up?"

"I'm going to object." Maxwell interrupted.

Margaret Banck began, "I play one –"

"Sustained." Judge Nobles ordered.

"—afternoon once every two weeks."[932] This odd question from Williams might have been an attempt to cast her as a gossip, to assassinate her character. Banck testified that she believed that Uncle Jimmy was intelligent. When asked if she thought he was competent, she testified, "Well, I couldn't tell you that, because I don't know how men act when women jump in their laps."

"I guess not. Thank you. I don't have any other questions, Ms. Banck." The bickering ended there.

286

Testimony of
Wanda Day

Wanda day started working for Uncle Jimmy after Otto Pridgen had taken over his power of attorney.[933] Wanda Day testified that she was a CNA I, and recently trained for her CNA II certification. She testified that she was employed full time for the past 12 years. She testified that she was hired to help Uncle Jimmy because his walking was slow, and he was hard of hearing, among other things. Maxwell asked her who she would report to in Uncle Jimmy's house. She testified, "Pat Jenkins." When asked how she knew that Wanda testified, "She made it clear, tell her everything that's going on..."[934] It's interesting to me that she wasn't told by Uncle Jimmy that Pat was in charge.

Maxwell asked her what the Pridgen's role was in the house. "The power of attorney" she testified. "Pat did mostly all the talking to them."[935]

What, if anything, did Ms. Jenkins tell you when you began working there about contact with Mister – Dr. Smith and his family?" Maxwell asked.

"For me not – she didn't want them to come in the house and, if they come, for me to be there, me and Carol. She would get upset if, you know, if things didn't go her way, basically. Ms. Day went on to testify that Pat wanted her to call whenever family was in the house. She testified that she would report to Pat, who would ask what they were talking about. "I mean Dr. Smith wasn't upset. They just was seeing how he was doing. That's the impression that I got."

Maxwell asked, "Did she ever ask you to do more than just simply report to her about what was going on?"

Wanda Day testified, "Well, she had that tape recorder at one point, because she was taping us... When I first started, we found the tape recorder and where she was taping us, and also noted that, if they come over, to tape their conversations..."[936]

Maxwell asked her if she ever heard the topic of a nursing home For Uncle Jimmy brought up. "From Pat" she testified. "She said, 'Only thing they want to do, Wanda, is put him in a nursing home, put him in a nursing home and take his money." She went on to testify that she witnessed Pat say that to Uncle Jimmy as well. When asked what Uncle Jimmy's reaction to this would be, she testified, "... he would like – you know, just give you a look. Wouldn't say nothing, wouldn't respond, or anything, because he had a voice box, but she would often say it."[937]

Maxwell asked her what Uncle Jimmy's relationship was like with Pat. "She [Pat] was good to him, you know, treated him real good." She testified, "Just demanding about – just controlling over him, you know. Would get upset about the least little things." She went on, "Certain times, she would say, 'Dr. Smith, you know, you'll just die if I leave here, you'll just die.'"[938]

Maxwell asked if she ever heard anyone discussing why Billy's power of attorney was revoked. Ms. Day testified that Carol Tucker and Pat Jenkins would say things like "... Billy wanted to put him in a nursing home. He put his name on the checkbook (a power of attorney might give authority to sign checks, but Billy's name was never put on any of Uncle Jimmy's accounts). Dr. Smith got upset and wanted to get rid of Billy for that reason, and we cannot let Billy in the house because he wants to get rid of all of us, all the CNAs, including you, too, Wanda." Wanda continued, "And I was like, I don't even know him. I didn't know him at that time."[939]

"Okay. And what was your impression of how he reacted when his family came to see him?" Maxwell asked.

"He was happy to see them, especially when the baby – the babies would come by, he was happy to see them. Billy, Jodie, it wasn't no animosity or no, you know, hostility. Just a family visit. That's what I took it."[940] It's interesting how different her testimony is than the other caregivers. It's also interesting to note that the caregivers who speak unkindly of Billy and his family stood to gain about a half-million dollars from the estate. Wanda day wouldn't get a penny from the estate, no matter which way the verdict fell.

Maxwell asked if Uncle Jimmy ever offered her tips. Wanda testified that she was involved in an auto accident, "... and he thought I didn't have transportation and he was like, Wanda, I got to get you a car. And I was like, no, Dr. Smith, I got it. It wasn't my fault, and I got insurance."[941] I wonder if Carol Tucker made an insurance claim on her car. I see this as evidence that Uncle Jimmy treated his nurses with equality, no matter what the color of their skin. Carol is white,

Wanda is black. He offered cars to both. Why were only white caregivers mentioned in the will?

Maxwell asked Wanda Day to describe the dispute between Dr. Bill Smith, his wife, and Pat Jenkins. "It was already going on once I got there..." She testified. "I just seen police cars. I was like, what I got myself into? Because I didn't know what was going on. And when I got in, the police officer was just saying he was just tired of coming here because that lady out there keeps calling him and they're sick and tired of coming out here. She's crazy. That's what the police officer said."[942]

Maxwell asked her if family members ever treated her with anything other than respect. "No. Always treated me nice." She testified. Maxwell asked her if he enjoyed going to his country club. "Yes" she testified. When asked why he stopped going, Wanda answered, "Pat said something about he left a tip, and that's all they want, to waste his money, and he's not going back anymore." Maxwell asked if she knew Linda Phillips. "No. she was already gone" she testified. "Only thing I got from that, Pat was like, we had to get rid of her."

An objection to that testimony from Williams was sustained. An off the record bench conference was held, and the direct examination continued. Ms. Day continued, "She [Pat] told me that Linda was employed with Dr. Smith and he wrote her a check, and we had to get rid of her. She claimed she didn't like her, anyway, but I didn't know anything about it. So she said they got rid of her..."[943]

Maxwell asked her about her relationship with Pat Jenkins. "It was hard, it really was." Ms. Day testified. "Not knowing whether you were going to come to work and not knowing just what to expect. Chaotic, sometimes. I mean, just not knowing. And, like I said, the least little thing would tick her off. If you don't agree with her, that's just it. I tried to be a sociable coworker and just try to give her a report and just let that be..."

She described Carol Tucker as "real nice, like scared to say the wrong thing, because she knew they wanted to get rid of her, too. Pat told me that also..."

When Maxwell asked about her relationship with Uncle Jimmy, she testified, "Oh, that was no problem. That was the best part of the job, taking care of Dr. Smith..."[944]

289

Maxwell asked her if she was there the last couple of days before Uncle Jimmy died. She testified, "Yes. That Saturday, I worked a double. I went in at 3:00 and got off at 8:00 Sunday morning, and I had to come back at 3:00 Sunday afternoon... When I came back that Sunday, Carol – and the look on her face, I was like, what? She couldn't say anything. So when I went in the room, Pat was giving him enemas, and it was already two empty ones on the bed. She was giving him a third one. I was listening. 'He's impacted Wanda. He's impacted.' And she started going up his rectum... I was like, he hadn't been eating that much to have three enemas, you know. A normal person doesn't even get three enemas, so I couldn't understand. And after that, it was just downhill. It was – I never seen that much blood in my life, just to come out of somebody. It just was running. It was running out, running out."[945]

Maxwell asked what Pat said about the enemas. "That's all." Wanda Day testified. "She was like, he's impacted, he's impacted, it needs to be taken out. But I know there's different ways you can go about it. As far as with Maxim, we could give enemas, a CNA I could give enemas. First of all, you got to have an order from the physician. Evan an RN can't give an enema, unless they have an order from a physician..."

Maxwell asked if she reported the blood to Maxim, and if such a report would be part of her routine. "Yes, it was, but she told me not to say anything. Pat told me not to say anything... But Monday morning when I went to the job, I told them, because it was so much blood to the point where my RN told me, don't move him, just don't move him anymore, because it was nothing else." She testified that Uncle Jimmy died shortly after that.[946] Maxwell ended there.

.....

Lisa Johnson-Tonkins cross examined first. She asked when she was employed full time. Johnson-Tonkins suggested that it would have been approximately October, of 2002, having worked part time for approximately three months before that. Day testified, "Yeah, sometime."[947] This would place her part time employment around the time that the will was being drafted and signed. She testified that he was very independent early in her service to him.[948]

Johnson-Tonkins asked if it would be acceptable practice in her industry to express thanks by giving a gratuity. "No" she testified. "We're not supposed to – well, I work for an agency, so we're not supposed to accept, you know.[949] She testified that she was away from work for two weeks after her second car accident, neither of which were her fault. She said that he offered her a car after that because he thought she wasn't coming back to work because she didn't have transportation. She said she did accept candy as a gift from Uncle Jimmy.[950]

She testified that he loved his church. Johnson-Tonkins asked a few more questions about his sleeping habits and visitation and ended her cross examination.[951]

…..

Lonnie Williams started by asking about the frequency of her work visits before she was hired part time. She testified that she worked about once a week, then shifted to a regular shift in October. She testified that Uncle Jimmy was nice, that he read a lot, and appeared to be intelligent.[952]

Williams asked, "Now, Wanda, you were present at the Smith house one day on 12/2 of '02 on shift, and at 4:50 that day, you called Jan Pridgen, did you not, and told her … 'Billy is at the house with Dr. Smith, saying that Pat had to be fired. She's rude to us. Dr. Smith said she is not going anywhere.' Didn't you call and report that…"

"… Pat was rude to Billy… But I don't remember that call." She testified.[953]

Williams asked, "Were you aware that Dr. Smith was not happy with the fact that the Smiths, Smith family, got his beach house when young Jimmy died, rather than it coming back to him?"

"Was I? No, I wasn't. They told me later on."

"Who told you?" Williams asked. "Alicia told you, Didn't she?"

"That Pat told her because Pat would tell Alicia things and Pat would tell me things" she testified.

Williams' fellow propounder, Bob Hunter, objected to that. There is no response from the Judge in the court transcript.[954]

Williams asked questions regarding the conversation she and Alicia had with Billy and his son Bill after the will was probated. "Wanda, you have a strong dislike for Pat Jenkins, don't you?" he pried.

"Not really." She testified. "She just – I just didn't like the way she was treating me and the other coworkers. I mean –"

291

"Excuse me, I'm sorry. I thought you had finished. Anything else?" Williams interrupted.

Ms. Day continued, "She used to talk down to Carol... She used to talk about O.K. and Jan. I mean, she used to often say, 'I'm sick and tired of doing that B's dirty work.' I didn't never know what she meant about dirty work, because I didn't ask her... I don't like how she treated Dr. Smith's family, you know, because it was – to me, it wasn't normal. I never been in that situation."[955]

Williams asked if Uncle Jimmy liked Pat, and if the affection between them was obvious. "Yes, he did... Mm-hmm. She didn't want anyone around Dr. Smith, the church... The church, the pastor, she used to often say about the pastor."[956]

Williams asked if she would be surprised that there were 58 visits from the Smith family from the time that Little Jimmy died to the time that Uncle Jimmy died. "No"[957] she testified. I'll note here that Ms. Day testified that Pat wanted to keep them out, not that Pat always succeeded in doing so.

Williams asked her if she ever heard a playback of the tapes Pat Jenkins made. She testified, "You couldn't hardly hear what the people were saying, but you can hear, like, little things. It was real low the way she had it."

"You couldn't understand anything? Williams interrupted.

"Let her finish. Let her finish. Go ahead." Judge Nobles ordered.

Wanda Day continued, "You couldn't really understand because the way she had it hid. It was just like you could hear TV going and, like people talking and stuff, but you couldn't really understand what was actually said."[958]

She mentioned the church earlier in her testimony, and Williams asked, "Do you say that Pat turned Dr. Smith against the First Baptist Church?"

"No, I didn't say she turned him against the First Baptist Church. She just didn't like – she was thinking they wanted his money, too, they just want his money, the pastor just want his money."[959]

Williams asked her if she ever made a note in her log about Pat's behavior. She testified that she did not, but she asked Maxim to find her other employment. When asked why she didn't make a log entry, Day testified, "... She took very good care of Dr. Smith. I don't have no complaint about her taking care of Dr. Smith, because she did."[960] I think that Wanda Day's concern was for his mind, not his body, right up to the point of the enemas.

Williams asked her about the enemas. She reiterated that she felt Pat should have contacted a doctor before giving enemas, and that she can't see a reason to give three.[961] As Williams wrapped up his questioning, she testified that she never saw Carol or the church do anything wrong. She testified that she didn't think he had Alzheimer's.[962] Williams ended there.

......

Maxwell asked her to reiterate that it is her health care agency's policy (Maxim) to prohibit caregivers from accepting tips. She did.[963]

......

Johnson-Tonkins asked Ms. Day if she believed Carol Tucker was influenced by Pat. "Was she influenced?" Day began. "She was scared. Carol used to cry all the time. Cry. Scared she was going to lose her job, scared if she say the wrong thing, scared to eat. Johnson-Tonkins asked if Uncle Jimmy was scared of members of the church who visited. "No" she testified.[964] Johnson would further widen the gap between her client, the church, and the other propounders.

......

After that day's testimony, the propounders offered a settlement.

293

29. The Aftermath

Put yourself in Billy Smith's shoes. There were still a lot of witnesses that would add more to the family's case. Putting Reverend Jim Everette on the stand, and questioning him about his handwritten notes, would reveal to the jury how deeply he was involved in Uncle Jimmy's affairs, so the church's involvement could be revealed to the jury. However, convincing a jury that a church has done something wrong might be easier said than done. Then there was Linda Phillips, who was mostly out of the picture when the will was signed. She was Lonnie William's golden ticket. If Billy fought to the last, she might walk away with everything. Billy had a heavy decision to make. He accepted the offer.

The parties signed an agreement not to discuss the terms of the settlement. You don't need to know the terms of the settlement to discover that only the farmhouse and approximately 20 acres around it were titled to the family. Why the church held on so tightly to the farmland is beyond me. If you want to know, ask Carlton Fisher. I suspect he knows. He was Chairman of Trustees of the First Baptist Church at the time. He is a realtor, and helped the church with the purchase of the New Hanover County Law Enforcement Center.[965]

Reverend James E. Everette wrote about the settlement in his book:

> Extended family members of Dr. Smith challenged his will by filing a caveat contesting its validity on the grounds that Dr. Smith was incapable of executing a will at age ninety-seven because he was not of sound mind.[39] However, in April of 2006, after weeks of testimony from dozens of witnesses in a court of law, an agreement was made between First Baptist Church, family members of Dr. Smith and care givers of the elderly dentist. The portion of Dr. Smith's estate that was realized by the church was in excess of four million dollars after all property was sold and liquidated into cash. This is the largest gift ever made to First Baptist Church. The majority of the

---

[39] Uncle Jimmy was actually 95 at the time he signed the will and the family's primary claim about the will was that it was procured by undue influence, not because Uncle Jimmy lacked competency.

assets the church received from the estate were used toward the expansion and renovation of the Activities Center.[966]

Every time I drive past the First Baptist Church Activities Center on Independence Blvd., I can't help thinking that it was funded by Uncle Jimmy's lack of independence. Now that you know more facts in this case, does this sound like a friendly settlement, or does it sound more like a powerful church bullied the family? Reverend Everette's book missed the mark. The local newspaper didn't do much better.

In the Wilmington Star News on April 25th, 2006, Ken Little wrote, "...Lawyers for Smith's family failed to meet their burden of proof..."[967] Given that the trial ended with a settlement, not a jury or judge's decision, Little's words seem ill informed. Where did Ken Little get that impression? In that same article Little wrote, "Lonnie Williams and Charles Meier represented the caregivers, who each received 10 percent of Smith's estate after taxes. 'The court entered an order and the case is dismissed. The will of James H. Smith is upheld in its entirety,' Meier said."[968] As you can see, relevant facts were left out of the public view.

…..

Jim Maxwell and the other attorneys returned to court on May 9, 2006, for an "on the record hearing" on the issue of awarding costs and fees.[969] Billy and Jodie Smith took some notes at that hearing, and among his notes they included:

> ...On the subject of OKP, Jim [Maxwell] said that he is not stupid, but just acts that way. Bob Hunter, First Baptist Church, described OKP as a "conniving crook." The judge said, "Jan Pridgen was behind everything." [Judge Nobles never got to see Jim Everette's deposition].

> Jim [Maxwell] met with the State Bar to file a case against OKP. When he went, there was already a file open on this case, which means that someone else had already filed against OKP based on our case...

The settlement was between the caregivers and the FBC and between the church and the family. Lonnie Williams wants to say he never gave the Smith's anything. (I still do not understand why the attitude toward the family has continued to be so mean.)...

Judge Nobles was concerned that we would be able to knock out the women and gain nothing for the family. If we had "knocked out" the women, the church would have gotten everything. The feeling was that FBC would have thanked us, period. Judge Nobles also said he had never tried a case so interesting. Some of his favorite parts, in no particular order, were: Wanda Day, the best witness; Bill Smith, who put a face on the family and demonstrated that the family was motivated, not by greed, but by a genuine concern for UJ's welfare; Margaret Banck, the most fun witness; and the exhibits that Jim Maxwell presented that Lonnie provided, and Lonnie almost objected to...

On a lighter note Bob Hunter said that [paraphrased] Jim Maxwell had probably had his greatest day in court when he had a black (Wanda Day), a society white (Margaret Banck), and a country redneck (Larry Fowler) all testifying for him and agreeing on their positions...

In a world so full of racial and ethnic tension, and a case that was filthy with it, the family found great comfort in the support of people like Wanda, Margaret, and Larry.

The hearing for awarding costs and fees brought more good news for the family. Trial costs were extensive. All the fees and much of the costs were paid out of the estate in addition to the settlement. Jim Maxwell asked for about $312,000 in fees to be paid out of the estate, and $43,000 in costs. Hunter and Johnson-Tonkins asked for about $110,000 in fees and $8,000 in costs. Williams and Meier asked for more than either of the other law firms. Their request for approximately $396,000 in costs and fees is interesting to me because of Maxwell's recollection from an early hearing in front of Judge Alford that Meier came to the hearing with no brief or notes except what he prepared as he sat in court waiting for the hearing to start, and where Lonnie Williams indicated that he did not know if he wanted to take any depositions. Per Maxwell's notes Williams stated that it was his preferred practice to not give witnesses an opportunity to "rehearse" their testimony, but to catch them "cold" in his examination at trial." (See chapter 19).

.....

In July of 2006, Billy Smith received a letter from the church letting him know that they received "a special gift" from Janice Pridgen, Carol Tucker, Patricia Jenkins, and Linda Phillips. [970] This was excruciatingly insulting to the family. After hearing testimony that Pat Jenkins gave Uncle Jimmy those enemas with Carol Tucker watching, and the Pridgens making notes in their billing records, the family believed that the church was trying to pass off a courtroom settlement as a charitable gift. Would you expect the family to just sit back and say, "Well, okay. We're all friends now."?

The drama didn't end there. Billy was the point-man for a home-owners association in which he owned property. The HOA hired a home inspector to evaluate the property, and Billy called him to meet and explain his report one day. When the inspector arrived, Billy recognized him as Gene McIntyre, a church member who had signed an affidavit against the family's case. Billy recalled his affidavit in a letter he wrote to Jim Maxwell before the trial:

> In his affidavit Gene McIntyre says 'His family members would not come in the room to join us' (for communion). This is the real story: McIntyre and George Nicklen arrived while Jodie and I were there. We greeted them, etc. Gene said they were there to give Dr. Smith communion. He had a small wooden tray or box with a lid on it. He took the lid off the box and there were four little glasses filled with communion grape juice. It was obvious that there was not enough to go around, so Jodie and I did the polite thing and remained in the kitchen while McIntyre, Nicklen and Pat Jenkins went into the den to have communion with Dr. Smith.
>
> It makes my blood boil to know the FIRST Baptist Church has stooped so low as to do such as this.
>
> It is also interesting that all these affidavits are basically the same except for a few words. [971]

In his personal notes, Billy described that meeting with the home inspector Gene McIntyre:

> ...After we went over the inspection I asked him if he was the GM [Gene McIntyre] that was a deacon at FBC. He flashed a big smile and said, "yes, are you a member at First Baptist?" I knew then that he did not recognize me, and later realized that he had little recollection of the Communion Sunday at UJ's house. My reply to him was, "No, I am not a member at FBC. I am Dr. Jimmy Smith's nephew." He then acted somewhat confused, but I think it was coming back to him. I said that I wanted to talk to him about the time he served communion to UJ and told UJ that I refused to participate. He said that he served communion to so many shut-ins that he couldn't remember the particular occasion... I reminded him that he had put it in the form of an affidavit, and reminded him that an affidavit is a sworn statement... He began to get nervous. He then said that he did not recall writing an affidavit... I told him that if he signed something that someone else had written for him, then his church had made a fool of him. He then became apologetic and said he was a Christian and would not hurt others. As we parted he offered a very sincere apology...[972]

For every person who treated the family badly during this case, there are dozens who offered their support. Local lawyers, who knew how difficult it was to get dragged through the mud congratulated Billy for standing up to them. Many people offered kind words during and after the trial. I've heard that there were some people inside the church who were trying to fight unethical behavior from the inside. These true friends make Wilmington a great place to live for Billy and the rest of our family. The rest can't take anything away from the family that we really need.

.....

To the NC Bar Association: The Bar's reputation will not be diminished if an attorney lies under oath, or lets a client lie under oath, or willfully evades taxes, as the evidence reported in this book suggests has happened. Only those individuals' reputations will be diminished.

But if the Bar fails to police itself, no one will respect any of you. In the words of Jim Maxwell, "A deaf, dumb and blind man with a 5th grade education, standing on a street corner in downtown Wilmington would have been suspicious of the circumstances leading up to and surrounding the making of this will." Yet you have not sanctioned anyone involved.

.....

To families facing similar tragedies: The best advice I can offer to you is this: Tell them you love them, every chance you get, in every way you can. Telephone them, text them, e-mail them, write them letters, and above all, visit them every chance you get. Know who is caring for them when you are away and try to ensure proper oversight. If you suspect abuse, seek council from true experts in the field of elder abuse. It is difficult to imagine these things happening when you are on the outside, so it is just as important to listen to others. If you hear about abuse in your community, take it seriously. Stand up for justice, and report crimes you suspect have been committed.

30. Thank You

After the trial Billy Smith wanted to offer some "thanks" to some people who truly deserved it. He was acutely aware that jurors spent two weeks of their lives listening to testimony. He asked Jim Maxwell if it would be appropriate to thank them for their service. Maxwell's paralegal forwarded Maxwell's advice, that it would be fine, but it would be unusual.[973] Billy felt awkward about it, and never sent his letter, but I'll extend a "thank you" on his behalf here:

To these jurors, and all who place human dignity ahead of personal consequences:

Thank you, and God bless you.

And last: Thank you, to my dad, Billy Smith; Who fought the good fight, who kept the faith, who finished the course...
-2 Timothy, 4:7

Preface

[1] National Research Council. (2003). Elder Mistreatment. *Abuse, Neglect, and Exploitation in an Aging America. Panel to Review Risk and Prevalence of Elder Abuse and Neglect.* Bonnie, R.J., and Wallace, R.B., Editors. Committee on National Statistics and Committee on Law and Justice, Division of Behavioral And social sciences and Education. Washington, D.C.: The National Academies Press, 9-10

[2] Cassidy, Thomas M. (Former Senor Special Investigator, NY State Attorney General's Office*).* *Elder Care. What to Look for, What to Look Out For!* Third Edition, Revised and updated. Far Hills, NJ, New Horizon Press, 2008, 2.

Main Body

[1] Transcript of the trial testimony of Wanda Day, In the General Court of Justice, Superior Court Division, 05 E 213, In the matter of the Will of James Henry Smith, Deceased. Reported by Katie K. Thomas, Official Court Reporter. April 10, 2006, 17-18.

[2] Polygraph examination of William T. Smith, Conducted By- Andrew Goldstein, LCPE, Forensic Polygraph Examiner, NC License #370-P, SC License #084, 10/6/2017.

[3] State of North Carolina, S.S. Warrantee Deed, September 15, 1942, Transferring property from W.T. Smith and wife Emma U. Smith, to James H. Smith.

[4] History.com, *Pope Urban II Orders First Crusade.* 2009. http://www.history.com/this-day-in-history/pope-urban-ii-orders-first-crusade Accessed June 27, 2017.

[5] History.com, *The Reformation.* 2009. http://www.history.com/topics/reformation Accessed June 27, 2017.

[6] Reformation500.csl.edu, *Pope Paul III.* http://reformation500.csl.edu/bio/paul-iii/ Accessed June 27, 2017.

[7] History.com, *Galileo Galilei.* 2010. http://www.history.com/topics/galileo-galilei Accessed June 27, 2017.

[8] Krieg, Robert A. Americanmagazine.org, *The Vatican Concordat with Hitler's Reich: The Concordat of 1933 was ambiguous in its day and remains so.* September 1, 2003. https://www.americamagazine.org/faith/2003/09/01/vatican-concordat-hitlers-reich-concordat-1933-was-ambiguous-its-day-and-remains Accessed June 27, 2017.

[9] USAToday30.usatoday.com, *Stephen Hawking Says Pope Told Him Not to Study Beginning of Universe.* June 15, 2006. USA Today http://usatoday30.usatoday.com/life/people/2006-06-15-hawking_x.htm Accessed June 27, 2017.

[10] Childres, Sarah, *What's the State of the Church's Child Abuse Crisis?* February 25, 2014 http://www.pbs.org/wgbh/frontline/article/whats-the-state-of-the-churchs-child-abuse-crisis/ Accessed June 27, 2017.

[11] Justice.gov, *Report to the Deputy Attorney General on the Events at Waco, Texas,* October 8, 1993. https://www.justice.gov/publications/waco/report-deputy-attorney-general-events-waco-texas Accessed June 27, 2017.

301

[12] Dailymail.co.uk, *Woman Who Was Forced to Marry an Elderly FLDS Leader When She Was Only 10 Speaks Out About Her Harrowing Escape from the Cult and the Decision to Testify Against her Stepson Warren Jeffs.* September 19, 2013, http://www.dailymail.co.uk/news/article-2424808/Rebecca-Musser-speaks-forced-marriage-Rulon-Jeffs.html Accessed June 27, 2017.

[13] Burke, Daniel, 380 Southern Baptist leaders and volunteers accused of sexual misconduct. https://www.cnn.com/2019/02/11/us/southern-baptist-abuse/index.html Updated February 11, 2019, Accessed February 18, 2019.

[14] Everette, James E. III, *A Heritage of Hope, A History of First Baptist Church, Wilmington, North Carolina, 1808-2008.* Nashville, TN, Fields Publishing, Inc. 2008. 183

[15] Ibid. 183-184

[16] Ibid.

[17] Digitalcollections.uncw.edu, UNCW Archives and Special Collections, Living history, Interview with Otto Pridgen, October 25, 2002, Interviewer: Hayes, Sherman, and Haas, Michael, 3. http://digitalcollections.uncw.edu/cdm/singleitem/collection/oralhistory/id/525/rec/11

[18] Ibid.

[19] Ibid, 4.

[20] Ibid, 6.

[21] Ibid, 10.

[22] Ibid, 8.

[23] Ibid, 8-9.

[24] Ibid, 7.

[25] Ibid, 5.

[26] Dobson, Helen E. *Our Living Strength*, Wilmington Printing Company, Wilmington, NC, 1958, Revised 1983, 14.

[27] Ibid 14.

[28] Ibid 14.

[29] Ibid 15.

[30] Ibid 15-16.

[31] Ibid 17.

[32] Ibid 11.

[33] Ibid 11.

[34] Ibid 18.

[35] Ibid 22.

[36] Ibid 23-24.

[37] Ibid 25.

[38] Ibid 25.

[39] Ibid 30.

[40] Ibid 40-41.

[41] Everette 9.

[42] Ibid 12.

[43] Ibid 10-11.

[44] History.ncdcr.gov *1898 Wilmington Race Riot Report*, May 31, 2006. http://www.history.ncdcr.gov/1898-wrrc/ Accessed June 27, 2017.

[45] Everette 97.
[46] Ibid 100.
[47] Ibid 100.
[48] Ibid 100-101.
[49] Ibid 145.
[50] Ibid 147.
[51] Ibid 145.
[52] Ibid 202-203.
[53] Ibid 148.
[54] Ibid 150.
[55] Ibid 151.
[56] Ibid 193.
[57] Ibid 193.
[58] Ibid 192.
[59] Ransbottom, Bernie, "'Bold Statement' to finally be heard..." Wilmington Star News, Aug. 5, 1979, p 1B.
[60] Talton, Trista, "Old jail could house homeless" Wilmington Star News, Aug 10, 2003, p 1B.
[61] Riesz, Charles W. Editorial page editor, "Sell it to the Marines" Wilmington Star News, May 23, 2003, p 8A.
[62] Talton, Trista, "Area developer plans to bid on old jail building" Wilmington Star News, Aug. 28, 2003, p 1A.
[63] Talton, Trista, "First Baptist makes offer on center" Wilmington Star News, Aug. 15, 2003, p 1A.
[64] Talton, Trista, "Old jail could house homeless" Wilmington Star News, Aug 10, 2003, p 1B.
[65] Ibid.
[66] Talton, Trista, "First Baptist makes offer on center" Wilmington Star News, Aug. 15, 2003, p 1A.
[67] Talton, Trista, "County counters offer on center" Wilmington Star News, Aug. 19, 2003, p 1A.
[68] Ibid.
[69] Talton, Trista, "Area developer plans to bid on old jail building" Wilmington Star News, Aug. 28, 2003, p 1A.
[70] Talton, Trista, and Little, Ken, "City may consider buying site" Wilmington Star News, Aug. 30, 2003, p 1A.
[71] Talton, Trista, and Fennell, Betty, "City OKs bid on county building" Wilmington Star News, Sep. 3, 2003, p 1A.
[72] Talton, Trista, and Little, Ken, "City may consider buying site" Wilmington Star News, Aug. 30, 2003, p 1A.
[73] Talton, Trista, and Fennell, Betty, "City OKs bid on county building" Wilmington Star News, Sep. 3, 2003, p 1A.
[74] Talton, Trista, "Church mum on LEC stance" Wilmington Star News, Sep. 10, 2003, p 1A.
[75] Ibid.

[76] Talton, Trista, "Church mum on LEC stance" Wilmington Star News, Sep. 10, 2003, p 1A., and Talton, Trista, and Fennell, Betty, "City OKs bid on county building" Wilmington Star News, Sep. 3, 2003, p 1A.

[77] Talton, Trista, "Boseman asks church to let loose LEC" Wilmington Star News, Sep. 9 2003, p 1A and "2 more ask church to relent", Wilmington Star News, Sep. 16 2003, p 1B.

[78] Talton, Trista, "County backs out of LEC deal" Wilmington Star News, Oct. 7, 2003 p 1A.

[79] Ibid.

[80] Talton, Trista, "County explores new future of LEC" Wilmington Star News, Oct. 8, 2003 p 1A.

[81] Talton, Trista, "Church says it won't sue – yet – over broken LEC promise" Wilmington Star News, Oct 17, 2003, p 1A.

[82] Riesz, Charles W. Editorial page editor, "Let's look at LEC one last time" Wilmington Star News, Jan. 31, 2005,

[83] Everette 202-203

[84] Ibid. 205

[85] Ibid 12.

[86] E-mail interview with Joyce Winstead, MSN, RN, FRE, Education and Practice Consultant, North Carolina Board of Nursing, Raleigh, NC, October 20, 2016.

[87] Letter from Carroll N. Herring, Herring Associates, Inc., Wilmington, NC, to James A. Smith, January 18th, 2002.

[88] Cassidy. 2.

[89] Copy of a will for James H Smith, February, 2002.

[90] Deposition of Dr. Michael Queen, In the General Court of Justice, Superior Court Division, 05 E 213, In the matter of the Will of James Henry Smith, Deceased. Reported by JoAnna M. Norton, with Norton, Schell, and Braswell. September 29, 2005, p 18.

[91] General Power of Attorney, State of North Carolina, County of New Hanover, granting William T. Smith, III power of attorney for James Henry Smith, April 16, 2002.

[92] Smith, William T. III, A July 13, 2004 memoir entitled Confidential Notes

[93] E-mail from William T. Smith III to family members and Reverend James Everette. February 22, 2003.

[94] Johnson, Ken, Investigative report from American Detective Services, Inc. Zebulon, NC. May 6, 2002. Also known as Caveator's exhibit 403, as numbered in the exhibit, 1-2.

[95] Ibid, 4.

[96] Ibid.

[97] Ibid, 5.

[98] Ibid, 5.

[99] Ibid.

[100] Ibid.

[101] Ibid, 5-14.

[102] Ibid, 14.

[103] Ibid, 15.

[104] Ibid, 16.

[105] Ibid, 19.
[106] Ibid, 19.
[107] Ibid, 20.
[108] Ibid.
[109] Ibid, 23.
[110] Ibid, 44.
[111] Ibid, 46.
[112] Ibid, 45.
[113] Ibid, 49.
[114] Ibid, 30.
[115] Ibid, 26.
[116] Ibid, 31.
[117] Ibid, 35-36.
[118] Ibid, 34.
[119] E-mail from William T. Smith III to family members and Bob Johnson and Anna Averette, attorneys at law. July 10, 2002.
[120] Johnson investigation
[121] Smith, William T. III, A July 13, 2004 memoir entitled Confidential Notes
[122] Durable Power of Attorney, State of North Carolina, County of New Hanover, for James Henry Smith, appointing O.K. Pridgen, II. Notarized by Jan Miller Pridgen, April 30, 2002, Registered by Rebecca T. Christian, Register of Deeds, May 1, 2002.
[123] William T. Smith III memo entitled "TEN THINGS." Not dated, and Phone conversation with William T. Smith III, October 24, 2016.
[124] Transcript of an interview of Wanda Day and Alicia Bethea by William T. Smith III and William T. smith IV, March 4, 2005. Also known as "Documents Produced in Response to Request for Production – No -1. Pages are not numbered.
[125] Mini mental exam and cover letter from Dr. Dewey H. Bridger, III, MD, to Otto K. Pridgen, May 1, 2002.
[126] Letter from Jodie Smith to James H. Smith's Sunday School class, May 30, 2002.
[127] E-mail from William T. Smith III to family members and Bob Johnson and Anna Averette, attorneys at law. July 10, 2002.
[128] E-mail from Jodie Smith to family members and Bob Johnson and Anna Averette, attorneys at law. July 10, 2002.
[129] Deposition of Linda Phillips, In the General Court of Justice, Superior Court Division, 05 E 213, In the matter of the Will of James Henry Smith, Deceased. Reported by Lois Redmond, Pace Reporting Service, Inc. August 29, 2005, p 38.
[130] Phone conversation with William T. Smith III, October 24, 2016.
[131] E-mail from Jodie Smith to family members and Bob Johnson and Anna Averette, attorneys at law. July 10, 2002.
[132] Neuropsychological report, Neuropsychological Services, Date of initial intake, 07/29/2002, Dates of evaluation, 08/13/2002 and 08/15/2002, Date of Dictation, 08/27/2002, Labeled "exhibit 3" for the court. p 1.
[133] Attachment to an e-mail from Jim Maxwell to William T. Smith III, cc William T. Smith IV and Jay Smith, Re: Trial prep, April 3, 2006, & e-mail from William T. Smith III to Charles Smith, Re: More, December 20, 2017.

[134] Phone conversation with William T. Smith III, October 24, 2016.

[135] Copy of a will for James H Smith, September 26, 2002

[136] Deposition of Robert A. O'Quinn, Volume Two, In the General Court of Justice, Superior Court Division, 05 E 213, In the matter of the Will of James Henry Smith, Deceased. Reported by JoAnna M. Norton, with Norton, Schell, and Braswell. August 30, 2005, p 14-28.

[137] Copy of a will for James H Smith, September 26, 2002

[138] Copy of a will for James H Smith, September 26, 2002

[139] Copy of a will for James H Smith, February, 2002

[140] E-mail from William T. Smith III to William T. Smith IV and Reverend James Everette. August 6, 2002.

[141] E-mail from William T. Smith III to family members and Bob Johnson, attorney at law, and forwarded to Reverend James Everette. August 6, 2002.

[142] Letter from John Newton of Squires Timber Co. Elizabethtown, NC, to Otto Pridgen regarding the timber on the Smith Tract in Columbus Co, NC. August 6, 2002.

[143] E-mail from William T. Smith III to family members and Bob Johnson, attorney at law, and Reverend James Everette. August 8, 2002.

[144] E-mail from William T. Smith III to family members and Bob Johnson, attorney at law, and Reverend James Everette. August 8, 2002.

[145] Letter from Otto K. Pridgen, attorney at law, to Robert Johnson, attorney at law, August 9, 2002.

[146] Letter from William T. Smith III to Otto K. Pridgen, attorney at law, October 1,2002.

[147] E-mail from William T. Smith III to family members, Anna Averette, attorney at law, and Reverend James Everette. February 4, 2003.

[148] Smith, William T. III, A March 4, 2004 memoir entitled Woodford Farm. Latest Events.

[149] Ibid.

[150] Ibid.

[151] Letter from Otto Pridgen, attorney at law, to Larry Fowler, June 14, 2004.

[152] Letter from William T. Smith IV to Otto Pridgen, attorney at law, December 2, 2002.

[153] Letter from William T. Smith III to Otto Pridgen, attorney at law, December 2, 2002.

[154] Letter from William T. Smith IV to Otto Pridgen, attorney at law, December 2, 2002.

[155] Letter from William T. Smith IV to Otto Pridgen, attorney at law, December 3, 2002.

[156] Letter from Otto Pridgen, attorney at law, to William T. Smith III, December 30, 2002.

[157] Letter from William T. Smith III to Otto Pridgen, attorney at law, December 31, 2002.

[158] Letter from William T. Smith IV to Otto Pridgen, attorney at law, December 2, 2002.

[159] Letter from Donna H. Mooney, RN, MBA, North Carolina Board of Nursing, director of Discipline, Raleigh, NC, to Patricia Jenkins. February 11, 2003.

[160] Smith, William T. III, A January 17, 2003 memoir with hand written title, Dr. Smith.

[161] Smith, William T. III, A January 17, 2003 memoir with hand written title, Dr. Smith.

[162] E-mail from Elizabeth S. Padget to family members, Robert Johnson, and Anna Averette, attorneys at law, and Reverend James Everette. May 11, 2003.

[163] E-mail from Robert Johnson, attorney at law to family members, and Reverend James Everette. May 12, 2003.

[164] E-mail from William T. Smith III to family members, and Robert Johnson (and his reply), attorney at law, January 11, 2005.

[165] E-mail from William T. Smith III to family members, and Robert Johnson (and his reply), attorney at law, January 11, 2005.

[166] North Carolina General Statute § 35A-1101, (7).

[167] E-mail from Alicia Smith to family members, Anna Averette and Robert Johnson, attorney at law, May 13, 2003.

[168] Letter from William T. Smith III to the congregation of the First Baptist Church of Wilmington, NC, with a cover letter addressed to Reverend Michael Queen, June 14, 2004.

[169] Smith, William T. III, An April 20, 2004 memoir. No Title.

[170] Smith, William T. III, An April 20, 2004 memoir. No Title.

[171] E-mail from Elizabeth S. Padgett to Otto K. Pridgen, attorney at law, January 3, 2005.

[172] Email from William T. Smith IV to family members, Jan 13, 2005, and reply by Carl Padgett, January 14, 2005.

[173] Ibid.

[174] Ibid.

[175] Wilson, Lacy, Real Estate Appraisal Report, Appraisal of James A. Smith's Estate, for Robert A. O'Quinn, Lacy Wilson Properties, April 10, 2002.

[176] Multiple forms of correspondence between Murchison, Taylor & Gibson, PLLC, attorneys at law, and family members. The memoranda describe guardianship procedures.

[177] Certificate of Death, New Hanover County Register of Deeds, Wilmington, NC, Died February 22, 2005, Recorded 25 February 2005, by Rebecca P. Smith, Register of Deeds.

[178] Email from Charles Smith to Reverend Michael Queen. February 25, 2005.

[179] Gurette, Ron T. Investigation Report on Interview with Joan Teer, February 13, 2006. Gurette Investigations, Charlotte, NC.

[180] Phone conversation with William T. Smith III, October 24, 2016.

[181] Smith, William, T. III, Untitled memoir dated March 1, 2005.

[182] Telephone conversation with Joseph Smith, December 20, 2017.

[183] Email from William T. Smith III to Reverend Michael Queen, and family members, and Rev. Queen's reply, March 2, 2005.

[184] Email from William T. Smith III to Reverend Michael Queen, and family members, and Rev. Queen's reply, March 2, 2005.

[185] Phone conversation with William T. Smith III, October 24, 2016.

[186] Email from William T. Smith III to Reverend Michael Queen, and family members, and Rev. Queen's reply, March 2, 2005.

[187] Smith, William, T. III, Untitled memoir dated March 1, 2005.

[188] E-mail from Joseph Smith to family members, March 3, 2005.

[189] Letter from William T. Smith III to David Whaley, accountant, March 3, 2005

[190] Law Enforcement Communication Record for Smith, James H, Dr., dated, March 4, 2005.

[191] Transcript of an interview of Wanda Day and Alicia Bethea by William T. Smith III and William T. Smith IV, March 4, 2005. Also known as "Documents Produced in Response to Request for Production – No -1. Pages are not numbered.

[192] Deposition of Dewey H. Bridger III, MD., In the General Court of Justice, Superior Court Division, 05 E 213, In the matter of the Will of James Henry Smith, Deceased. Reported by Betty W. Pace Thorne, Pace Reporting Service, Inc. March 2, 2006, p 67.

[193] Facsimile from Jim Maxell's office to William T. Smith III, dated March 4, 2005.

[194] Email from William T. Smith III to Reverends Michael Queen, and James Everette, March 2, 2005

[195] Letter from Carlton Fisher to Billy Smith, March 7, 2005.

[196] Smith Family list of Questions to be asked at March 7, 2005 meeting with MAXWELL FREEMAN & BOWMAN.

[197] Letter from Jim Maxwell, attorney at law, to Bob Johnson, attorney at law, March 7, 2005.

[198] Letter from Jim Maxwell, attorney at law, to Otto K. Pridgen, II, attorney at law, March 7, 2005.

[199] Email from Joseph Smith to family members and Robert Johnson, attorney at law, March 7, 2005.

[200] Email from William T. smith IV to Jim Maxwell, attorney at law, and William T. Smith III, March 8, 2005.

[201] Fax from Lonnie B. Williams, attorney at law, to James B. Maxwell, attorney at law, March 17, 2005.

[202] Deposition of Dr. Michael Queen, In the General Court of Justice, Superior Court Division, 05 E 213, In the matter of the Will of James Henry Smith, Deceased. Reported by JoAnna M. Norton, with Norton, Schell, and Braswell. September 29, 2005, p 107.

[203] Everette, 193.

[204] Everette, 199.

[205] Email from Robert Johnson, attorney at law, to William T. Smith III, March 21, 2005.

[206] Phone conversation with William T. Smith III, October 24, 2016.

[207] Ibid.

[208] E-mail from Jack Shelhart, to family members, May 2, 2005.

[209] Memo from James Maxwell to the Estate of James H. Smith File, Re: Conference/First Baptist Church, April 27, 2005.

[210] Ibid

[211] E-mail from Lonnie Williams Sr. to Jim Maxwell, Subject: depositions postponement, April 22, 2005.

[212] From Wikipedia, the free encyclopedia, Amos "n" Andy, https://en.wikipedia.org/wiki/Amos_%27n%27_Andy, Accessed December 13, 2017.

[213] Email from James Maxwell to Lonnie Williams, Re: Sale Saturday, May 4, 2005.

[214] E-mail from Lonnie Williams Sr. to Jim Maxwell, cc Jan Pridgen, Subject: Smith estate, April 27, 2005, and e-mail from Lonnie Williams Sr. to Jim Maxwell, May 4, 2005.

[215] Phone conversation with William T. Smith III, October 24, 2016.

[216] E-mail from Jim Maxwell to William T. Smith III, cc William T. Smith IV, Subject: Farm Management, June 21, 2005.

[217] Memorandum from James B. Maxwell, to Octavia Smith, Christine Shelhart, Lisa Padgett [Sic, Shelhart], Jack W. Smith Jr., Frederick Smith, and John Shelhart, Re: Status of Caveat to the Will of James H. Smith, May 2, 2005.

[218] Letter from James Maxwell to William Thomas Smith III, Re: Estate of James H. Smith, May 10, 2005.

[219] Notice of deposition, Duces Tecum, from the general court of justice, Superior Court Division, before the clerk, file number 05-E-213, to Patricia Jenkins, Carol Tucker, Linda Phillips, Otto K. Pridgen, David Whaley, and Jack Richardson, May 12, 2005.

[220] Memo from Billy Smith to Jim Maxwell, Re: Errors in Bob Hunter's REQUEST FOR ADMISSIONS, Stamped, May 20, 2005, and Letter from James B. Maxwell to Robert T. Hunter Jr. Re: In the matter of the Will of James Henry Smith, Deceased, New Hanover County Superior Court: 05 E 213, dated May 17, 2005.

[221] E-mail from James Maxwell to family members, Re: update, June 14, 2005.

[222] Ibid

[223] Phone conversation with William T. Smith III, October 24, 2016.

[224] E-mail from James Maxwell to family members, Re: update, June 14, 2005.

[225] Ibid.

[226] Memorandum from James B. Maxwell, to Octavia Smith, Christine Shelhart, Lisa Padgett [Sic, Shelhart], Jack W. Smith Jr., Frederick Smith, and John Shelhart, Re: Status of Caveat to the Will of James H. Smith, May 2, 2005.

[227] Memo from James Maxwell to the Estate of James H. Smith File, Re: Conference/First Baptist Church, April 27, 2005.

[228] Ibid

[229] Telefax (and mailed) letter from Lonnie B. Williams, to James B. Maxwell, and Robert N. Hunter, Re: In the matter of the will of James Henry Smith, Deceased, Our file No. 010941, July 1, 2005.

[230] Letter from James B. Maxwell, to William T. Smith III, William T. Smith IV, and Anna R. Smith, July 5, 2005.

[231] Pridgen, Otto K. Statement for Services Rendered, Re: Estate of James H. Smith, Jun 29, 2005.

[232] Ibid

[233] Ibid

[234] Hearing [regarding O.K. Pridgen's fees], In the general court of justice, Superior Court Division, before the clerk, file number 05-E-213, August 30, 2005.

[235] Transcript of the trial testimony of Patricia C. Jenkins, In the General Court of Justice, Superior Court Division, 05 E 213, In the matter of the Will of James Henry

Smith, Deceased. Reported by Katie K. Thomas, Official Court Reporter. April 10, 2006, p 79.

[236] Pridgen, Otto K. Statement for Services Rendered, Re: Estate of James H. Smith, Jun 29, 2005.

[237] Ibid

[238] Wilson, Lacy, Real Estate Appraisal Report, Appraisal of James A. Smith's Estate, for Robert A. O'Quinn, Lacy Wilson Properties, April 10, 2002.

[239] McKenzie, William, and Alleman, Heidi, Complete Appraisal – Summary Report of The James A. Smith Tract, Approximately 622 Acres, Ingram, McKenzie and Associates, Inc., July 12, 2005.

[240] Pridgen, Otto K., Response to Caveator's first set of interrogatories and first request for production of documents, In the general court of justice, Superior Court Division, before the clerk, file number 05-E-213, July 29, 2005.

[241] Memorandum from James B. Maxwell, to 11 family members, August 8, 2005.

[242] Neuropsychological report, Neuropsychological Services, Date of initial intake, 07/29/2002, Dates of evaluation, 08/13/2002 and 08/15/2002, Date of Dictation, 08/27/2002, p 2.

[243] Ibid, 3.

[244] Ibid, 3.

[245] Ibid, 3.

[246] Ibid, 3.

[247] Ibid, 4.

[248] Ibid, 4.

[249] Neuropsychological report, Neuropsychological Services, Date of initial intake, 07/29/2002, Dates of evaluation, 08/13/2002 and 08/15/2002, Date of Dictation, 08/27/2002, p 1.

[250] Ibid, 2.

[251] Ibid, 2.

[252] Deposition of Linda Phillips, In the General Court of Justice, Superior Court Division, 05 E 213, In the matter of the Will of James Henry Smith, Deceased. Reported by Lois Redmond, Pace Reporting Service, Inc. August 29, 2005, p 12.

[253] Ibid, 21.

[254] Ibid, 10.

[255] Ibid, 21,22.

[256] Ibid, 16,26.

[257] Ibid, 46.

[258] Ibid, 25,54.

[259] Ibid, 35,54.

[260] Ibid, 39.

[261] Ibid, 40.

[262] Phone conversation with William T. Smith III, October 24, 2016.

[263] Deposition of Linda Phillips, In the General Court of Justice, Superior Court Division, 05 E 213, In the matter of the Will of James Henry Smith, Deceased. Reported by Lois Redmond, Pace Reporting Service, Inc. August 29, 2005, p 62-64.

[264] Deposition of Dr. Frank Reynolds, In the General Court of Justice, Superior Court Division, 05 E 213, In the matter of the Will of James Henry Smith,

Deceased. Reported by Lois Redmond, Pace Reporting Service, Inc. August 29, 2005, p 62-64. 9

[265] Ibid, 13-14.

[266] Ibid, 15,30.

[267] Ibid, 15-16.

[268] Ibid, 39.

[269] Deposition of Edward A. Rusher, Jr., In the General Court of Justice, Superior Court Division, 05 E 213, In the matter of the Will of James Henry Smith, Deceased. Reported by Lois Redmond, Pace Reporting Service, Inc. August 30, 2005, p 9-10

[270] Ibid, 8.

[271] Ibid, 17.

[272] Ibid, 18.

[273] Deposition of Otto K. Pridgen, Volume One., In the General Court of Justice, Superior Court Division, 05 E 213, In the matter of the Will of James Henry Smith, Deceased. Reported by Lois Redmond, Pace Reporting Service, Inc. August 29, 2005, p 5-6.

[274] Ibid, 6-7.

[275] Ibid, 7.

[276] Ibid, 8.

[277] Ibid, 8-9.

[278] Ibid, 14.

[279] Ibid, 17.

[280] Ibid, 17.

[281] Ibid, 19.

[282] Deposition of Otto K. Pridgen, Volume Two., In the General Court of Justice, Superior Court Division, 05 E 213, In the matter of the Will of James Henry Smith, Deceased. Reported by Lois Redmond, Pace Reporting Service, Inc. August 31, 2005, p 112-113

[283] Ibid, 32-33.

[284] Ibid, 33.

[285] Ibid, 34.

[286] Ibid, 35.

[287] Ibid, 37-38.

[288] Neuropsychological report, Neuropsychological Services, Date of initial intake, 07/29/2002, Dates of evaluation, 08/13/2002 and 08/15/2002, Date of Dictation, 08/27/2002, p 2.

[289] Deposition of Otto K. Pridgen, Volume One., In the General Court of Justice, Superior Court Division, 05 E 213, In the matter of the Will of James Henry Smith, Deceased. Reported by Lois Redmond, Pace Reporting Service, Inc. August 29, 2005, p 42.

[290] Ibid, 21,42.

[291] Ibid, 47.

[292] Ibid, 69-71.

[293] Ibid, 45.

[294] Pridgen, Otto K., Response to Caveator's first set of interrogatories and first request for production of documents, Interrogatory #9, In the general court of

justice, Superior Court Division, before the clerk, file number 05-E-213, July 29, 2005.

[295] Deposition of Otto K. Pridgen, Volume One., In the General Court of Justice, Superior Court Division, 05 E 213, In the matter of the Will of James Henry Smith, Deceased. Reported by Lois Redmond, Pace Reporting Service, Inc. August 29, 2005, p 67-68

[296] Deposition of Otto K. Pridgen, Volume Two., In the General Court of Justice, Superior Court Division, 05 E 213, In the matter of the Will of James Henry Smith, Deceased. Reported by Lois Redmond, Pace Reporting Service, Inc. August 31, 2005, p 97.

[297] Caveator's exhibit 421.

[298] Deposition of Otto K. Pridgen, Volume One., In the General Court of Justice, Superior Court Division, 05 E 213, In the matter of the Will of James Henry Smith, Deceased. Reported by Lois Redmond, Pace Reporting Service, Inc. August 29, 2005, p 62.

[299] Ibid, 61,63.

[300] Ibid, 76-86.

[301] Pridgen, Otto K. Statement for Services Rendered, Re: Estate of James H. Smith, Jun 29, 2005.

[302] Deposition of Otto K. Pridgen, Volume One., In the General Court of Justice, Superior Court Division, 05 E 213, In the matter of the Will of James Henry Smith, Deceased. Reported by Lois Redmond, Pace Reporting Service, Inc. August 29, 2005, p 61-62.

[303] Pridgen, Otto K. Statement for Services Rendered, Re: Estate of James H. Smith, Jun 29, 2005.

[304] Deposition of Otto K. Pridgen, Volume One., In the General Court of Justice, Superior Court Division, 05 E 213, In the matter of the Will of James Henry Smith, Deceased. Reported by Lois Redmond, Pace Reporting Service, Inc. August 29, 2005, p 85-86.

[305] Jack Richardson depo p9

[306] Ibid, 22-24.

[307] Ibid, 25,59.

[308] Ibid, 75.

[309] Deposition of Jack Richardson, Volume Two, In the General Court of Justice, Superior Court Division, 05 E 213, In the matter of the Will of James Henry Smith, Deceased. Reported by Lois Redmond, Pace Reporting Service, Inc. August 31, 2005, 109

[310] Ibid, 103.

[311] Neuropsychological report, Neuropsychological Services, Date of initial intake, 07/29/2002, Dates of evaluation, 08/13/2002 and 08/15/2002, Date of Dictation, 08/27/2002, p 4.

[312] Deposition of Jack Richardson, Volume One, In the General Court of Justice, Superior Court Division, 05 E 213, In the matter of the Will of James Henry Smith, Deceased. Reported by Lois Redmond, Pace Reporting Service, Inc. August 29, 2005, p 35.

[313] Deposition of Jack Richardson, Volume Two, In the General Court of Justice, Superior Court Division, 05 E 213, In the matter of the Will of James Henry Smith,

Deceased. Reported by Lois Redmond, Pace Reporting Service, Inc. August 31, 2005, p 94.

[314] Ibid, 69

[315] Ibid, 72

[316] Deposition of Jack Richardson, Volume One, In the General Court of Justice, Superior Court Division, 05 E 213, In the matter of the Will of James Henry Smith, Deceased. Reported by Lois Redmond, Pace Reporting Service, Inc. August 29, 2005, p 20-21.

[317] Deposition of Jack Richardson, Volume Two, In the General Court of Justice, Superior Court Division, 05 E 213, In the matter of the Will of James Henry Smith, Deceased. Reported by Lois Redmond, Pace Reporting Service, Inc. August 31, 2005, p 51-52, and interview with Reverend James Everette, 4/6/2020.

[318] Deposition of Jack Richardson, Volume One and Two, In the General Court of Justice, Superior Court Division, 05 E 213, In the matter of the Will of James Henry Smith, Deceased. Reported by Lois Redmond, Pace Reporting Service, Inc. August 29-31, 2005, p 18,72,115.

[319] Deposition of Jack Richardson, Volume Two, In the General Court of Justice, Superior Court Division, 05 E 213, In the matter of the Will of James Henry Smith, Deceased. Reported by Lois Redmond, Pace Reporting Service, Inc. August 31, 2005, p 54.

[320] Ibid, 77.

[321] Ibid, 54.

[322] Ibid, 70.

[323] Ibid, 117.

[324] Deposition of Robert A. O'Quinn, Volume One, In the General Court of Justice, Superior Court Division, 05 E 213, In the matter of the Will of James Henry Smith, Deceased. Reported by Lois Redmond, Pace Reporting Service, Inc. August 30, 2005, p 20-21.

[325] Ibid, 7.

[326] Pridgen, Otto K., Response to Caveator's first set of interrogatories and first request for production of documents, Interrogatory #9, In the general court of justice, Superior Court Division, before the clerk, file number 05-E-213, July 29, 2005.

[327] Deposition of Robert A. O'Quinn, Volume One, In the General Court of Justice, Superior Court Division, 05 E 213, In the matter of the Will of James Henry Smith, Deceased. Reported by Lois Redmond, Pace Reporting Service, Inc. August 30, 2005, 23-24

[328] Ibid, 24,48.

[329] Ibid, 26,27,30.

[330] Ibid, 24-25.

[331] Ibid, 39.

[332] Ibid, 40-41.

[333] Deposition of Otto K. Pridgen, Volume One and Two, In the General Court of Justice, Superior Court Division, 05 E 213, In the matter of the Will of James Henry Smith, Deceased. Reported by Lois Redmond, Pace Reporting Service, Inc. August 31, 2005, p 114-115.

[334] Deposition of Robert A. O'Quinn, Volume One, In the General Court of Justice, Superior Court Division, 05 E 213, In the matter of the Will of James Henry Smith, Deceased. Reported by Lois Redmond, Pace Reporting Service, Inc. August 30, 2005, p 47.

[335] Deposition of Robert A. O'Quinn, Volume Two, In the General Court of Justice, Superior Court Division, 05 E 213, In the matter of the Will of James Henry Smith, Deceased. Reported by JoAnna M. Norton, with Norton, Schell, and Braswell. August 30, 2005, p 14.

[336] Ibid, 15.

[337] Deposition of Robert A. O'Quinn, Volume One, In the General Court of Justice, Superior Court Division, 05 E 213, In the matter of the Will of James Henry Smith, Deceased. Reported by Lois Redmond, Pace Reporting Service, Inc. August 30, 2005, p 27.

[338] Ibid, 28.

[339] Attachment to an e-mail from Jim Maxwell to William T. Smith III, cc William T. Smith IV and Jay Smith, Re: Trial prep, April 3, 2006, & e-mail from William T. Smith III to Charles Smith, Re: More, December 20, 2017.

[340] Deposition of Robert A. O'Quinn, Volume One, In the General Court of Justice, Superior Court Division, 05 E 213, In the matter of the Will of James Henry Smith, Deceased. Reported by Lois Redmond, Pace Reporting Service, Inc. August 30, 2005, p 62.

[341] Deposition of Robert A. O'Quinn, Volume Two, In the General Court of Justice, Superior Court Division, 05 E 213, In the matter of the Will of James Henry Smith, Deceased. Reported by JoAnna M. Norton, with Norton, Schell, and Braswell. August 30, 2005, p 10.

[342] Ibid, 10.

[343] Ibid, 18.

[344] Deposition of Robert A. O'Quinn, Volume One, In the General Court of Justice, Superior Court Division, 05 E 213, In the matter of the Will of James Henry Smith, Deceased. Reported by Lois Redmond, Pace Reporting Service, Inc. August 30, 2005, p 52.

[345] Deposition of Patricia Jenkins, In the General Court of Justice, Superior Court Division, 05 E 213, In the matter of the Will of James Henry Smith, Deceased. Reported by Betty W. Pace Thorne, Pace Reporting Service, Inc. September 28, 2005, p 76.

[346] Ibid, 5.

[347] Ibid, 96.

[348] Ibid, 96-98.

[349] Ibid, 98-102.

[350] Ibid, 96.

[351] Letter from Carroll N. Herring, Herring Associates, Inc., Wilmington, NC, to James A. Smith, January 18th, 2002.

[352] Deposition of Patricia Jenkins, In the General Court of Justice, Superior Court Division, 05 E 213, In the matter of the Will of James Henry Smith, Deceased. Reported by Betty W. Pace Thorne, Pace Reporting Service, Inc. September 28, 2005, 44.

[353] Ibid, 32,64,140.

[354] Ibid, 141-145.
[355] Ibid, 151-53.
[356] Ibid, 155.
[357] Memorandum from Jim Maxwell to 9 family members, October 10, 2005.
[358] Ibid, 26.
[359] Ibid, 18.
[360] Ibid, 28.
[361] Ibid, 48.
[362] Ibid, 16.
[363] Ibid, 31.
[364] Ibid, 49-50, 163.
[365] Ibid, 51-52.
[366] Ibid, 53.
[367] Ibid, 56-57.
[368] Ibid, 58.
[369] Ibid, 66.
[370] Ibid, 67.
[371] Ibid, 68-76.
[372] Ibid, 6, 81.
[373] Ibid, 82-86.
[374] Ibid, 91.
[375] Ibid, 115.
[376] Ibid, 125.
[377] Deposition of Carol Tucker, In the General Court of Justice, Superior Court Division, 05 E 213, In the matter of the Will of James Henry Smith, Deceased. Reported by Betty W. Pace Thorne, Pace Reporting Service, Inc. September 28, 2005, 6.
[378] Ibid, 11.
[379] Ibid, 11-12.
[380] Ibid, 18.
[381] Ibid, 20.
[382] Ibid, 53.
[383] Transcript of the trial testimony of Patricia C. Jenkins, In the General Court of Justice, Superior Court Division, 05 E 213, In the matter of the Will of James Henry Smith, Deceased. Reported by Katie K. Thomas, Official Court Reporter. April 10, 2006, p 79-80.
[384] Ibid, 29.
[385] Ibid, 30-32.
[386] Ibid, 33.
[387] Ibid, 35.
[388] Deposition of Jan Pridgen, In the General Court of Justice, Superior Court Division, 05 E 213, In the matter of the Will of James Henry Smith, Deceased. Reported by Betty W. Pace Thorne, Pace Reporting Service, Inc. September 28, 2005, p 4.
[389] Ibid, 9.
[390] Ibid, 12.
[391] Ibid, 14.

[392] Ibid, 15.

[393] Ibid, 15.

[394] Ibid, 17.

[395] Deposition of Dr. Michael Queen, In the General Court of Justice, Superior Court Division, 05 E 213, In the matter of the Will of James Henry Smith, Deceased. Reported by JoAnna M. Norton, with Norton, Schell, and Braswell. September 29, 2005, p 5.

[396] Ibid, 84.

[397] Ibid, 6.

[398] First Baptist Church record of pastor visits to James H. Smith's address, marked Exhibit 14 for the court.

[399] Talton, Trista, "Church mum on LEC stance" Wilmington Star News, Sep. 10, 2003, p 1A.

[400] Deposition of Dr. Michael Queen, In the General Court of Justice, Superior Court Division, 05 E 213, In the matter of the Will of James Henry Smith, Deceased. Reported by JoAnna M. Norton, with Norton, Schell, and Braswell. September 29, 2005, p 54.

[401] Ibid, 8.

[402] Ibid, 16.

[403] Ibid, 16-17.

[404] Ibid, 16-17.

[405] Ibid, 26.

[406] Ibid, 17-18.

[407] Ibid, 18.

[408] Ibid, 19-20.

[409] Ibid, 21.

[410] Ibid, 24-25.

[411] Ibid, 28.

[412] Deposition of Dr. Michael Queen, In the General Court of Justice, Superior Court Division, 05 E 213, In the matter of the Will of James Henry Smith, Deceased. Reported by JoAnna M. Norton, with Norton, Schell, and Braswell. September 29, 2005, p 28-31.

[413] Ibid, 28-31.

[414] Ibid, 31-32.

[415] Ibid, 33.

[416] Ibid, 39.

[417] Ibid, 39.

[418] Ibid, 41.

[419] Ibid, 48.

[420] Ibid, 48,62.

[421] Ibid, 5.

[422] First Baptist Church record of pastor visits to James H. Smith's address, marked Exhibit 14 for the court.

[423] Deposition of Dr. Michael Queen, In the General Court of Justice, Superior Court Division, 05 E 213, In the matter of the Will of James Henry Smith, Deceased. Reported by JoAnna M. Norton, with Norton, Schell, and Braswell. September 29, 2005, p 92

[424] Ibid, 75.

[425] Ibid, 65.

[426] Deposition of Dr. James Everette, In the General Court of Justice, Superior Court Division, 05 E 213, In the matter of the Will of James Henry Smith, Deceased. Reported by JoAnna M. Norton, with Norton, Schell, and Braswell. September 29, 2005, p 5.

[427] Ibid, 6.

[428] Ibid, 9.

[429] First Baptist Church record of pastor visits to James H. Smith's address, marked Exhibit 14 for the court.

[430] Deposition of Dr. James Everette, In the General Court of Justice, Superior Court Division, 05 E 213, In the matter of the Will of James Henry Smith, Deceased. Reported by JoAnna M. Norton, with Norton, Schell, and Braswell. September 29, 2005, p 10-11.

[431] Ibid, 10.

[432] Ibid, 17.

[433] Ibid, 18.

[434] Ibid, 35.

[435] Ibid, 109.

[436] Ibid, 28.

[437] Ibid, 55.

[438] Ibid, 28.

[439] Deposition of Jack Richardson, Volume Two, In the General Court of Justice, Superior Court Division, 05 E 213, In the matter of the Will of James Henry Smith, Deceased. Reported by Lois Redmond, Pace Reporting Service, Inc. August 31, 2005, p 51-52, and interview with Reverend James Everette, 4/6/2020.

[440] Deposition of Dr. James Everette, In the General Court of Justice, Superior Court Division, 05 E 213, In the matter of the Will of James Henry Smith, Deceased. Reported by JoAnna M. Norton, with Norton, Schell, and Braswell. September 29, 2005, p 105.

[441] Ibid, 109.

[442] Ibid, 61.

[443] Deposition of Jack Richardson, Volume Two, In the General Court of Justice, Superior Court Division, 05 E 213, In the matter of the Will of James Henry Smith, Deceased. Reported by Lois Redmond, Pace Reporting Service, Inc. August 31, 2005, p 94.

[444] Deposition of Dr. James Everette, In the General Court of Justice, Superior Court Division, 05 E 213, In the matter of the Will of James Henry Smith, Deceased. Reported by JoAnna M. Norton, with Norton, Schell, and Braswell. September 29, 2005, p 62.

[445] Deposition of Jack Richardson, Volume Two, In the General Court of Justice, Superior Court Division, 05 E 213, In the matter of the Will of James Henry Smith, Deceased. Reported by Lois Redmond, Pace Reporting Service, Inc. August 31, 2005, p 77.

[446] Deposition of Dr. James Everette, In the General Court of Justice, Superior Court Division, 05 E 213, In the matter of the Will of James Henry Smith, Deceased.

Reported by JoAnna M. Norton, with Norton, Schell, and Braswell. September 29, 2005, p 28.

[447] Ibid, 41.

[448] Ibid, 39, 41, 44.

[449] Ibid, 105

[450] Ibid, 109

[451] Ibid, 22

[452] Ibid, 67

[453] Phone conversation with William T. Smith III, October 24, 2016.

[454] Deposition of Dr. James Everette, In the General Court of Justice, Superior Court Division, 05 E 213, In the matter of the Will of James Henry Smith, Deceased. Reported by JoAnna M. Norton, with Norton, Schell, and Braswell. September 29, 2005, p 74-75.

[455] Ibid, 63.

[456] Deposition of Jack Richardson, Volume One and Two, In the General Court of Justice, Superior Court Division, 05 E 213, In the matter of the Will of James Henry Smith, Deceased. Reported by Lois Redmond, Pace Reporting Service, Inc. August 31, 2005, p 20-21.

[457] Deposition of Dr. James Everette, In the General Court of Justice, Superior Court Division, 05 E 213, In the matter of the Will of James Henry Smith, Deceased. Reported by JoAnna M. Norton, with Norton, Schell, and Braswell. September 29, 2005, p 56-57.

[458] Ibid, 57-58.

[459] E-mail from Jim Maxwell to R.N. Hunter Jr., cc William T. Smith III, Re: Smith Estate, September 13, 2005.

[460] Amended Motion for Partial Summary Judgment, In the General Court of Justice, Superior Court Division, 05 E 213, In the matter of the Will of James Henry Smith, Deceased. From the firm Hunter, Higgins, Miles, Elam & Benjamin, PLLC, October 12, 2005, & e-mail from Jim Maxwell to Lonnie Williams, Sr., cc R. N. Hunter, October 12, 2005.

[461] E-mail from Lonnie Williams, Sr. to Jim Maxwell, Re: Faxed Notice of Hearing, October 12, 2005

[462] E-mail from Lonnie Williams, Sr. to Jim Maxwell, Re: Faxed Notice of Hearing, October 12, 2005, & e-mail from Jim Maxwell to Lonnie Williams, Sr., cc R. N. Hunter, October 12, 2005.

[463] Notice of Hearing on a petition for fees, In the General Court of Justice, Superior Court Division, 05 E 213, In the matter of the Will of James Henry Smith, Deceased, from Lonnie Williams, October 21, 2005, & Memorandum from Jim Maxwell to nine family members, Re: Upcoming Schedule, October 24, 2005.

[464] Facsimile from Robert N. Hunter Jr., to Lonnie Williams and Jim Maxwell, Re: In the matter of the Will of James Henry Smith, Deceased (05-E-213), In the matter of the estate of Iris Smith (02-E-082).

[465] Deposition of Herbert Carlton Fisher, In the General Court of Justice, Superior Court Division, 05 E 213, In the matter of the Will of James Henry Smith, Deceased. Reported by Nancy L. Richie, November 9, 2005, p 4-5.

[466] Ibid, 5

[467] WWAY News, Feb 23, 2017, A-6 "Two Wilmington attorneys plead guilty to tax charges" https://www.wwaytv3.com/2017/02/23/two-wilmington-attorneys-plead-guilty-to-tax-charges/, accessed December 15, 2017.

[468] Deposition of Herbert Carlton Fisher, In the General Court of Justice, Superior Court Division, 05 E 213, In the matter of the Will of James Henry Smith, Deceased. Reported by Nancy L. Richie, November 9, 2005, p 5.

[469] Ibid, 7.

[470] Ibid, 9.

[471] Ibid, 12-15.

[472] Ibid, 36.

[473] Ibid, 37-38.

[474] Ibid, 39.

[475] Ibid, 40.

[476] Ibid, 39-40.

[477] Executor and propounders' motions to dismiss and motion for summary judgment, In the General Court of Justice, Superior Court Division, In the matter of the Will of James Henry Smith, Deceased (05-E-213), filed by Charles D. Meier and Lonnie B. Williams, October 27, 2005.

[478] Ibid

[479] Affidavits, In the General Court of Justice, Superior Court Division : In the matter of the Will of James Henry Smith, Deceased (05-E-213), by Christy Jones, PhD., October 27, 2005, Dewey Bridger III, MD., October 27, 2005, Hyton W. Babson, October 28, 2005, Charles E. ("Bud") Davis, October 28, 2005, and Gene L. McIntyre, e-mail from William T. Smith III to Jim Maxwell, Re: Gene McIntyre, November 1, 2005.

[480] E-mail from Jim Maxwell to seven family members, cc Bob Johnson, Re: First Baptist Church Brief in Support of Motion for Summary Judgment, November 4, 2005.

[481] Court Order, In the General Court of Justice, Superior Court Division, In the matter of the Will of James Henry Smith, Deceased (05-E-213), Signed by William A. Cobb Jr., December 5, 2005.

[482] E-mail from Jim Maxwell to William T. Smith III, cc 10 family members, Re: Mediation and beyond, January 24, 2006.

[483] E-mail from William T. Smith III to 16 family members, Re: Potential Agreement with Church, March 5, 2006.

[484] E-mail from Jim Maxwell to William T. Smith III, cc 16 family members, Re: Go for it, January 24, 2006.

[485] Ibid.

[486] Deposition of Dewey H. Bridger III, MD., In the General Court of Justice, Superior Court Division, 05 E 213, In the matter of the Will of James Henry Smith, Deceased. Reported by Betty W. Pace Thorne, Pace Reporting Service, Inc. March 2, 2006, p 4.

[487] Ibid, 27.

[488] Smith, James, Medical Record, patient of Dewey H. Bridger, III MD., May 1, 2002, (page numbered for the court) p 305.

[489] Ibid, 302.

[490] Cassidy, 2.

[491] Smith, James, Medical Record, patient of Dewey H. Bridger, III MD., May 1, 2002, (page numbered for the court) p 305.

[492] Ibid, 298.

[493] Deposition of Dewey H. Bridger III, MD., In the General Court of Justice, Superior Court Division, 05 E 213, In the matter of the Will of James Henry Smith, Deceased. Reported by Betty W. Pace Thorne, Pace Reporting Service, Inc. March 2, 2006, p 80.

[494] Transcript of the trial testimony of Janice M. Pridgen, In the General Court of Justice, Superior Court Division, 05 E 213, In the matter of the Will of James Henry Smith, Deceased. Reported by Katie K. Thomas, Official Court Reporter. April 10, 2006, 29.

[495] Smith, James, Medical Record, patient of Dewey H. Bridger, III MD., May 1, 2002, (page numbered for the court) p 351.

[496] Ibid, 351.

[497] Ibid, 351.

[498] Ibid, 281.

[499] Ibid, 273.

[500] Ibid, 272.

[501] Ibid, 268.

[502] Ibid, 267.

[503] Deposition of Dewey H. Bridger III, MD., In the General Court of Justice, Superior Court Division, 05 E 213, In the matter of the Will of James Henry Smith, Deceased. Reported by Betty W. Pace Thorne, Pace Reporting Service, Inc. March 2, 2006, 68

[504] Smith, James, Medical Record, patient of Dewey H. Bridger, III MD., May 1, 2002, (page numbered for the court) p 261.

[505] Ibid, 302.

[506] Neuropsychological report, Neuropsychological Services, Date of initial intake, 07/29/2002, Dates of evaluation, 08/13/2002 and 08/15/2002, Date of Dictation, 08/27/2002, Labeled "exhibit 3" for the court. p 1.

[507] Smith, James, Medical Record, patient of Dewey H. Bridger, III MD., May 1, 2002, (page numbered for the court) p 308.

[508] Ibid, 307.

[509] Ibid, 310.

[510] Ibid, 310.

[511] Ibid, 306.

[512] Ibid, 362.

[513] Ibid, 305.

[514] Ibid, 360-361.

[515] Ibid, 305,303.

[516] Ibid, 300.

[517] Ibid, 359.

[518] Ibid, 302.

[519] Transcript of the trial testimony of Janice M. Pridgen, In the General Court of Justice, Superior Court Division, 05 E 213, In the matter of the Will of James Henry Smith, Deceased. Reported by Katie K. Thomas, Official Court Reporter. April 10, 2006, 29.

[520] Smith, James, Medical Record, patient of Dewey H. Bridger, III MD., May 1, 2002, (page numbered for the court) p 302.

[521] Ibid, 302.

[522] Neuropsychological report, Neuropsychological Services, Date of initial intake, 07/29/2002, Dates of evaluation, 08/13/2002 and 08/15/2002, Date of Dictation, 08/27/2002, Labeled "exhibit 3" for the court. p 1.

[523] Ibid, 1.

[524] Ibid, 1.

[525] Smith, James, Medical Record, patient of Dewey H. Bridger, III MD., May 1, 2002, (page numbered for the court) p 302.

[526] Ibid, 298.

[527] Ibid, 358.

[528] Neuropsychological report, Neuropsychological Services, Date of initial intake, 07/29/2002, Dates of evaluation, 08/13/2002 and 08/15/2002, Date of Dictation, 08/27/2002, Labeled "exhibit 3" for the court. p 1.

[529] Smith, James, Medical Record, patient of Dewey H. Bridger, III MD., May 1, 2002, (page numbered for the court) p 317.

[530] Ibid, 320

[531] Ibid, 298

[532] Ibid, 292

[533] Ibid, 351

[534] Ibid, 315

[535] Ibid, 281

[536] Ibid, 278

[537] Ibid, 341

[538] Ibid, 273

[539] Ibid, 273

[540] Ibid, 341

[541] Ibid, 273

[542] Ibid, 272

[543] Ibid, 272

[544] Ibid, 272

[545] Ibid, 269-270

[546] Deposition of Dewey H. Bridger III, MD., In the General Court of Justice, Superior Court Division, 05 E 213, In the matter of the Will of James Henry Smith, Deceased. Reported by Betty W. Pace Thorne, Pace Reporting Service, Inc. March 2, 2006, p 67, & Smith, James, Medical Record, patient of Dewey H. Bridger, III MD., May 1, 2002, (page numbered for the court) p 270.

[547] Smith, James, Medical Record, patient of Dewey H. Bridger, III MD., May 1, 2002, (page numbered for the court) p 267.

[548] Ibid, 267.

[549] Ibid, 267.

[550] Ibid, 261.

[551] Healthline.com, Organic Brain Syndrome. http://www.healthline.com/health/organic-brain-syndrome#Overview, Accessed December 18, 2017

[552] Deposition of Christy L. Jones, PhD., In the General Court of Justice, Superior Court Division, 05 E 213, In the matter of the Will of James Henry Smith, Deceased. Reported by Betty W. Pace Thorne, Pace Reporting Service, Inc. March 3, 2006, p 4.

[553] Ibid, 6.

[554] Ibid, 10, and addendum.

[555] Ibid, 10-11.

[556] Ibid, 11.

[557] Ibid, 11.

[558] Ibid, 11-12.

[559] Ibid, 13.

[560] Ibid, 12.

[561] Ibid, 18.

[562] Neuropsychological report, Neuropsychological Services, Date of initial intake, 07/29/2002, Dates of evaluation, 08/13/2002 and 08/15/2002, Date of Dictation, 08/27/2002, Labeled "exhibit 3" for the court. p 1.

[563] Deposition of Christy L. Jones, PhD., In the General Court of Justice, Superior Court Division, 05 E 213, In the matter of the Will of James Henry Smith, Deceased. Reported by Betty W. Pace Thorne, Pace Reporting Service, Inc. March 3, 2006, p 16.

[564] Ibid, 21.

[565] Ibid, 22-23.

[566] Ibid, 33.

[567] Ibid, 33.

[568] Ibid, 68.

[569] Ibid, 24-25.

[570] Ibid, 37-38.

[571] Ibid, 27.

[572] Ibid, 65.

[573] Ibid, 56.

[574] Ibid, 57.

[575] Ibid, 58.

[576] Neuropsychological report, Neuropsychological Services, Date of initial intake, 07/29/2002, Dates of evaluation, 08/13/2002 and 08/15/2002, Date of Dictation, 08/27/2002, Labeled "exhibit 3" for the court. p 1.

[577] Deposition of Christy L. Jones, PhD., In the General Court of Justice, Superior Court Division, 05 E 213, In the matter of the Will of James Henry Smith, Deceased. Reported by Betty W. Pace Thorne, Pace Reporting Service, Inc. March 3, 2006, p 57-58.

[578] Deposition of Dewey H. Bridger III, MD., In the General Court of Justice, Superior Court Division, 05 E 213, In the matter of the Will of James Henry Smith, Deceased. Reported by Betty W. Pace Thorne, Pace Reporting Service, Inc. March 2, 2006, p 52-53.

[579] Memorandum, To: Smith Estate File, From J.B. Maxwell, RE: telephone conversation with E.B. Poucher, juror April 26, 2006.

[580] Deposition of Dewey H. Bridger III, MD., In the General Court of Justice, Superior Court Division, 05 E 213, In the matter of the Will of James Henry Smith,

Deceased. Reported by Betty W. Pace Thorne, Pace Reporting Service, Inc. March 2, 2006, p 67.

[581] Deposition of Christy L. Jones, PhD., In the General Court of Justice, Superior Court Division, 05 E 213, In the matter of the Will of James Henry Smith, Deceased. Reported by Betty W. Pace Thorne, Pace Reporting Service, Inc. March 3, 2006, p 58.

[582] Gurette, Ron T., Investigative Report for James B. Maxwell, Client, Estate of James Henry Smith, Re: Joan Teer, 1/22/2006 to 2/13/2006.

[583] Gurette, Ron T., Investigative Report for James B. Maxwell, Client, Estate of James Henry Smith, Re: Theresa Hondros, 1/22/2006 to 2/13/2006.

[584] Gurette, Ron T., Investigative Report for James B. Maxwell, Client, Estate of James Henry Smith, Re: Shirley Lovitt, 1/22/2006 to 2/13/2006.

[585] Gurette, Ron T., Investigative Report for James B. Maxwell, Client, Estate of James Henry Smith, Re: Beverly Boykin, 1/22/2006 to 2/13/2006.

[586] Gurette, Ron T., Investigative Report for James B. Maxwell, Client, Estate of James Henry Smith, Re: Clyde "Bill" Gentry, 1/22/2006 to 2/13/2006.

[587] Gurette, Ron T., Investigative Report for James B. Maxwell, Client, Estate of James Henry Smith, Re: Todd Allen Mozingo, 1/22/2006 to 2/13/2006.

[588] E-mail from Jim Maxwell to William T. Smith III, cc nine family members, Re: Smith Estate, March 31, 2006.

[589] Ibid.

[590] Little, Ken,, "Witnesses: Dentist wasn't reckless with money" Wilmington Star News, April 13, 2006 p 1A.

[591] Ibid, A1.

[592] Deposition of Robert A. O'Quinn, Volume One, In the General Court of Justice, Superior Court Division, 05 E 213, In the matter of the Will of James Henry Smith, Deceased. Reported by Lois Redmond, Pace Reporting Service, Inc. August 30, 2005, p 23-24.

[593] Transcript of the trial testimony of Robert A. O'Quinn, In the General Court of Justice, Superior Court Division, 05 E 213, In the matter of the Will of James Henry Smith, Deceased. Reported by Katie K. Thomas, Official Court Reporter. April 10, 2006, p 21.

[594] Ibid, 24.

[595] Ibid, 27.

[596] Ibid, 29.

[597] Ibid, 32.

[598] Ibid, 33.

[599] Ibid, 33.

[600] Ibid, 34.

[601] Ibid, 36.

[602] Ibid, 39-40.

[603] Ibid, 41.

[604] Ibid, 43.

[605] Ibid, 54-55.

[606] Ibid, 42.

[607] Ibid, 50-51.

[608] Ibid, 81.

[609] Ibid, 47.

[610] Defendant's exhibit 414 In the General Court of Justice, Superior Court Division, 05 E 213, In the matter of the Will of James Henry Smith, Deceased.

[611] Ibid, 59.

[612] Ibid, 113, 117-119.

[613] Ibid, 129.

[614] Deposition of Robert A. O'Quinn, Volume One, In the General Court of Justice, Superior Court Division, 05 E 213, In the matter of the Will of James Henry Smith, Deceased. Reported by Lois Redmond, Pace Reporting Service, Inc. August 30, 2005, p 23-24.

[615] Deposition of Jack Richardson, Volume Two, In the General Court of Justice, Superior Court Division, 05 E 213, In the matter of the Will of James Henry Smith, Deceased. Reported by Lois Redmond, Pace Reporting Service, Inc. August 31, 2005, p 77.

[616] Transcript of the trial testimony of Robert A. O'Quinn, In the General Court of Justice, Superior Court Division, 05 E 213, In the matter of the Will of James Henry Smith, Deceased. Reported by Katie K. Thomas, Official Court Reporter. April 10, 2006, p 148.

[617] Ibid, 129.

[618] Little, Ken, "Sides dispute where Smith's money went" Wilmington Star News, Apr. 14, p 1B & 2B.

[619] Ibid, 1B & 2B.

[620] Transcript of the trial testimony of Otto K. Pridgen, In the General Court of Justice, Superior Court Division, 05 E 213, In the matter of the Will of James Henry Smith, Deceased. Reported by Katie K. Thomas, Official Court Reporter. April 10, 2006, p 7.

[621] Ibid, 7-8.

[622] Ibid, 13.

[623] Ibid, 14-15.

[624] Ibid, 15-16.

[625] Ibid, 16.

[626] Ibid, 19.

[627] Ibid, 27.

[628] Ibid, 28.

[629] Ibid, 30.

[630] Ibid, 31.

[631] Ibid, 34-35.

[632] Ibid, 27.

[633] Ibid, 35.

[634] Ibid, 37.

[635] Ibid, 37.

[636] Ibid, 38.

[637] Phone conversation with William T. Smith IV, October 11, 2012.

[638] Transcript of the trial testimony of Otto K. Pridgen, In the General Court of Justice, Superior Court Division, 05 E 213, In the matter of the Will of James Henry Smith, Deceased. Reported by Katie K. Thomas, Official Court Reporter. April 10, 2006, p 47.

[639] Ibid, 56.

[640] Ibid, 61-2.

[641] Ibid, 55.

[642] Defendant's exhibit 424 In the General Court of Justice, Superior Court Division, 05 E 213, In the matter of the Will of James Henry Smith, Deceased. Handwritten note from Pat Jenkins to Carol, dated 7/10/02.

[643] Transcript of the trial testimony of Otto K. Pridgen, In the General Court of Justice, Superior Court Division, 05 E 213, In the matter of the Will of James Henry Smith, Deceased. Reported by Katie K. Thomas, Official Court Reporter. April 10, 2006, p 65-66.

[644] Ibid, 76-89.

[645] Ibid, 90.

[646] Ibid, 97-98.

[647] Ibid, 101.

[648] Ibid, 111.

[649] Ibid, 114.

[650] Ibid, 115.

[651] Ibid, 117.

[652] Ibid, 116.

[653] Ibid, 118-119.

[654] Ibid, 127.

[655] Ibid, 131.

[656] Ibid, 149.

[657] Ibid, 139.

[658] Ibid, 146.

[659] Ibid, 152.

[660] Ibid, 161.

[661] Deposition of Jack Richardson, Volume Two, In the General Court of Justice, Superior Court Division, 05 E 213, In the matter of the Will of James Henry Smith, Deceased. Reported by Lois Redmond, Pace Reporting Service, Inc. August 31, 2005, p 51-52.

[662] Transcript of the trial testimony of Otto K. Pridgen, In the General Court of Justice, Superior Court Division, 05 E 213, In the matter of the Will of James Henry Smith, Deceased. Reported by Katie K. Thomas, Official Court Reporter. April 10, 2006, p164.

[663] Ibid, 165-166.

[664] Ibid, 168.

[665] Transcript of the trial testimony of Linda Phillips, In the General Court of Justice, Superior Court Division, 05 E 213, In the matter of the Will of James Henry Smith, Deceased. Reported by Katie K. Thomas, Official Court Reporter. April 10, 2006, p 6-7.

[666] Ibid, 9.

[667] Ibid, 10.

[668] Ibid, 23-24.

[669] Ibid, 32.

[670] Ibid, 32.

[671] Ibid, 37-38.

[672] Ibid, 40.

[673] Ibid, 42.

[674] Ibid, 44.

[675] Ibid, 46.

[676] Phone conversation with William T. Smith III, October 24, 2016, and Polygraph examination of William T. Smith, Conducted By- Andrew Goldstein, LCPE, Forensic Polygraph Examiner, NC License #370-P, SC License #084, 10/6/2017.

[677] Transcript of the trial testimony of Linda Phillips, In the General Court of Justice, Superior Court Division, 05 E 213, In the matter of the Will of James Henry Smith, Deceased. Reported by Katie K. Thomas, Official Court Reporter. April 10, 2006, p 51-52.

[678] Ibid, 47.

[679] Ibid, 48.

[680] Ibid, 54.

[681] Ibid, 57.

[682] Ibid, 58.

[683] Ibid, 59-61.

[684] Ibid, 62.

[685] Ibid, 64.

[686] Ibid, 68.

[687] Ibid, 70.

[688] Ibid, 71.

[689] Ibid, 71.

[690] Ibid, 74.

[691] Ibid, 75.

[692] Ibid, 76.

[693] Ibid, 78.

[694] Ibid, 82.

[695] Ibid, 89.

[696] Transcript of the trial testimony of Christy L. Jones, In the General Court of Justice, Superior Court Division, 05 E 213, In the matter of the Will of James Henry Smith, Deceased. Reported by Katie K. Thomas, Official Court Reporter. April 10, 2006, p 4-5.

[697] Ibid, 7.

[698] Ibid, 10-11.

[699] Ibid, 11-12.

[700] Ibid, 14.

[701] Ibid, 16.

[702] Ibid, 19.

[703] Ibid, 20.

[704] Checking account statements for Dr. James H. Smith, account number ending in 158031, First Union, Commercial interest checking, January 2002 through December 2002.

[705] Transcript of the trial testimony of Christy L. Jones, In the General Court of Justice, Superior Court Division, 05 E 213, In the matter of the Will of James Henry Smith, Deceased. Reported by Katie K. Thomas, Official Court Reporter. April 10, 2006, p 23.

[706] Ibid, 23.
[707] Ibid, 24-25.
[708] Ibid, 25.
[709] Cassidy 1-2.
[710] Transcript of the trial testimony of Christy L. Jones, In the General Court of Justice, Superior Court Division, 05 E 213, In the matter of the Will of James Henry Smith, Deceased. Reported by Katie K. Thomas, Official Court Reporter. April 10, 2006, p 27.
[711] Ibid, 29.
[712] Ibid, 30.
[713] Ibid, 30-31.
[714] Ibid, 31-35.
[715] Ibid, 38.
[716] Ibid, 41-42.
[717] Ibid, 43-50.
[718] Ibid, 51.
[719] Ibid, 51-52.
[720] Ibid, 55-56.
[721] Ibid, 57.
[722] Ibid, 58.
[723] Ibid, 60.
[724] Ibid, 61-62.
[725] Ibid, 62.
[726] Ibid, 64.
[727] Ibid, 65.
[728] Ibid, 66.
[729] Ibid, 66-71.
[730] Ibid, 72.
[731] Ibid, 73.
[732] Ibid, 82-84.
[733] Ibid, 84-85.
[734] Ibid, 86.
[735] Ibid, 87.
[736] Transcript of the trial testimony of Kristine Herfkens, In the General Court of Justice, Superior Court Division, 05 E 213, In the matter of the Will of James Henry Smith, Deceased. Reported by Katie K. Thomas, Official Court Reporter. April 10, 2006, p 3-6
[737] Ibid, 7-11.
[738] Ibid, 14-15.
[739] Ibid, 16.
[740] Ibid, 16-19.
[741] Ibid, 12.
[742] Ibid, 19-21.
[743] Ibid, 23.
[744] Ibid, 24.
[745] Ibid, 25.
[746] Ibid, 26.

[747] Ibid, 27-29.
[748] Ibid, 27-39.
[749] Ibid, 39.
[750] Ibid, 40.
[751] Ibid, 43.
[752] Ibid, 44.
[753] Ibid, 45.
[754] Ibid, 48.
[755] Ibid, 50.
[756] Ibid, 51.
[757] Ibid, 51-53.
[758] Ibid, 57.
[759] Transcript of the trial testimony of Michael Queen, In the General Court of Justice, Superior Court Division, 05 E 213, In the matter of the Will of James Henry Smith, Deceased. Reported by Katie K. Thomas, Official Court Reporter. April 10, 2006, p 3.
[760] Ibid, 4.
[761] Ibid, 6.
[762] Ibid, 9.
[763] Ibid, 9-10.
[764] Ibid, 10-11.
[765] Ibid, 13-14.
[766] Ibid, 14-15.
[767] Ibid, 17-19.
[768] Ibid, 25-26.
[769] Ibid, 27.
[770] Ibid, 33.
[771] Ibid, 33.
[772] Ibid, 36.
[773] Ibid, 39.
[774] Ibid, 43.
[775] Ibid, 44-47.
[776] Ibid, 47.
[777] Ibid, 49.
[778] Ibid, 50.
[779] Ibid, 53.
[780] Ibid, 54-57.
[781] Ibid, 60.
[782] Ibid, 63.
[783] Little, Ken, "Grandnephew testifies in fight over will" Wilmington Star News, April 20, 2006, p 2B.
[784] Ibid, 2B.
[785] Ibid, 2B.
[786] Transcript of the trial testimony of Janice M. Pridgen, In the General Court of Justice, Superior Court Division, 05 E 213, In the matter of the Will of James Henry Smith, Deceased. Reported by Katie K. Thomas, Official Court Reporter. April 10, 2006, p 4.

[787] Ibid, 4-5.
[788] Ibid, 5.
[789] Ibid, 8-9.
[790] Ibid, 11.
[791] Ibid, 12.
[792] Ibid, 24-25.
[793] Ibid, 29.
[794] Ibid, 32.
[795] Ibid, 35.
[796] Ibid, 35.
[797] Ibid, 35.
[798] Ibid, 40.
[799] Ibid, 42.
[800] Ibid, 43.
[801] Ibid, 48-49.
[802] Phone conversation with Lisa Shelhart, January 8, 2017.
[803] Transcript of the trial testimony of Janice M. Pridgen, In the General Court of Justice, Superior Court Division, 05 E 213, In the matter of the Will of James Henry Smith, Deceased. Reported by Katie K. Thomas, Official Court Reporter. April 10, 2006, p 52.
[804] Ibid, 59.
[805] Ibid, 60-76.
[806] Ibid, 75-77.
[807] Ibid, 77-79.
[808] Ibid, 80-81.
[809] Ibid, 85.
[810] Ibid, 87-92.
[811] Ibid, 59.
[812] Ibid, 93.
[813] Ibid, 95.
[814] Ibid, 96.
[815] Ibid, 102.
[816] Ibid, 105.
[817] Ibid, 107-108.
[818] Ibid, 109.
[819] Ibid, 113-114.
[820] Ibid, 115.
[821] Ibid, 116-117.
[822] Ibid, 117.
[823] Ibid, 126- 132.
[824] Ibid, 130.
[825] Ibid, 139.
[826] Ibid, 145.
[827] Ibid, 148-149.
[828] Ibid, 155-160.
[829] Ibid, 162-163.
[830] Ibid, 167.

[831] Ibid, 170.

[832] Ibid, 179-180.

[833] Ibid, 184-186.

[834] Ibid, 187-188.

[835] Ibid, 188-190.

[836] Transcript of the trial testimony of Patricia C. Jenkins, In the General Court of Justice, Superior Court Division, 05 E 213, In the matter of the Will of James Henry Smith, Deceased. Reported by Katie K. Thomas, Official Court Reporter. April 10, 2006, p 4.

[837] Ibid, 5.

[838] Ibid, 36-38.

[839] Ibid, 16.

[840] Ibid, 63.

[841] Ibid, 69.

[842] Ibid, 70.

[843] Ibid, 71.

[844] Ibid, 7.

[845] Ibid, 8-9.

[846] E-mail interview with Joyce Winstead, MSN, RN, FRE, Education and Practice Consultant, North Carolina Board of Nursing, Raleigh, NC, October 20, 2016.

[847] Transcript of the trial testimony of Patricia C. Jenkins, In the General Court of Justice, Superior Court Division, 05 E 213, In the matter of the Will of James Henry Smith, Deceased. Reported by Katie K. Thomas, Official Court Reporter. April 10, 2006, p 10.

[848] Ibid, 11-13.

[849] Ibid, 28-29.

[850] Ibid, 29-30.

[851] Ibid, 29-30.

[852] Ibid, 32-35.

[853] Ibid, 39.

[854] Ibid, 40.

[855] Ibid, 41.

[856] Ibid, 42.

[857] Ibid, 45.

[858] Ibid, 58.

[859] Ibid, 55-56.

[860] Ibid, 60.

[861] Ibid, 60.

[862] Ibid, 60.

[863] Ibid, 71-72.

[864] Ibid, 79-81.

[865] Ibid, 82.

[866] Ibid, 83.

[867] Ibid, 86.

[868] Ibid, 86-87.

[869] Ibid, 88.

[870] Ibid, 92.

[871] Ibid, 96.

[872] Ibid, 96.

[873] Ibid, 97-103.

[874] Ibid, 106.

[875] Ibid, 111.

[876] Ibid, 112-113.

[877] Ibid, 113.

[878] Ibid, 116.

[879] Transcript of the trial testimony of Carol S. Tucker, In the General Court of Justice, Superior Court Division, 05 E 213, In the matter of the Will of James Henry Smith, Deceased. Reported by Katie K. Thomas, Official Court Reporter. April 10, 2006, p 5

[880] Ibid, 8-9.

[881] Ibid, 12-13.

[882] Ibid, 14.

[883] Ibid, 14-16.

[884] Ibid, 14-16.

[885] Ibid, 17.

[886] Ibid, 20.

[887] Ibid, 21.

[888] Ibid, 21-22.

[889] Ibid, 26-27.

[890] Ibid, 29-30.

[891] Ibid, 31.

[892] Ibid, 32-35.

[893] Ibid, 35.

[894] Ibid, 37.

[895] Ibid, 37-40.

[896] Ibid, 41.

[897] Ibid, 42.

[898] Ibid, 43.

[899] Ibid, 44.

[900] Ibid, 45.

[901] Ibid, 48-49.

[902] Ibid, 49-50.

[903] Ibid, 49-50.

[904] Ibid, 53-54.

[905] Ibid, 58.

[906] Ibid, 59.

[907] Transcript of the trial testimony of Larry Fowler, In the General Court of Justice, Superior Court Division, 05 E 213, In the matter of the Will of James Henry Smith, Deceased. Reported by Katie K. Thomas, Official Court Reporter. April 10, 2006, p 4.

[908] Ibid, 5.

[909] Ibid, 6.

[910] Ibid, 7.

[911] Ibid, 8-9.

[912] Ibid, 10-11.

[913] Ibid, 12-13.

[914] Ibid, 13-14.

[915] Ibid, 15-16.

[916] Transcript of the trial testimony of Otto K. Pridgen, In the General Court of Justice, Superior Court Division, 05 E 213, In the matter of the Will of James Henry Smith, Deceased. Reported by Katie K. Thomas, Official Court Reporter. April 10, 2006, p 153.

[917] Transcript of the trial testimony of Larry Fowler, In the General Court of Justice, Superior Court Division, 05 E 213, In the matter of the Will of James Henry Smith, Deceased. Reported by Katie K. Thomas, Official Court Reporter. April 10, 2006, p 19-20.

[918] Ibid, 20-21.

[919] Ibid, 21-22.

[920] Ibid, 24.

[921] Ibid, 25-27.

[922] Ibid, 31.

[923] Transcript of the trial testimony of Margaret Banck, In the General Court of Justice, Superior Court Division, 05 E 213, In the matter of the Will of James Henry Smith, Deceased. Reported by Katie K. Thomas, Official Court Reporter. April 10, 2006, p 3.

[924] Ibid, 4-5.

[925] Ibid, 6.

[926] Ibid, 8-9.

[927] Ibid, 13.

[928] Ibid, 14.

[929] Ibid, 14.

[930] Ibid, 16.

[931] Ibid, 16.

[932] Ibid, 16-17.

[933] Transcript of the trial testimony of Wanda Day, In the General Court of Justice, Superior Court Division, 05 E 213, In the matter of the Will of James Henry Smith, Deceased. Reported by Katie K. Thomas, Official Court Reporter. April 10, 2006, p 10.

[934] Ibid, 4-6.

[935] Ibid, 6.

[936] Ibid, 8.

[937] Ibid, 9.

[938] Ibid, 9.

[939] Ibid, 11.

[940] Ibid, 12.

[941] Ibid, 13.

[942] Ibid, 13-14.

[943] Ibid, 14-16.

[944] Ibid, 16-17.

[945] Ibid, 17-18.

[946] Ibid, 18-19.

947 Ibid, 20-21.
948 Ibid, 21.
949 Ibid, 23.
950 Ibid, 25.
951 Ibid, 26-27.
952 Ibid, 27-29.
953 Ibid, 30-31.
954 Ibid, 32.
955 Ibid, 32-33.
956 Ibid, 33-34.
957 Ibid, 35.
958 Ibid, 35-36.
959 Ibid, 36.
960 Ibid, 37-38.
961 Ibid, 38-39.
962 Ibid, 41.
963 Ibid, 42.
964 Ibid, 42.
965 Everette, 203.
966 Ibid, 205.
967 Little, Ken, "Agreement ends trial contesting Smith's will" Wilmington Star News, April 25, 2006, p 6A & 6B.
968 Ibid, 6A & 6B.
969 E-mail from Jim Maxwell to William T. Smith III, cc Lori Rosemond, Re: Some questions, May 8, 2006.
970 Notification letters from First Baptist Church to William T. Smith III, that Patricia Jenkins, Linda Phillips, Janice Miller Pridgen, and Carol Tucker made contributions to the "Smith Fund" at First Baptist Church, circa July, 2006.
971 E-mail from William T. Smith III to Jim Maxwell, Re: Gene McIntyre.
972 Personal notes of W. T. Smith dated July 15, 2007.
973 Letter from Lori Rosemond to William T. Smith III, July 6, 2006.

CPSIA information can be obtained
at www.ICGtesting.com
Printed in the USA
FSHW020630130221
78471FS